TEACHING WITH STUDENT TEXTS

TEACHING WITH STUDENT TEXTS

Essays Toward an Informed Practice

Edited by

JOSEPH HARRIS
Duke University

JOHN D. MILES
Wofford College

CHARLES PAINE
University of New Mexico

UTAH STATE UNIVERSITY PRESS
Logan, Utah
2010

Utah State University Press
Logan, UT 84322

Manufactured in the United States of America
Cover calligraphy and design by Barbara Yale-Read

ISBN: 978-0-87421-785-8 (paper)
ISBN: 978-0-87421-786-5 (e-book)

Library of Congress Cataloging-in-Publication Data

Teaching with student texts : essays toward an informed practice / edited by Joseph Harris, John D. Miles, Charles Paine.
      p. cm.
   Includes bibliographical references and index.
   ISBN 978-0-87421-785-8 (pbk. : alk. paper) – ISBN 978-0-87421-786-5 (e-book)
   1. Report writing–Study and teaching (Higher)–Evaluation. 2. Teachers–In-service training. 3.
Teaching. I. Harris, Joseph (Joseph D.) II. Miles, John Dodge. III. Paine, Charles.
   PE1404.T398 2010
   808'.0420711–dc22

                                        2010015479

To

STUDENTS,

whose writing drives the work of our field

CONTENTS

Acknowledgments   *ix*

Introduction   *1*

   Joseph Harris, John D. Miles, and Charles Paine

ONE   VALUING STUDENT TEXTS

1   Re-Valuing Student Writing   *9*

   Bruce Horner

2   Revealing Our Values: Reading Student Texts with Colleagues in High School and College   *24*

   Nicole B. Wallack

3   "What Do *We* Want in This Paper?" Generating Criteria Collectively   *35*

   Chris M. Anson, Matthew Davis, and Domenica Vilhotti

4   Teaching the Rhetoric of Writing Assessment   *46*

   Asao B. Inoue

TWO   CIRCULATING STUDENT TEXTS

5   Ethics, Student Writers, and the Use of Student Texts to Teach   *60*

   Paul V. Anderson and Heidi A. McKee

6   Reframing Student Writing in Writing Studies Composition Classes   *78*

   Patrick Bruch and Thomas Reynolds

7   Students Write to Students about Writing   *88*

   Laurie McMillan

8   The Low-Stakes, Risk-Friendly Message-Board Text   *96*

   Scott Warnock

9   Product as Process: Teaching Publication to Students   *108*

   Karen McDonnell and Kevin Jefferson

10 Students' Texts beyond the Classroom: *Young Scholars in Writing*'s Challenges to College Writing Instruction   *118*

   Doug Downs, Heidi Estrem, and Susan Thomas

11 The Figure of the Student in Composition Textbooks   *129*

   Mariolina Rizzi Salvatori and Patricia Donahue

THREE CHANGING CLASSROOM PRACTICES

12 Workshop and Seminar   *145*
    Joseph Harris

13 What Do We Talk about When We Talk about Workshops? Charting the First Five Weeks of a First-Year Writing Course   *154*
    Maggie Debelius

14 Texts to Be Worked on and Worked with: Encouraging Students to See Their Writing as Theoretical   *163*
    Chris Warnick

15 Writing to Learn, Reading to Teach: Student Texts in the Pedagogy Seminar   *171*
    Margaret J. Marshall

16 The Writer/Text Connection: Understanding Writers' Relationships to their Writing   *181*
    Muriel Harris

17 Learning from Coauthoring: Composing Texts Together in the Composition Classroom   *190*
    Michele Eodice and Kami Day

18 Inquiry, Collaboration, and Reflection in the Student (Text)-Centered Multimodal Writing Course   *200*
    Scott L. Rogers, Ryan Trauman, and Julia E. Kiernan

19 Workshopping to Practice Scientific Terms   *210*
    Anne Ellen Geller and Frank R. Cantelmo

20 Bringing Outside Texts In and Inside Texts Out   *220*
    Jane Mathison Fife

21 Embracing Uncertainty: The *Kairos* of Teaching with Student Texts   *229*
    Rolf Norgaard

    Afterword: Notes toward an Informed Practice   *243*
    Charles Paine and John D. Miles

    References   *256*
    Index   *264*
    Contributors   *268*

ACKNOWLEDGMENTS

This project began with a problem we three editors faced as mentors of new writing teachers: How could we help them use student texts in the writing classroom? But this initial vision soon evolved into something much larger, more interesting, and more useful—a book that we hope will inform the practice of any teacher who teaches with student texts. (It has certainly informed ours.) Like many such projects, this one has required far more time and effort than we anticipated but has also been far more fun and rewarding than we could have imagined. We are of course very pleased to see this work reach an audience but a little sorry to see this deeply collaborative effort come to an end. There are many people we need to thank for making this project so rewarding and for helping this book find its vision and direction.

First, we thought we should thank the builders of web-based collaboration tools like Google Docs, Skype, and others. This collaboration—involving over 30 editors, contributors, and readers scattered across the United States and beyond—would not have been possible without them.

Our contributors deserve special thanks for patiently and repeatedly revising their work (sometimes starting almost from scratch), meeting every one of our deadlines as the project found its shape. We also thank the ninety-plus scholars who responded to our call for proposals. Their ideas also contributed to this book's ultimate direction.

Two anonymous readers of the initial manuscript were enormously helpful in helping us understand and articulate what this volume of essays could achieve. In response to their criticism, we were able to reshape the book and give better direction to our contributors as we asked them (yet again) for revisions. We'd also like to thank Barbara Yale-Read for an elegant book cover and Judith Martin for a comprehensive and useful index.

Finally, Michael Spooner, the director of Utah State University Press, deserves thanks for the enthusiasm and intellectual leadership he has shown in sponsoring not only this project but so much important work in our field during the last decade.

INTRODUCTION

Joseph Harris
Duke University

John D. Miles
Wofford College

Charles Paine
University of New Mexico

"It changes everything." That's how a new teacher described what happened when he started to work in class with the texts his students were writing. We began this project out of the desire to share that epiphany—to show how experienced teachers work with student texts in the writing classroom and why that practice can be so transformative. We imagined a collection of essays that, as we put it in our call for proposals, would describe "how teachers can use texts written by the students they are working with to illustrate the moves, strategies, principles, and forms of critical reading and academic writing."

In putting this book together, we strove to make that *how* visible. We asked our contributors not merely to theorize or explain but to illustrate in some detail how they actually go about teaching with student texts. A few of our early readers found this focus a bit of a throwback. Didn't teachers of writing decide years ago that our main work was with student texts, they asked? So what's new here? Well, to be sure, our field does center around pedagogy. This is shown in the very texts we work with and circulate among ourselves. We have textbooks, handbooks, rhetorics, anthologies—almost every sort of advice on writing that one could imagine. We have examples of actual student writing, and of teacher comments on them. We have handouts for teaching: questions for discussion, assignments for writing, and guidelines for response. Historians have uncovered curricula, syllabi, and some precious few student texts from the past, along with the theories of writing and language that drove them. As a field, then, we have thought hard about what we do in the classroom and why, and we have been generous in sharing the materials of our work with one another.

But still something remains mysterious. Or at least that has been our experience working with teachers of writing—both new and experienced—who often seem to find it remarkably hard to picture in useful detail what they might actually *do* with student texts in the classroom. How do you select student drafts to talk about? How do you lead a seminar or workshop about a student text that is respectful and engaging but also prompts meaningful reflection and revision? How do you relate that sort of in-class discussion to the ongoing work that students are doing as writers? We have seen many teachers who, unsure of how to answer such questions, either turn their courses into a series of unconnected tips on revising, leading one class after the next on how this or that writer might improve this or that draft, or who use student texts as mere springboards to discussion of other issues or topics, or much worse, who find ways of not talking about student texts at all.

And so we have tried in this book to assemble a portfolio of teachers working with student texts, a set of snapshots showing classroom moves that teachers can make with student writing. We realize that others have covered this ground before us. Indeed, we're struck by how several of the pedagogies in our field have a kind of ur-text that presents a certain kind of classroom practice in compelling detail. To offer a few quick examples: Surely part of the hold that workshop pedagogies have had on our field can be traced to Peter Elbow's lucid and specific descriptions of his work with writing groups in his 1973 *Writing Without Teachers*. But William E. Coles, Jr., models an alternate tradition of working with student texts—something that feels less like a workshop than a graduate seminar—in the class-by-class narrative of his 1978 *The Plural I*. And Ira Shor turns the hopes and ideals of critical pedagogy into a concrete practice in his detailed accounts of how he works with student writers in his 1987 *Critical Teaching and Everyday Life*. But precisely what makes these books so powerful also limits their usefulness to new teachers—as each is, in the end, a brief for a particular way of working with student texts. Our goal here instead has been to document a *range* of teaching moves and practices that provide both generative examples and specific activities that others can adopt and adapt.

You will thus find that the essays in this book do not form a unified whole. This was partly deliberate, partly a happy surprise. Rather than beginning as editors with a grid of topics and approaches we wanted to fill in, we instead genuinely wanted to find out what our fellow writing teachers were doing and why. The result is that the authors in this book offer a varied set of approaches to teaching with student texts. Sometimes these approaches align, sometimes they diverge, sometimes they conflict. We hope that this diversity proves useful to teachers as they reflect on the sorts of work they want to do with student writers. We also believe that it accurately reflects the current state of teaching in our field—which in our view is defined less by a set of agreed-upon methods than by a series of driving questions and concerns.

One such concern has been how to center a writing course on the work of the students in it. In the last fifty years, two competing responses to this concern have emerged. One has been to focus on the writing *process*. In process-centered courses, the teacher tends to function as a kind of coach, guiding students through the ongoing labor of prewriting, drafting, revising, and editing their work. Now there can be no question that all of us today are, to one extent or the other, process teachers. But what strikes us is that you can teach the writing process while paying fairly little attention to the content of the texts that students write. Indeed, the injunction to *teach writers not writing* can encourage teachers, paradoxically, to focus so much on processes that they may downplay what students actually have to say. And an interest in student texts can become associated with the current-traditionalist practices of the bad old pre-process days—with a focus, that is, on eradicating errors and legislating proper forms and genres.

But we have titled this book *Teaching with Student Texts*, not teaching student writing or teaching student writers. This distinction—between *texts* and *writing*—is a key one for us. We are not current-traditionalists, nor are the contributors to this book. But we do wish to speak for a pedagogy that puts students at the center of a writing course by making the texts they produce the material focus of our work together. In the kind of course we are imagining, and that our contributors describe in various ways, student texts are *on the table*—they are what the class is talking about and working on. Perhaps we can define our focus by negation: There are courses, good ones, that teach the process of writing—that ask students to turn in proposals, then drafts, then revisions, to confer with their teacher, and to read their work aloud in small groups. But such courses don't necessarily make student texts the focus of class work—or to put this another way, they don't necessarily make student texts what students spend their time together in class reading, analyzing, debating, criticizing, and learning from. We are interested in what happens when a teacher makes that curious, reflective, inward-looking move—when the texts written by students in a class become the materials for that class. As varied as the contributions to this book are, they all describe courses in which student texts are a visible and central focus of the work that a class does together. This book coheres, that is, around an interest not simply in *students writing* but in *student writings* (or texts) as a teaching focus.

A second concern that drives this book is expressed in our subtitle: *Essays toward an Informed Practice*. We are drawn to the field of writing and rhetoric in strong part by its commitment to blurring the lines between theory and practice. We like how people in our field identify themselves as teachers as well as scholars or researchers, and by their insistence that knowledge is produced not just in the archive or lab but in the classroom. But, frankly, we have also been discouraged by how many attempts to merge theory and practice have seemed to err, as it were, on the side of theory—that articles and books that begin as promising analyses of the complex intellectual work of teaching often shift to a (perhaps easier) discussion of the theoretical principles or hopes underlying such work. We aim here to promote work that counters this emphasis—that offers not a simple set of tips or lore, but that clearly centers on an account of a particular *teaching practice*.

We've also tried hard to make this a collection of *essays*. Given our interest in showcasing a range of teaching moves and practices, we've asked the contributors to this book to cut to the chase—to center their pieces on the work they do with student writers, and to describe that work in clear and accessible terms. We've also asked them to be brief: almost all the essays in this book run under 4,000 words. We think the intellectual and political commitments of the authors ring clearly throughout these essays, but clarifying those commitments is not their principle aim. Rather, we've asked our contributors to be as clear as they can about the actual work that goes on in their courses, so that other teachers—with varying scholarly, political, and theoretical commitments—can reuse, revise, or resist their methods.

And the essays collected here do just that—and very well indeed. But we think they also do something more. In reading and talking about the essays that make up this book, we have become convinced that working closely with student texts is not simply a classroom move but a defining practice for the field of writing and rhetoric. Working with student texts is what writing teachers *do*. But what we also realized, as we read and reread these essays, is that the practice of teaching with student texts is not only defining but dynamic—that it is a part of our work that is being constantly reinvented and retooled.

We thus decided to structure this book to highlight what we learned from working with these essays. The first section, Valuing Student Texts, brings together a set of essays that look at the need to rethink the uses and meanings of student texts when they are seen not simply as work to be graded by the instructor but as the central focus of a course. These pieces show how teaching with student texts makes questions of assessment, of what we really value, central to the intellectual work of our courses. The second section, Circulating Student Texts, consists of essays that look at the multiple forms student texts can take, the various ways they can circulate, and the different readerships they can address. When we started this project, we had not anticipated that such questions of value and circulation would become so central to this book, but we now think they offer a necessary and compelling context for the last and longest section, Changing Classroom Practices, which consists of essays that speak forcefully to our original aims for this book—that show how bringing student texts to the table can transform the kinds of everyday work that go on in writing courses. We want to stress that these categories overlap with each other. Our groupings are simply meant to highlight emphases and to suggest recurring issues of concern.

Each of the three sections of this book begins with our brief summary of the essays in it. We also invited a few authors—Bruce Horner, Paul V. Anderson and Heidi A. McKee, Mariolina Rizzi Salvatori and Patricia Donahue, Rolf Norgaard—to write the somewhat longer essays we've used to frame each section. And this volume ends with an afterword in which Charles Paine and John D. Miles offer an alternative thematic table of contents intended to help readers gain an overall sense of teaching with student texts. We hope these reflective pieces help us better see teaching with student texts not simply as a classroom technique but as an informed practice that needs to be argued for, questioned, and revised.

Finally, we'd like to note a small difficulty we had in editing this volume, because we think it points to larger issues in how our field deals with student writers and student texts. All of the contributors to this book who quote student texts have obtained written permission to do so from the students involved. But the exact terms of that permission— and especially whether student authors are to be named or kept anonymous—vary from chapter to chapter. Similarly, we have discovered there is no set protocol in our field for how to refer to student writers. Do we say, "As Elizabeth writes," or "As Elizabeth Smith writes," or "As Smith (2009) writes"? And what about references to comments in class, or brief or informal writings? The rules of thumb we have decided upon for this volume are these: In citing student texts, we have respected the terms of the agreements our contributors have negotiated with students. If student authors expected to be cited by name, we have included those citations in our list of references. If students expected to be given pseudonyms or kept anonymous, we have done so. In referring to class-room conversations, our practice has been to refer to a speaker—either teacher or student—by first and last name when they are first noted in a text, and by first name alone afterwards. (And so, for instance, we would first write, "As John D. Miles noted," and then after, "John continued to say.") These are in some ways technical matters, but we suspect they also point towards important questions about how to acknowledge the intellectual work of students—and of colleagues when their work takes a form other than that of a published article or book. We very much believe that we need to cite and analyze such work—that is what this book is about. But we are also convinced that, as a field, we need to think more about how we value student writing, how we represent student writers and their texts in our own discourse, and how we support the work students do as intellectuals.

PART ONE
Valuing Student Texts

The four essays in this first section examine the ways the value of students' texts is established, or (more often) is simply allotted with little deliberation or reflection. They also describe ways students and teachers can participate in and critique the process of valuing, thus moving this usually unexamined process toward something like an "informed" practice for both students and teachers.

Bruce Horner's "Re-Valuing Student Writing" identifies perhaps the most significant motivation for teaching with student texts: placing student texts in the center of a class makes student writing matter by making the issue of student writing—and writing generally—a legitimate area of academic inquiry. Horner explains that although the field of rhetoric and composition has explored three main tactics for conferring various kinds of value on student texts, finding a legitimate value for students' texts has remained a significant and intractable problem. Advocating an approach that has students examining the ways in which their writing and others' writing is situated and valued in the academy, Horner argues that student writing can move beyond having mere "exchange value," exchanging student writing for display or grades, what he calls "notwriting." Rather, students can rework academic knowledge so their writing does real work and attains legitimate "use value."

The remaining three essays provide rich descriptions of specific methods for students and teachers to explore the ways student writing is and can be valued in various situations and by various readers. In "Revealing Our Values: Reading Student Texts with Colleagues in High School and College," Nicole B. Wallack focuses not on a college classroom but on a summer workshop where teachers share their expectations, values, and practices with their colleagues from across the high school/college divide. Teachers read student texts in order to name their values about writing, test those values against those of their colleagues, and use them to design effective assignments. With better mutual understanding, Wallack argues, high-school teachers can avoid teaching aspects of writing that college teachers do not value, and college faculty can help students transfer their knowledge and skills to college work.

Chris M. Anson, Matthew Davis, and Domenica Vilhotti describe a similar method for naming and examining their values in "'What Do *We* Want in this Paper?' Generating Criteria Collectively." They describe a method designed to help undergraduate students articulate and internalize readers' expectations for their assigned writing. Students collectively create criteria based on "interestingly problematic" drafts responding to the same assignment. This process, because it engages the students themselves in formulating the standards for the texts they will produce, reflects a constructivist model of teaching and learning. Three specific examples of the process—two from sections of first-year composition courses and one from a graduate course on teaching writing—show students' collective development of criteria from sample student texts.

Asao B. Inoue's "Teaching the Rhetoric of Writing Assessment" provides a fitting bookend for this section. Inoue extends Bruce Horner's call for pedagogical practices that examine how writing is situated and valued in the academy and, like Wallack, and Anson, Davis, and Vilhotti, describes his approach in rich detail. In Inoue's writing class, students reflect on their writing as they theorize rhetorics of assessment. Quoting and citing his students' insights about the relationships between creating and assessing written work, Inoue makes a strong case that this pedagogy—which has students writing, assessing others' writing, assessing their own writing, and "habitually, chronically" reflecting on assessment—helps students become better writers who have greater control over their writing decisions. He ends with a list of ideas for encouraging students to consider the rhetorics of assessment.

1

RE-VALUING STUDENT WRITING

Bruce Horner
University of Louisville

There is now a well-established tradition of complaint about student writing in composition. I refer here not to the much longer-standing tradition of complaint that students today can't write, or write poorly, and/or don't write as well as they used to. That tradition, a robust one, continues apace, part of a larger tendency to displace onto literacy what are, in fact, social anxieties—what John Trimbur has argued is a "discourse of crisis" (1991). Those of us in the field of composition studies, in combination with our colleagues in the broader field of literacy studies, have been assiduous in using historical research to challenge myths of a current decline from a golden age of high literacy standards invoked by that tradition of complaint (Brandt 2001; Resnick and Resnick 1977).

But while scholars have been combating those myths, there remains within composition studies itself a tradition of complaint about a putative lack of value to the work student writing can accomplish *qua* "student writing" with an extremely limited range of circulation—restricted almost entirely to a readership of those attending or teaching a single section of a first-year composition course. In this tradition, the problem resides not with the quality of the writing but with the fact of its location within the academy and, more specifically, the first-year composition course. That location, at least within first-year composition courses as ordinarily constituted, is understood to significantly restrict what the writing can be and do, and hence its value. As a consequence, those attempting to increase the value of this writing, in the eyes of teachers and students, have directed their efforts toward either broadening the circulation of that writing or asking students to produce writing that goes against conventions for student writing. The hope driving such efforts is that they will somehow render students "authors" rather than mere "students," and thus their writing as something other than simply "student writing."

In this chapter, I argue that this tradition rests on limited, if dominant, cultural understandings of the work that can be accomplished by writing circulating only within academic institutional settings. As a consequence, attempts to resist restrictive notions of the work of student writing end up reinforcing those dominant understandings that account for the denigration of student writing to begin with. As an alternative to this tactic, I argue for ways we might work with student writing in composition courses that would offer a valuing of it countering dominant notions of the work of those courses and their students. I will begin by outlining three of the primary trajectories and tactics of this tradition in order to identify its assumptions regarding student writing as what I will call "notwriting." These trajectories identify the problem of student writing with either the students' selves, the academic conventions to which their writing is expected to conform, or the location of the students and their writing in the first-year writing course, and they address the problem in these terms: through pedagogies focused on the authenticity or ethical integrity of the selves expressed in the writing, or on breaking with academic conventions, or on removing the students and their writing from the first-year writing course. In defining the problem in these ways, they implicitly accede to dominant conceptions of the Real to which students and their writing are to aspire that are, in fact, problematic. I then consider alternatives to this tradition presented by Anis Bawarshi (2003) and John Trimbur (2000), alternatives aimed at shifting from a "compositional" to a "rhetorical" orientation to allow for the potential of first-year writing students to engage in critique of problematic conceptions of the Real. In points of tension in Bawarshi's and Trimbur's arguments, I identify three challenges in revaluing the work of student writing, and explore ways of treating student writing in the specific location of the first-year college writing course as, in fact, legitimate academic work.

STUDENT WRITING AS "NOTWRITING" VERSUS WRITING THE REAL

Susan Miller's critique (1991) of the "intransitive" nature of student writing, at least as it is organized in many first-year composition courses, provides one touchstone in this tradition of complaint. Miller argues that the production of such "intransitive" writing has "no particular products as results" (97). The purpose of such writing, instead, is performance for evaluation: to illustrate the writer's ability to produce particular forms (e.g., mirroring conventionally "correct" writing), and even to adopt an ideological stance recognizable by instructors as acceptably "educated." Students are positioned as "presexual, preeconomic, prepolitical" and as always "emerging . . . but never as actually responsible 'authors'" (87, 196). Such a positioning of the students and their writing is understood as both an effect and cause of the low status of both and of composition generally insofar as it is identified solely with courses for such students and their writing (196).

Miller's critique hinges on a chain of binaries in terms of which students *qua* students and those they teach are doomed: they are not authors, not members of the *polis*, not yet responsible beings, hence their writing is effectively "notwriting." At best it is a display, or "performance" (in the non-"performative" sense of speech-act theory) for instructor evaluation, of students' ability to produce writing that conforms to dominant expectations for notational practice (e.g., Standard Written English), ideological stance, (and) or interpretations of assigned readings. As intransitive, student writing has no real effects, no real purpose, and performs no real work (and hence is not "performative"). It is, instead, a "bastard" discourse peculiar to the academy.

In earlier manifestations of this tradition, many of them associated in composition studies with "expressivists" such as Ken Macrorie, William E. Coles, and Roger Sales (though the expressivist credentials of the last two have been challenged), such writing was derided as "themewriting" or "Engfish." In these manifestations of complaint, the problem of student writing was defined largely, though not exclusively, in terms of the authenticity, maturity, or ethical integrity of the student's self as displayed in his or her writing, though it might be more accurate to say that teachers in this tradition adopted the pedagogical tactic of turning students' extant concern about the presentation of self in their writing against the contradictions that the institutional demands for such presentation inevitably entailed. The writing deemed praiseworthy by these participants in the tradition was often writing which deliberately defied conventional expectations for student themes while still being recognizable as themes rather than as, say, research reports or newspaper editorials. As commentators (e.g., France 1993) have observed, this praise of writing for its authenticity, indexed by its defiance of conventional expectations for students, is the burden of many of the contributions to Coles and Vopat's collection of composition teachers' arguments for *What Makes [Student] Writing Good* (1985).

Later manifestations of this tactic have encouraged writing that appears to break with academic conventions, on the assumption that those conventions themselves constrain what it is possible for the work of student writing to accomplish. Here the problem with student writing is identified less with the students themselves than with the formal conventions and media that are imagined to dominate academic writing and constrain what it is possible for that writing to do—both for students and for academics generally (Elbow 1991). Those adopting this tactic have encouraged students to produce writing that is recognizably "alternative" to academic discourse as a means of breaking past those constraints (Bridwell-Bowles 1992; Bridwell-Bowles 1995; Hindman 2001; Yancey 2004). But this move mistakes the notations produced through the work of writing with its actual work, which has to include not simply the notations but also, as Raymond Williams has argued, "the nature of a practice and . . . its conditions" (1980, 47). In other words, it fetishizes formal features as in themselves constituting the work of writing rather than recognizing the contributions that reading practices make toward determining what, in fact, the work, and value, of that writing might be. That is, it fails to recognize writing as a material social practice.

A different set of tactics within this tradition of complaint appears to take Williams' advice: it defines the problem of student writing not in terms of the students' selves, except insofar as these are "subjectivities," nor in terms of the textual conventions of academic writing *per se*, but with the location of the writing in the academy generally and, more specifically, within the first-year composition course. Those defining the problem in this way view that location as restricting the writing produced there to "bastard" discourse whose accomplishments, or work, are (again) of no real value, though here value is measured in terms of the work's use to other disciplines, to students' future employers, or to the nation and world. One tactic to solving the problem, when understood this way, is to deny the location of the writing by assigning students to write in an imaginary role to an imaginary audience for an imaginary purpose, a denial that in practice fools no one (Bartholomae 1985; Ong 1975; Petraglia 1995b). Alternatively, it is argued that student writing can accomplish "real" work only by taking it, and/or the students, outside the location of the first-year composition course to venues where it is imagined writing accomplishes real work.

For example, many of the arguments for incorporating service learning into the teaching of composition claim that doing so engages students in real writing with real effects in the (of course) real world (Dorman and Dorman 1997; Heilker 1997), in assumed opposition to the writing, effects, and place of the first-year composition course. By taking students and their writing outside the confines of the first-year composition course, it is claimed, students no longer work as students in the bastard discourse of first-year composition but instead write brochures and the like with effects in the world. Aligned arguments call for replacing first-year composition (FYC) courses of instruction altogether with writing-across-the-curriculum (WAC) or writing-in-the-disciplines (WID) programs. These arguments hold that FYC pretends to teach "general writing skills" which, in fact, do not "transfer" to the "real" writing undertaken in academic disciplines and the workplace. The general writing skills taught in FYC are thus deemed bogus, suitable only for the artificial site of FYC, which is deemed to be void of any legitimate academic or work-related discursive context that would make the writing produced there meaningful (Petraglia 1995b, 91–92; Freedman 1995, 137; Hill and Resnick 1995).

FROM COMPOSITIONAL TO RHETORICAL ORIENTATIONS TO STUDENT WRITING

Those arguing for retaining the first-year composition course in spite of the apparent paucity of its potential as a site of legitimate writing have done so largely in terms of shifting the focus of the course from what is imagined to be its "composition" orientation to a "rhetorical" orientation. In one of the smartest of the recent arguments in this vein, Anis Bawarshi (2003) accepts that the first-year composition course (identified as "First-Year Writing" or "FYW" in his text) cannot "re-create the various ideological and discursive formations that underwrite disciplinary and professional contexts," but he rejects the notion that this limitation justifies eliminating the FYW course. Instead, he argues, the FYW course can function "as a kind of rhetorical promontory from which we teach students how to read and negotiate the boundaries of various disciplinary and professional contexts," thereby becoming "the site in which students learn how to access, interrogate, and (re)position themselves as writers within these disciplinary and professional contexts" using analyses of genres as the "passports" for doing so (155).

Likewise, albeit from a quite different point of departure, John Trimbur calls for courses in which students both examine and engage in "translations" of knowledge from, say, specialized scientific journals to newspaper accounts to advice columns to the texts of legislation (2000, 212–13). The aim of such course designs is to problematize "expertise in the circulation of academic and professional writing" (212), and "[m]ore specifically, . . . to [help] students to see that the shift in register and genre between a journal article and a news report amounts to a shift in modality . . . that marks journal articles as 'original' contributions and news reports as secondary and derivative" (213). As in the kind of FYW course for which Bawarshi calls, such courses would engage students in analyzing, and thereby better grasping and presumably learning to subsequently intervene effectively in, the ways in which particular genres carry particular meanings and effects for writers and readers, with special attention to the modes by which genres circulate. For the assignments in the course Trimbur describes (which he acknowledges as "works in progress" [212]), students would engage in critical analyses of the mediation effected by modes of circulation as a means toward the end of producing "socially useful knowledge," in the form, for example, of "public health publicity on teen or college-age sexuality" (214).

While both Bawarshi's and Trimbur's arguments arise out of composition's tradition of complaint about student writing, they also suggest ways to turn against that tradition. Admittedly, both appear to assign a primarily preparatory role to their courses, whether that preparation is for work in the genres of academic disciplines or in the texts circulating in the public sphere. But there are points of tension in their arguments that suggest an alternative stance to take toward student writing. For example, Bawarshi, while seeing "FYW as possibly a prerequisite" to writing in the disciplines, also sees it as "a site within the structure of the university that enables students to reflect critically on and at the same time to write about the university's disciplinary structures" (155). And in a final footnote, Bawarshi cautions that he intends his pedagogy not to promote "*assimilation* into genred sites of action" but to promote "critical understanding and participation," finding that students develop "the desire to change" genres as they "begin to uncover the desires, subjectivities, and activities embedded in a genre's rhetorical conventions" (185, n. 6, emphasis added). Thus, in these calls Bawarshi identifies the work of his students and the FYW course not as preparatory for but contributing to the work of academic genres, in alignment with James Slevin's call for an "interpretive pedagogy" for first-year composition in which students and teachers work "collaboratively . . . to interpret educational practices and to work for educational reform" (2001, 2).

For his part, Trimbur cautions that while it is not possible to "get out of the relations of *in loco parentis* that encompass the work of teaching writing" (2000, 194), he does not want to suggest "that there is *no* social good that comes from the higher learning, advanced research, and the specialized practices and vocabularies of the disciplines and professions," as opposed to more widely circulating writing (212). That is, Trimbur recognizes that while, on the one hand, academic writing, by students or "professionals," remains, well, academic writing, it is also the case that there may well be "social good" to works not recognized by the dominant culture as having such value.

CHALLENGES IN RE-VALUING STUDENT WRITING: WORKING FYC

I see these tensions pointing to three challenges. First, there is the challenge of seeing past the official duties assigned by the dominant to particular sites to the full range of work that might be accomplished at those sites. Second, there is the challenge of not allowing the exchange value ordinarily assigned the work conducted at those sites to occlude from view the potential use values to be realized from that work. And third, there is the challenge of recognizing that the work accomplished at those sites is not contained by or in the textual forms by which that work ordinarily is seen as circulating—that is to say, the challenge of not fetishizing the textual form of writing, student or otherwise. In suggesting that FYW students might, in fact, not simply acquire agility with the genres other academic disciplines demand but also critique these, Bawarshi (2003) resists the purely preparatory role the dominant assigns to the site of FYW. In calling attention to the "social good" that might arise from work the dominant might ordinarily deride as "merely academic," Trimbur (2000) rejects both mistaking the ordinary exchange value of academic writing for its potential use value, and calculations of the value of work purely in terms of the circulation of particular textual forms. The textual forms and modes of circulation of "higher learning, advanced research, and the specialized practices and vocabularies of the disciplines and professions" do not in themselves fully determine the work these might accomplish (212).

These tensions point to both the possibilities and the difficulties of treating student writing as something more and other than simple (intransitive) "performance." On the one hand, both students and instructors in FYC courses must contend with the *in loco parentis* dynamics and strictly "preparatory" role assigned to FYC arising from the FYC requirement itself (often as a prerequisite to other courses and to graduation) and the official institutional demands for assigning of credit and merit in the form of grades, but also with the individual and institutional histories of (low) expectations for the students and the writing that students in such settings are assigned to produce (from, e.g., past schooling and the mass media, including training in writing five-paragraph themes and inculcated beliefs about what constitutes "good" and "correct" writing). It is against all these that we might pursue work by students that is "critical" (in the senses both of engaging in critique and of being significant) and that might bring social good.

But what would this mean in practice? Dominant cultural definitions of what might constitute critical work by student writers would head us toward the tactics discussed above: moving students, and/or their writing, outside the location of FYC, and/or change the kind of writing they are asked to engage in from more academically conventional forms to those with recognizable currency in the public sphere. At best, this leaves the site of FYC, and its inhabitants, to be sites of precursion to and for this other kind of writing. As an alternative, I would argue for having FYC students and teachers use the site of FYC to explore the potential uses of writing

- whose range of circulation is restricted to participants of the FYC site itself,

- that takes the form, often enough, of readings of other texts familiar to others at the site, and

- that is produced within the confines of the *in loco parentis* relations characteristic of FYC.

The course design I have in mind here would do all these in open acknowledgement and investigation of these material conditions. In other words, we can have students address the material conditions of the FYC site and FYC student writing, not as dooming any projects to be pursued there, but as working conditions to be *worked* by teachers and students both: to be put to use, that is, despite the low exchange value ordinarily assigned to activities conducted in such conditions. The alternative, in fact, is spurious in its literal im-materiality: to assume either that any other kind of writing can or does take place free from social, institutional, and historical circumstances, or that student writing is somehow removed from these—that students, their writing, and the first-year writing courses where they are found are somehow imaginary. But, as Charles Bazerman has wryly observed, "If we start analyzing the first-year writing course[,] we find it is a very real place" (1995b, 254).

Confronting this material reality involves overcoming two ideological challenges. First, while, as Trimbur acknowledges (2000), there is no escaping the *in loco parentis*, intimate domestic character of social relations obtaining in the FYC course, we need to recognize that this character does not entirely determine those relations or the work produced there. Counter to what is implied by the invocation, familiar to anyone moderately steeped in composition scholarship and teacher-corridor talk, that "the teacher, after all, has the power of the grade," such power does not, in fact, eliminate all possible value or authenticity to student writing and the kinds of social relations that might obtain in an FYC course. There are two problematic assumptions to claiming otherwise. On the one hand, there is the assumption that the *in loco parentis* situation itself obtains only within the rarefied sphere of the academy, rather than being a characteristic of all writing. But it is manifestly the case that display, after all, or the desire to display and "perform" for evaluation, operates in virtually all writing, in and outside the academy. On the other hand, despite *in loco parentis*, good work can be accomplished. Students, like the rest of us, can accomplish useful work *despite* the fact that doing so might earn them good grades, just as academics can produce useful writing that gets published despite the fact that publications inevitably add lines to their vitas, and just as professional writers can produce valuable books despite the fact that doing so adds to their incomes (Brandt 2009). To think otherwise is to assume that a commodity's exchange value negates any possible use value it might have.

The notion that the academic setting of FYC restricts the value of what it is possible for students to accomplish in their writing points to a second challenge teachers face in attempting to engage their students in useful work as FYC students: the sense that conventionally academic writing of the sort frequently assigned in FYC courses is by definition of no "real" value (signaled by its denigration as being "merely 'academic'"). There is a long history of compositionists responding to academic institutions' denigration of composition by returning the favor and denigrating academic work. This leads to valorizing writing that is recognizably non-academic in its formal conventions and to denigrating the value of writing assignments that have students take on conventional tasks, such as producing readings of published texts (France 1993).

But such responses fetishize particular forms or genres for the work accomplished in their production. Those who valorize writing recognizably nonacademic in its formal conventions (and who doubt the value of writing conforming to academic formal conventions) confuse the work of those involved in the writing with the forms themselves: it is only by doing so that they can conclude that changing the forms will by itself change the value of the work the writing accomplishes. Likewise, those who reject the value of student work taking the form of "readings" accept the dominant's denial of the contributions that the labor of reading makes to the production of the use value of writing by assuming instead that the value of writing resides in the textual commodity. Alan France (1993), for example, complains that pedagogies asking students to be "textual critics" place students in a "discursive position . . . divorced from political praxis, or in terms of traditional rhetorical education, from democratic agency in the public forum," a position he derides as "no more politically enabling than the [role of] experiential soothsayer," a role he sees expressivist pedagogies assigning to students (594, 602). Ironically, however, such arguments accede to the dominant's seizure of what constitutes political praxis and democratic agency. For they reproduce what Michel de Certeau (1984) calls the "ideology of consumption-as-a-receptacle" which "distinguishes and privileges authors, educators, revolutionaries, in a word, 'producers,' in contrast with those who do not produce [e.g., readers]" by assuming that "[t]o write is to produce the text; to read is to receive it from someone else without putting one's own mark on it, without remaking it" (167, 169). Conversely, we may treat the reading students "perform" (in their student writing) as in fact an activity of remaking the text and so, in effect, an engagement in production. However limited the circulation of that production, it ultimately has effects on the noetic economy, just as the readings professional academics perform of data, phenomena, and other texts have effects on the culture at large, despite the tenuous and distanciated relation of those effects to the site of their immediate production.

The standard rebuttal to claims that student readings have significance takes two forms. First, it is said that these readings do not circulate beyond the FYC classroom. This argument locates the work of reading only in the textual commodities students produce, as if the students themselves, with their complicated consciousnesses, never leave the classroom. Moreover, it assumes a limited notion of productive forces, forgetting what Raymond Williams reminds us is Marx's "central notion of productive forces, in which . . . the most important thing a worker ever produces is himself, himself in the fact of that kind of labour" (1980, 35). Readings participate in just such production, hence the concern with the particular kinds of consciousness and social relations that particular ways of reading and writing may encourage the production of. Second, it is argued that student readings do not, in fact, deserve to circulate because students, especially FYC students, have little to say worth broad circulation. After all, it is argued, there is a difference between the average FYC student and recognized "authors" that merits distinguishing the former from the latter. Note, however, that this rebuttal, in line with the first, aligns itself with a view of the production of knowledge that denies its sociality, locating production strictly with individuals ("authors") and at a point discrete from circulation and consumption. This denies the role social relations and conditions play in knowledge production, circulation, and consumption simultaneously. Conversely, we may say that (1) even those writers recognized as "authors" do not produce, by themselves alone, what merits circulation (and indeed, many produce plenty that arguably does not merit it); (2) even when students might appear to rehearse already existing knowledge, that rehearsal contributes to the (re)production of that knowledge, effectively re-making it through rehearsal; and (3) similarly, particularly by virtue of not being yet effectively disciplined academically, students are well positioned to contribute to the remaking of knowledge through their reading-reworking of representations of it. In other words, this rebuttal fails to recognize the interdependent relationship between the production of knowledge and its consumption and distribution and, concomitantly, its social character.

Paradoxically, that same failure to recognize the social character of knowledge production manifests itself in teachers' efforts to encourage and honor students' potential to contribute to knowledge. I have in mind here standard advice to writing teachers and tutors that in their comments and suggestions, they should honor students' own purposes and ideas in their writing, however inchoate these may appear to be, and be wary of imposing their own ideas on their students. But while it seems appropriate to avoid transforming the activity of student writing into the equivalent of taking dictation, acknowledging the social character of "authorship" of knowledge requires that we acknowledge specifically the role that teachers and tutors (as well as peers and the culture at large) must inevitably play in shaping the knowledge, and knowing, produced in and through student writing.

This does not mean teachers should tell students what to think, but it does mean they can play a more legitimate role as readers—in the de Certeauian sense discussed above—of student writing by adopting that stance. That is, they can recognize, and encourage students to recognize, that teachers' readings do, in fact, remake what students say in the process of reading (and commenting on) the students' writing (and vice versa). When, for example, I suggest alternative perspectives to my students in response to their texts, it is true I may run the risk of overwriting their texts (thereby limiting the knowledge produced, as editors sometimes do). But it is also possible that I can thereby contribute more responsibly to our inevitable collaboration in the production of knowledge, in the same way that teams of investigators collaborate in the production of academic knowledge (marked in science journals by the lengthy number of designated authors of single articles). The difficulty here is resisting, and helping students to resist, sliding from such collaboration into mere "performance" whereby the students take my suggestions as is, without, in turn, reworking them in revising their texts in response. This is a difficulty that any teacher faces in making comments, written or spoken, on student work. It is a problem not simply of the *in loco parentis* situation but of the genre of such comments and of collaboration in general. But (fortunately) it is also the case that even the most ardent student efforts to engage in such mere "performance" will inevitably rework what is taken, as teachers hoping to "improve" their students' texts discover (sometimes to their dismay).

At least some of the course practices aligned with "social-epistemic" approaches to the teaching of composition are conducive to valuing the work of student writing as academic, in the best sense of that word

(Berlin 1989; Rankin 1990). These include (1) sequencing assignments to give students chances and directions for building, and building on by revising, the knowledge they (re)produce in their writing, (2) discussing and commenting on student writing in terms of the kind of (re)working of knowledge it accomplishes, and the strategies by which such reworking is accomplished, and (3) making all practices with student and other writing—including how it is produced, circulated, discussed, read, and commented on by both peers and teachers—the subject of inquiry for the ways they might be taken up that would be more productive of learning and knowledge. Even the significance of the practice of restricting the circulation of students' writing to the course, rather than being treated as a settled matter, can itself be the subject of inquiry for what that circulation might allow for as well as disallow.

David Bartholomae and Anthony Petrosky's account of a course for "basic" writing students in *Facts, Artifacts, Counterfacts* illustrates some of these practices (1986). Revised versions of some of the students' writings are gathered, edited, and published to become one of the primary texts for student analysis. That text circulates only within the confines of the course. However, contrary to conventional FYC practice, its contents are analyzed not for whether they conform to generic conventions of, say, Standard Written English but for what they contribute to knowledge about the course subject of adolescent growth and change (on this distinction in the reading of student writing, see Salvatori and Donahue in this volume). Other published writings are discussed only in terms of the meanings students are able to make of them in their writing about them. Student writing and what it accomplishes are not sentimentalized; instead, students come to see the ways in which, at least initially, their own knowledge is circumscribed by the ways their writing simply reproduces conventional discourse, and it is revised not to mask this reproduction but to break from it, often by explicit acknowledgment of the writer's inscription by it. More generally, the course positions those students officially occupying the extreme margins of the academy—basic writing students—in a role akin to graduate students in producing knowledge and examining the means of its production.

Beyond such features of course design, I will mention just two other tactics teachers have devised to encourage the valuing of student work as academic:

- incorporating into individual assignments and assignment sequences occasions for students to respond dialogically to the contributions of others, and asking students to develop ways by which they can cite from each others' work in doing so (and investigating why conventions for such citations are not readily available in handbooks)

- treating course "authorized" texts, including textbook chapters, teachers' written comments, and assignments (a.k.a. "prompts") as subject to questioning to render the inevitable reworking of such texts manifest and hence subject to revision (Dryer 2008, Malcolm 2008)

Through these kinds of gestures, teachers can help students accomplish more in their writing than the mere display of knowledge by acknowledging the students' engagement in the reworking of knowledge through the material social practices of their writing. Other contributors to this volume offer additional, and more detailed, curricular and pedagogical strategies by which the work of student writing is both acknowledged and supported. While contributors' specific strategies and arguments for them are understandably, necessarily, and rightly varied, they are united in aiming to treat student texts as sites for students' and teachers' collaborative engagement in legitimate academic inquiry: as real writing, not "notwriting." Thus the contributors themselves forward such work by reworking the site of first-year writing to better, more productive ends.

The admittedly academic sphere of FYC—domestic, intimate, rarefied—need not preclude the accomplishment of legitimate work there. Instead, the material conditions of that site—a regular time and space for a small number of colleagues to meet, read and reread common texts; to share and work on their writings and rewritings in response to the readings and their own writings; to have opportunities to do library research—make possible certain kinds of work that can contribute to the revision, in the process of reproduction, of society and knowledge: work that dominant culture tends to denigrate as un-useful, as merely academic, even as unreal, because of its distance from writing, and writers, conventionally recognized as useful and real. But teachers need not yield to such denigrating valuations of their work and the work of their students. Instead, they can pursue the potential for resistance afforded by the marginal material and institutional position and precursory role dominant culture has assigned FYC by exploring, with their students, the academic use of student writing.

2

REVEALING OUR VALUES
Reading Student Texts with Colleagues in High School and College

Nicole B. Wallack
Columbia University

I guess I would like to ask a broad cross section of college professors what they are actually looking for [in academic writing]. . . . I remember that one of my wife's professors—one whom she admired greatly—told her class to "forget everything they learned in high school," which is of course pretty disheartening. It's also a ludicrously small sample size, though, which is why I guess I want to know if what I'm teaching actually helps kids at the next level.

High-school teacher

Why do you [high-school teachers] teach things that are NOT true? Why do you put ideas in their heads that will limit [students'] thinking rather than enhance [it]?

College teacher

Scholars in composition and writing studies are demonstrating a growing interest in how students transfer what they learn about writing from one educational setting to another. Recent longitudinal studies examine the degree to which students apply knowledge and skills from first-year composition classes to their upper-level, discipline-based courses (Beaufort 2007; Bergmann and Zepernick 2007; Sommers 2008; Wardle 2007). However, in professional development workshops for teachers, we tend to overlook one of the most fraught educational territories: where our expectations for high-school student writing meet those for college writing. In this essay I argue not only that there is a need to fill this gap in the data, but also a need to consider what happens to teachers across educational levels in its absence: we invent. We assume what our colleagues want on either side of the divide, what they value, and what they teach. We mythologize, and myths tend to invoke demons as well as heroes. We "triangulate" (in the parlance of psychology) with our students against a common foil: high-school teachers sometimes explain that students need to avoid the first person in order to satisfy their future college teachers; college teachers sometimes tell their students that their high-school teachers should not have only taught them to write five-paragraph essays.

I hope some playful hyperbole does not obscure a genuine problem and a serious proposition I am trying to name. Without considerable effort to bridge educational levels, high-school teachers will prepare students to write and read in ways that many college faculty do not value. At the same time, college teachers will miss opportunities to reinforce and build on writing and reading habits of mind and practice that students learned from their middle- and high-school teachers. Most of us know all too well what it feels like to be held accountable for our students' lack of preparation for The Future, whatever that means, and so we might try to conserve the rhetoric of blame for when and where we really need it. I propose that the relatively simple act of reading student writing with colleagues across educational levels can help us name and analyze our assumptions about one another's teaching priorities. Fostering these professional encounters can help teachers close gaps in our knowledge, identify our blind spots, and improve how we teach students to write and read.

In the remainder of this essay, I demonstrate how the problem I have named arises in professional development workshops for teachers at Bard College's Institute for Writing and Thinking (IWT). I suggest how we can work productively in these collaborative workshops to read student writing across educational levels, and to identify where our expectations for academic writing coincide and conflict with our colleagues who work at different educational levels. I draw from the results of surveys I conducted of IWT workshop participants in the summer of 2008, and report briefly on the data they provide about teachers' expectations and practices for writing in high school and college. Finally, I offer some thoughts about directions for future research in this area, and consider both the social and educational benefits of pursuing it.

ENCOUNTERING STUDENT TEXTS WITH COLLEAGUES: A WORKSHOP

Bard College's Institute for Writing and Thinking was established in 1981 by Peter Elbow and Paul Connelly to provide teachers across disciplines and educational levels with professional development workshops and conferences that can help them to more fully integrate writing into their lives inside and outside the classroom. The Institute (IWT) continues to realize this mission both on the Bard campus and on site at middle schools, high schools, and colleges. Teachers come to the Institute's workshops from across the United States and abroad in order to work in a professional development setting that emphasizes experiential rather than didactic approaches to teaching writing. The workshops vary in length from one to seven days long, and participants meet for three or four ninety-minute workshops a day. It is an immersion experience for all concerned.

On workshop evaluations, participants often mention how illuminating and pleasurable it is for them to be able to write and to think about how to teach writing with a diverse group of colleagues. Disciplinary differences create one kind of obvious meaningful difference among teachers, but often participants are equally surprised by how varied their colleagues' notions of writing can be within their disciplines, particularly across grade levels. Middle-school, high-school, and college English teachers note that they are struck by how their expectations, values, and requirements for student writing intersect and diverge with those of other English teachers. These moments of surprise—and opportunity—arise most vividly and explicitly when working with student texts. For this reason, I incorporate at least one ninety-minute session in which participants bring their own students' writing to explore with the group.

Here is an overview of the workshop process:

- Ask participants to bring texts with them.
- Select a text or two for the whole group to work with (and reproduce it).

  Provide guidance for reading the text (individually and collaboratively).
- Provide a framework for analyzing our discussion of the text.

Ask Teachers to Bring Student Texts with Them to the Workshop

I ask teachers who attend the workshop to bring a copy of a student text they would like to work with. Depending on the focus of the workshop, I might either invite them to choose a text that represents something particularly strong and compelling to them, or a text that reflects what an average student is able to do on a particular assignment. Whichever text they choose, it should be one that interests them. I discourage teachers from bringing very troubling or problematic student texts. Certainly there are times when working with such texts is important, but especially when teachers work in mixed groups, they can get caught up in the reading challenges created by struggling student texts. Although it is important for teachers to have choice about the degree to which they share their students' writing with colleagues, I want to make sure they are prepared for the possibility that it will be read by the whole group—with their permission.

Select a Text or Two for the Whole Group to Work with

Once teachers arrive at the workshop, I gather the texts and read through them for one or two samples to work with. Generally speaking, I look for a student text that fulfills the following criteria:

> *Format and length:* Typed; will take no more than fifteen minutes to read in its entirety (i.e., in the 1000–1200 word range). Essays without any comments or grades from the teacher are preferable.
>
> *Genre:* Nonfiction prose; a piece of expository writing; an essay or an academic paper such as observation notes with discussion sections.
>
> *Qualities:* The writer is able to, or *attempts to*
>
> - pursue an argument of some kind, develop a thesis, or explore an idea
>
> - present, analyze, and reflect on sources, particularly written ones, and cite them
>
> - follow structural, syntactical, and grammatical conventions of standard written English.

With the criteria in mind, it is not difficult to read through seven to ten student papers very quickly and make a suitable choice within fifteen minutes. However, it also can be useful to have more time to review the texts; in that case, I might ask participants to email copies to me in advance. When I choose this option, I offer some explanation for how the text will be used. It is important to reassure participants that the group is not going to be critiquing anyone's assignment design. To pro-tect the student writer, I invite the teacher to create a pseudonym for him or her, and I remove all other information that might identify the student. Although the group comments on the student's work, the aim is not to identify the particular student's strengths and weaknesses, but rather to help participants to name, explain, and test their own expecta-tions and values for student writing.

Provide Guidance tor Reading the Text (Individually and Collaboratively)

I give the group ten to fifteen minutes to read through the student text, marking its strengths and weaknesses. A "strength" is any textual feature that demonstrates what the student knows how to do, reflects some degree of purposefulness and control, or indicates that the writer is attempting something difficult (e.g., offering a counterargument, or defining a complex key term). A "weakness" may certainly be an error, but it also might be something that is missing from the text locally or as a whole. Usually, I ask participants to think of weaknesses as those aspects of student writing that give us clues about what the student writer prob-ably needs to learn how to do next.

I advise participants not to spend a great deal of energy trying to imagine what the teacher had in mind for this assignment or whether the student has fulfilled it. I offer this advice because students often misperceive their teachers' expectations for writing assignments (see Anson, Davis, and Vilhotti in this volume for a strategy to help remedy those misperceptions). In the workshop I am describing here, it is more important for participants to focus not on what they guess about the teacher's expectations but on what they can see in the student's writing.

After we read and mark the text, we gather some of the strengths and weaknesses on a board in two columns. I ask for strengths alone first, without caveats, and then invite participants to add weaknesses to the list after the strengths side of the board is quite full. Sometimes a strength is paired with a weakness, but just as often, once it is named as a strength, teachers can leave an issue without qualifying it later on. Figure 2.1 offers an example of the kind of chart we generate.

After we have assembled these lists, I ask teachers to identify one or two strengths and weaknesses they would want to focus on that would not only help the student improve his or her performance on the partic ular paper we are reading, but would also make a qualitative difference

Strengths (what student can do)	Weaknesses (what student needs to learn next)
sense of voice	moves between registers and pronouns (third and first person)
good questions (genuine, not just rhetorical)	omits signal phrases for many quotations (dropped in) or uses generic verbs, such as "writes," "says," "talks about"
chooses apt quotations	
provides context for quotations	
sentence-level correctness	tends not to analyze quotations
makes use of powerful concepts derived from readings	quotes in places where paraphrase would be more appropriate
thesis is more than a claim of fact	thesis comes at the end of the paper
gestures towards transitions between most paragraphs	too many questions (some could be claims)
title reflects/includes key concepts from the paper	repetitiveness
MLA citation formatting consistent	does not define key terms

Figure 2.1. Sample chart of strengths and weaknesses.

to the student's future writing. Teachers jot notes for a few moments to say what they have selected as the most important issues to work on and why. I also ask them to hypothesize about why the student may be strong in the area(s) they have chosen, and may need to learn in the others.

Provide a Framework for Analyzing Our Discussion of the Text

In terms of naming our values, the workshop comes to fruition at this moment and in the discussion that follows the individual writing, when the participants share their diagnoses and name their priorities about working with the student and the text. Impromptu assessment of student writing is a common feature of professional development workshops, so participants usually find it both easy and pleasurable to draw on their expertise. However, it is often much more difficult for teachers to offer their *hypotheses* about why the student may be demonstrating the particular strengths and weaknesses they have identified. More telling, too. In these conversations, both high-school and college teachers tend to ascribe too much (or not enough) agency to the student writer, to the student's writing teachers, to the assignment, and to the student's writing context. Therefore, I have started to ask for one or two teachers to take notes during these discussions in which they try to keep track of our hypotheses as close to verbatim as they can make them. As a final writing prompt for this workshop, I ask the scribes to read our hypotheses back to the group, and we "believe and doubt" the most compelling or provocative hypothesis that we heard about the student text during the workshop (on "believing and doubting," see Elbow 1973).

Up to this point, I have described a problem I have detected in working with high- school and college teachers when they read student writing together. I have also sketched the basic outline and rationale for a workshop in which teachers read student texts together in order to name what they value. Against this backdrop I offer a few specific insights gleaned from the research that emerged as I sought to examine formally teachers' attitudes and myth making about their colleagues' approaches to teaching writing.

The impetus for my research into teachers' expectations and values about student writing across disciplines and education levels has been shaped by listening to exchanges among workshop participants. As they voice their hypotheses during this workshop, teachers often move quickly from trying to name the intellectual and formal challenges that might have prompted the student's performance to giving those issues not just an individual cause (one teacher's idiosyncratic desires, one student's individual struggles and successes), but a collective or even systemic one. That is, teachers generate relatively negative pedagogical and/or sociological myths about their colleagues' assumptions and values for writing.

In one recent workshop, for example, we analyzed an essay from a student in a first-year composition course that featured a close reading of a novel by Zora Neal Hurston. Almost immediately, participants noticed that the writer appeared to be employing a five-paragraph argumentative structure, which both helped her to organize her ideas and hampered her from fully developing the compelling claims with which she concluded her essay. Some of the teachers hypothesized that the student learned the form in high school and was continuing to apply this approach in her early attempts at college writing.

In the ensuing conversation the participants began to articulate other, more problematic hypotheses. Some of the college teachers posited that because students learn *only* the five-paragraph essay in high school, they are all rule-bound, inflexible writers who need to "unlearn" the form in college ("they" in this instance could refer to both high-school students and their teachers). Reasonably, the high-school and middle-school teachers around the table protested, letting their college colleagues know that their own practice was not exclusively devoted to teaching the five-paragraph form. Then it was the high-school teachers' turn to voice their assumptions. One suggested that she taught the five-paragraph form because she was trying to get students to learn how to "prove a thesis," which is what she believed college teachers wanted. A college teacher quipped, "Not the kind of thesis this student is writing," which drew some appreciative laughter all around the table. Again, the problem was that the high-school teachers—all thoughtful, dedicated veterans of the profession—did not really know what their colleagues in college settings expected from a thesis or how it differed from the form of thesis they were used to teaching.

I ended this particular workshop asking the teachers to pair up with a colleague from another educational level and design two exercises for the student writer we had read: one to help the student do more of what she needed to be successful in high school, another to help her fulfill the college teacher's expectations. It was fine with me if those values were the same, but I also wanted to give the teachers room to differentiate those goals given their own teaching contexts.

DIRECTIONS FOR FUTURE STUDIES AND INITIATIVES

There is only so much work teachers can accomplish together in a single professional development context, even with fruitful questions to pursue. Therefore, in the summer of 2008, I invited 700 teachers who had all participated in workshops at Bard's IWT to take one of two possible online surveys—one designed for high-school teachers, the other for college teachers. Fifty-five high-school and thirty-seven college teachers responded to the invitation. Although I cannot discuss all of my findings here, three are worth raising in this discussion:

- High-school and college teachers largely agree about what aspects of writing are most important for success in college: analysis, argument, clarity, evidence, and reflection.

- High-school and college teachers claim to teach their students strikingly similar things in their writing classes: critical thinking; devising theses or arguments; choosing, evaluating, and "working with" evidence; revision and other writing processes.

- High-school and college teachers express a desire to know more about what their colleagues "on the other side" of the educational divide are teaching students about writing. College teachers tend to speculate more about why and how their high-school colleagues teach. High-school teachers tend to ask more questions about their college colleagues' expectations for incoming students' writing.

Across all of the questions, assumptions, pleas, complaints, and corrections they voiced in this survey, high-school and college teachers clearly signal that they know less than they need (and want) to know about what their colleagues expect and value. However, the degree to which they already agree on what is fundamentally important when teaching students to write in academic contexts suggests we could all be teaching much more purposefully than we do right now. Even though there are opportunities for high-school and college teachers to work with one another at conferences through our professional organizations, we do not do so very often. When we do have these opportunities, a college teacher typically takes on the role of the expert who comes to work with high-school teachers during inservice days.

In some school districts, administrators are attempting to alter that paradigm. For the past eleven years, the English department at Suffolk County Community College in Brentwood, New York, has invited high-school teachers from surrounding school districts to fulfill some of their inservice training obligations by participating alongside Suffolk faculty in writing-across-the-curriculum workshops. These workshops feature student writing from both the college and the high schools, and since many teachers have returned to the workshop over time, the group has been able to learn about one another's expectations and apply these insights as they plan their curricula.

Teachers in high school and college do attempt to gather data on their own about their students' writing experiences. Some college teachers of writing ask students to bring papers from high school into their first week of class, and some high-school teachers bring college assignments into their high-school courses. These exercises can provide a glimpse over the educational divide, and help us determine whether the work we are doing has any relationship to what is happening at the other level. Writing studies and composition scholars are beginning to examine this area more closely. Patrick Sullivan and Howard Tinberg's collection (2006) explores what "counts" as college-level writing from the perspective of high-school and college teachers as well as students. Stephen Acker and Kay Halasek (2008) report on the results of a collaborative effort by Ohio State University and two high schools to read and evaluate student writing using digital portfolios (ePortfolios); students received feedback from high-school and college teachers on the same pieces of writing (2). Although the primary focus for their study was to determine whether using ePortfolios improved students' writing, the study underscores that both high-school and college writing faculty benefit from working collaboratively (10).

The effects of dual-credit English courses for high school are also garnering some scholarly attention. Kara Taczak and William Thelin (2009) report on the mixed success for fourteen- and fifteen-year-old students in a dual-credit program in the Midwest. However, without more formalized initiatives at schools, in school districts, or even at the federal level to foster collaboration (with incentives for both college faculty and high-school teachers, such as service points for college teachers and inservice credit for high-school teachers), we are likely to continue groping in the dark.

Fundamentally, we must value writing in high school enough for its own sake to make it worth building on in college. Collectively, we teachers, parents, administrators, and students do not have a strong sense what writing is really for in high school right now—aside from a very imperfect form of standardized assessment. Faculty within or across departments in high schools should have time to work with their colleagues to answer this question: what roles does (and should) writing play in the curriculum? Portfolio initiatives can offer one method for teachers to gather data about the writing students are already doing. Teachers will be more likely to pursue such initiatives if schools foster teachers' collaborations with one another as readers and responders to student writing. Were departments to commit to making student writing the centerpiece of faculty meetings and inservice days for one year, teachers and administrators would have a rich set of data with which to refine and revise curricula. More important, faculty would gain profound insights into how their own values influence their reading of student writing, and they could become more reflective and efficient responders to student work.

At the college level, faculty, administrators, and students would benefit from doing similar work together. In the first chapter of this book, Bruce Horner makes a strong case for reclaiming students' work in their first-year composition courses as "real writing." Beyond first-year courses, college faculty need to know more about what we ask of students as writers in two or four years, particularly if we would like students to be better prepared for their transition from high school.

Writing-across-the-curriculum and writing-in-the-disciplines programs certainly fulfill some of these goals. Perhaps more simply, were every college department to publish an online collection of excellent student writing, students and faculty could assess what students know how to do and what they need to learn. Writing programs and writing centers can support departments as they begin this work.

Finally, it is worthwhile to consider the role of writing-based teaching in schools of education, and in other areas of graduate student education. If—as it seems—there is a discrepancy between what teachers want from student writing and what we teach, then it is likely we are not training teachers at all levels to incorporate writing in rich ways into their daily teaching in high school and college.

Work among colleagues inside our institutions is a crucial part of being able to collaborate with colleagues across education levels with a clearer sense of our own goals. Encountering our students' work with colleagues from across the educational divide between high school and college can help us all learn how to traverse these borderlands more surely, and to teach our collective group of students the satisfactions of a writing life from kindergarten through college.

3

"WHAT DO *WE* WANT IN THIS PAPER?"

Generating Criteria Collectively

Chris M. Anson
North Carolina State University

Matthew Davis
Florida State University

Domenica Vilhotti
Mastery Charter School

When students are asked to read and discuss each others' drafts in progress or review and revise their own drafts, they often work in a rhetorical vacuum, not really knowing what makes a successful response and guessing at whatever (often implicit or unexplained) criteria the instructor will use to judge their papers. Even when students use revision prompts or guides, or descriptive criteria against which they are supposed to judge their developing texts, they usually have little opportunity to understand, work with, or internalize those criteria. Instead, they continue to labor under a trial-and-error model of learning that fails to engage them fully in the process of critically considering their structural, rhetorical, informational, and linguistic choices.

In this essay, we describe a method designed to help students articulate and internalize readers' expectations for their assigned writing. This method, which resembles dynamic criteria mapping (Broad 2003) on a student level, involves the collective creation of criteria based on what we call "interestingly problematic" student drafts responding to the same assignment. Because it engages the students themselves in formulating the standards for the texts they will produce, it reflects a constructivist model of teaching and learning (see Honebein 1996; Jonassen 1991; N. Nelson 2001). After describing and rationalizing the general approach, we provide examples—from sections of first-year composition courses and from a graduate course on teaching writing—that show students' collective development of criteria from sample student texts.

CREATING CRITERIA FROM SAMPLE STUDENT TEXTS

It is almost impossible to write something meaningful for other readers without having a mental map of socially constructed expectations that includes choices of appropriate structure, lexis, persona or authorial representation, and a host of other features. In many academic settings, students must derive the standards for successful performances of complex tasks inductively, using both explicit and implicit cues embedded in a writing assignment, a teacher's oral explanations and admonitions, and the course syllabus, readings, and other sources of information. For developing writers enrolled in courses taught by instructors who have highly idiosyncratic instructional preferences, this process of figuring out expectations presents a serious challenge, and the resulting papers often end up displaying guesswork ("Is this what you wanted?") more than they reflect an understanding of the broader rhetorical, stylistic, structural, and other conventions associated with the genre they are practicing (see Anson 2007).

Students bring into their writing courses prior knowledge of how certain texts work, so that when they write familiar genres, they can use memory to guide many of their decisions. Most students' experiences with narrative, for example, give them a sense of what "makes a good one" without access to actual narratives. But when they are asked to write less familiar kinds of academic texts, or unique varieties of familiar texts, they often work in an experiential void. To help students explore, negotiate, and articulate the standards that define a successful response to a writing task, we use a process focusing on the drafts of previous students who responded to the same task. The general process, from which each of us has developed individual variations described below, is quite simple.

- *Instructor provides the writing assignment.* Students consider a fully articulated writing assignment or project, which will usually include information about its genre or type of writing and its goals, content, length, use of sources, and the like.

- *Instructor distributes "interestingly problematic" student draft(s).* Usually before they have written a full rough draft, the students are given one or more student papers or sections of papers responding to the same assignment in a previous course. (We recommend collecting permission forms and keeping archives of papers for future use; see Anderson and McKee's essay in this volume.) Such drafts should represent neither stellar nor dreadful responses; rather, they should be "interestingly problematic" in order to engage students in a discussion of both obvious and more subtle issues and concerns. Carefully chosen, they offer deviations from what might be expected in a good response as well as features that are effective. For most formal assignments, it's important that students spend time working through the papers carefully, so we recommend that they be read and analyzed beforehand, as homework that is counted in some way, even informally using simple checkmarks. Prompts for analysis and response can be given to students so they focus on particular features of the drafts, and these can be tied to evidence of certain learning goals or processes embedded into the assignment.

- *Students individually analyze draft(s).* Individually, students analyze the papers and reach conclusions about what specific features work or don't work, what choices are problematic or successful, what sentences or sections "flow" or "read badly," and so on.

- *Students collectively (with or without instructor) derive principles and criteria.* In some form (via blog, class discussion, small-group work, worksheet, etc.), students derive principles, criteria, or generalizations from their specific impressions, a process that requires significant orchestration and instructional intervention.

- *Instructor publishes final criteria for students to use.* After continued work on the criteria, the instructor publishes them in final form (as a rubric, scale, checklist, or set of descriptive standards). The criteria can then be used formatively by the students as they draft, discuss, and revise their responses to the assignment, and summatively by the teacher when grading students' work.

THREE APPLICATIONS

To demonstrate ways in which the principles of student-generated criteria can be adapted to specific courses, we offer three examples, two from standard first-year composition courses and one from a graduate-level course for new teachers of writing.

Example 1: A Guided, Small-Group Approach to Student-Generated Rubrics

To help her first-year composition students take ownership of the traits of good writing, Domenica Vilhotti employs a highly structured, small-group approach to the creation of student-generated rubrics. The activity guides students to analyze and critique sections of sample student papers, such as the introduction or body paragraphs. Using key words previously studied in class, such as *coherence, provable,* and *specific,* each group creates standards for its assigned paper section.

Domenica begins by carefully selecting interestingly problematic, yet quite competent sections of student papers. Before students enter the class, tables or groups of desks have been assembled and labeled to serve as stations representing each major paper section. Because Domenica focuses on the fundamentals of essay structure in her first few assignments, typical stations might be labeled Introduction, Analysis (body of the paper), Conclusion, and Overall Presentation. Domenica stocks each station with several different appropriate excerpts for groups to investigate, such as four interestingly problematic student conclusions. Each station is also supplied a blank rubric that Domenica has already structured based on the four prefabricated categories.

As students arrive, they are directed to the stations in groups of three. It is essential to keep group size small to maximize each student's contribution, although this may require that some stations have the same focus. Domenica explains the flow of the activity and emphasizes the group norms of paper critique, such as academic distance, evidence-based commentary, and substantive criticism with a focus on revision.

After Domenica's briefing, the groups begin reading and critiquing their paper excerpts. Note that while the categories Introduction, Analysis, Conclusion, and Overall Presentation may seem constricting, they are accessible the first time students encounter this activity. To ensure that students consider higher-order concepts such as audience, structure, or linguistic choice, Domenica provides keywords within the categories (see fig. 3.1 below for an example).

Stations are given approximately ten minutes to read aloud, discuss, and analyze the sample student documents. Alternatively, they may be more comfortable reading the documents silently, commenting in the margins or via track changes, and then regrouping to discuss. Students mark elements of their sections that "sound good" or "feel awkward." If possible, they should articulate why something is powerful or ineffective, but if they cannot, the next step in the activity provides further guidance to aid their articulation.

After all group members have been given a chance to read and analyze several of the student excerpts, they collaboratively list the characteristics of effective writing in their assigned category. Group members are encouraged to make full use of the class Web site and all previous notes, handouts, and textbook readings. Students in Domenica's classes, for example, repeatedly return to the essay's assignment sheet, their handout on effective topic sentences and thesis statements, and their notes on paragraph development and use of evidence.

Because Domenica chooses to teach longer classes, she has the student groups rotate clockwise to the next station. Based on their analysis and discussion of the samples, the new groups attempt to revise or add information to the first group's completed rubric section, which has been left at the station. When the entire activity ends, each group submits to Domenica (by email or hard copy) the rubric created at their station so she can compile all of them into a complete rubric for the paper. In debriefing the activity, Domenica asks the class to reflect on what they learned and provide feedback about the process. The next time the class meets, Domenica leads a discussion of the complete rubric she has pieced together between classes, and it undergoes further revision if necessary. The compiled and approved rubric is then immediately posted to the web site.

Figure 3.1 shows a worksheet, focusing on introductions, that Domenica placed at one of the stations, along with excerpts from sample student papers. Figure 3.2 shows a student-created rubric for the same dimension (introductions) of this writing assignment.

Example 2: Deriving Principles from Sample Texts

In his graduate course, Teaching Writing in College, Chris Anson uses student-generated criteria to help new teachers of composition to learn how to write effective assignments. At this point in the course (as students begin focusing on assignment design), Chris has deliberately not provided any criteria or other evaluative information about assignment design—no rubrics, scales, or descriptions—the goal of the activity being to pull that information out of students' existing experience and judgment. He then asks the students to read one or more sample

Criteria	Excellent	Fair	Poor
Introduction			
Keywords to consider: lead, thesis statement, specificity, comprehensive, analytical, provable, diction, context, argument, stance, general-to-specific			
For more information, go to: [a Web link to resources is included here]			
[Example] "Introduction provides a general introduction to and background context of the topic that is the subject of the author's articles."			
[Your criteria go here . . .]			

Figure 3.1. Worksheet section that focuses on introductions. Students use this section of the worksheet to help them generate criteria as they examine example introductions at the introduction workstation.

Scientific Argument: Criteria	Excellent	Fair	Poor
Introduction			
Courtesy of [students' names]			
Strong opening sentences, not cute, overly dramatic or weak; opening sentences should capture the essence of the whole paper.			
Introduction is not too specific, but captures just the major points; don't write the whole paper in the intro. However, the reader should not be confused as to what is to come in the paper; enough should be presented so they know what they're reading.			
The author's argument should be clearly made in the intro, not just "previewed."			
Assignment is explained; audience knows that these two sources are different and that they will be compared. Also included is what makes the articles credible.			
Uses all information in context; points are not made arbitrarily and should be able to relate with the rest of the introduction.			
Thesis statement is not excessively long, drawn-out, or hard to find. Not incomplete or too general. Make sure thesis is specific, comprehensive, analytical and provable.			
Introduction includes title of article and authors and year written. Include context of authors and their agenda if either is relevant.			
Strong transitions within introduction and into 1st body paragraph.			

Figure 3.2. Completed introduction section for the student-created rubric. After generating rubric sections like these for all parts, students participate in a class discussion about their criteria, followed by the instructor's posting of the final rubric on the class website.

assignments written by students in a previous class who were preparing to teach a typical introductory composition course. Each sample is interestingly problematic in that it might contain some elements that engage or motivate first-year students but give confusing instructions or lack any statement of learning goals, or it might be well organized but too intellectually challenging for a class of freshmen.

When students come to class prepared to discuss the sample assignment, they first compare their responses briefly in small groups, discussing what worked well, what was problematic, what stood out for them, and so on. Then, reconvening the class, Chris leads a detailed discussion of the draft, soliciting the responses of the groups. Chris makes it clear that the discussion will move between two levels: the text (based on the students' analysis of the samples' strengths and weaknesses), and the more abstract *principles* derived from the specific instances. These principles can take the form of answers to these questions: How do we know a good first-year composition assignment when we see it? What does this specific weakness or problem or strength that you noticed in the sample tell us more generally about how we would create or recognize a successful writing assignment? What qualities define a *good* or *successful* assignment?

At first it is difficult even for graduate students to move between the levels, so Chris usually coaches them with targeted questions: We've all agreed that this assignment constrains students inappropriately, but how would we frame a principle here? Should assignments never be constraining? Soon, however, students catch on to the process and begin offering general principles, showing how those principles are derived from specific instances in the text. In order to create a list of criteria or expectations, Chris records all suggestions on a computer projected to a screen, and often these are negotiated and renegotiated, drafted and revised, as the discussion proceeds.

At the end of the session, Chris saves the final principles electronically. Because they have been created with some spontaneity, sometimes at different levels (rhetorical, stylistic, informational, etc.), the principles need to be consolidated, reorganized, reworded, or clarified, and made more like criteria. At home, Chris adds any crucial criteria that may not have emerged from the discussion or that may have been only partly articulated. In the main, however, the resulting criteria represent the collective work of the class, having been generated from students' own impressions of other students' or teachers' assignment drafts.

After a brief class discussion of the near-final draft and some further tinkering, if necessary, Chris posts the criteria online. In some cases, the graduate students may be asked to apply the criteria—now that they have been formalized—to yet another sample assignment, to give them practice looking for specific features and to help them further internalize the standards for successful responses. The students then use the criteria to draft their own assignments, to discuss each other's assignments in small revision groups, and to reflect on their final drafts.

One class of graduate students created a bullet list of twenty-two formalized criteria for successful assignments that included provisions such as "has clearly articulated learning goals," "has activities that reflect the goals of the assignment," "provides support (preteaching) for stages of the assignment," and "clearly describes evaluation standards."

Another class decided to create a checklist (shown in figure 3.3) against which teachers can consider drafts of assignments.

Example 3: Creating Rubrics for Specific Genres

Students' familiarity with the formal genres of the natural sciences is often severely limited—their most common experience is with high-school biology lab reports. Therefore, student-generated criteria for assignments that require writing within a scientific genre are especially helpful in allowing students to understand and internalize evaluative expectations. For a participant-observation study report (POSR) assignment in his first-year introduction to Academic Writing course, Matt Davis has students create, amend, and reorganize a grading rubric devised from a sample student paper. After reviewing an interestingly problematic student paper as a group, the class refers to the assignment sheet for grounding in a local context and fashions a descriptive rubric chart through class discussion. Matt steers but does not lead the discussion, finding that the structure of the rubric comes to reflect the structure of the scientific report being analyzed. The students then create three evaluative categories for each expectation: Poorly Demonstrated, Somewhat Demonstrated, and Well Demonstrated.

Matt makes copies of the in-class rubric and gives each student the task of amending at least one of the evaluative categories for homework. He explains to the students that their changes can be either local or global—from requesting a clearer definition of a word to refashioning the entire document. Matt then collects these changes and compiles them into a final version of the rubric, which the class approves by vote.

Checklist: Components of Successful Writing Assignments

____ *Statement of purpose, learning goals, and/or outcomes*

____ *Assignment description*

Audience (actual or invoked, if any besides the teacher)

Genre or type of writing

Voice or style

Disciplinary format, reference style, if appropriate

Scope of paper (formality, length, complexity)

Materials to be used or consulted

Processes to be used or practiced

Constraints and options

____ *Supporting work*

Projected episodes/work sequence (what happens when)

Classroom support of processes to be used

Peer-group work; supported revision cycles

Provisions for other forms of feedback or response on drafts

Formative use of criteria

____ *Evaluation criteria or expectations*

Rubric or grading guide

Description of standards and expectations

Accompanying samples or models (annotated or graded)

Format and presentational requirements (font, margins, references, etc.)

Due date(s)

____ *Other considerations*

Level of engagement or interest for students

Creativity

Enthusiasm reflected

Intellectual challenge

Openness to many responses (no "right answer")

Structure of assignment description (based on processes, most to least important elements, or some other clear rationale)

Quality of writing (of assignment itself)

Appropriate level of detail (balance of general and specific)

Figure 3.3. Checklist-style set of criteria created by graduate students. Some classes may choose to create a formalized list of criteria, and others (like this one) can choose other options for describing the criteria they have developed.

After grading the assignment according to the student-created rubric, Matt collects student feedback on the process.

In a recent class that went through this process, twenty-two students made a total of forty-two changes to the in-class rubric, although each student was charged with making only one change (some of the changes were duplicates). Each element of the assignment (Introduction, Methods, Results, Discussion, and Conclusion) received between three and seven changes, and Style, with eight, received more commentary than any other category. Additionally, students often provided unsolicited explanations with their changes, and one student extended his commentary to describe his ideas for using the rubric for shaping an upcoming peer-review session. Although students in this particular instance made few changes to the structure of the rubric itself, another section of the course voted in favor of a narrative rubric and changed the evaluative categories to correspond with the traditional grading scale.

This process can provide instructors with formative assessment that guides their decisions about the course's shape and content. For instance, in terms of local issues, students were especially sensitive to definitions of terms (especially interested in the appearance and content of "sophisticated" prose). Therefore, Matt devoted a portion of a future class session to style. Additionally, student comments showed a desire to negotiate the role of personal opinion in the scientific report. To the suggestion that students include possibilities for future research in their reports, one student asked, "Isn't further research a personal opinion?" This prompted a lively discussion of the role of subjectivity in the sciences that dialogued in interesting ways with the discussion on formal style and objectivity.

The process can also result in students developing relatively nuanced and sophisticated insights completely on their own. For instance, on a more global scale, students were able to distinguish important markers of genre and categorize them in ways suited to their particular inquiry. Several students' comments concerned the relationship of Results to Discussion. Using the genre models available, students quite correctly suggested the movement of data interpretation from Results to Discussion, and two students articulated specific reasoning behind their thoughts on this move. One remarked that in the Results, "only the data showing patterns needs to be included," while another suggested that writers "only mention results that pertain to the topic, not to other topics." Furthermore, several students suggested ways that the Results topics." Furthermore, several students suggested ways that the Results and Discussion could be effectively merged, a move resulting from their understanding of genre as a flexible category. In particular, students were concerned with relating later sections back to their hypotheses, and one student even noted that the Conclusion should "restate the hypothesis and relate it to the rest" of the sections. Although the specific conventions they suggest are not always appropriate to the POSR genre, these comments show that students are actively engaged in negotiating the ways that generic conventions influence textual choices about data collection, presentation, and interpretation. The changes and additional explanatory notes demonstrate not only students' willingness to become involved in the creation of evaluative criteria, but also their confidence and facility in doing so.

When students produce a sample rubric together, they rely primarily on reflection and their experience with scientific texts to produce the final version. This reflection allows both articulation of their changes and internalization of the evaluative criteria, although this latter process usually needs continued reinforcement. More importantly, when students analyze sample texts with the goal of trying to explain, to themselves and others, what it means to produce such texts successfully, they are learning skills and strategies useful in other discursive settings where texts, and their standards, may be unfamiliar to them.

4

TEACHING THE RHETORIC OF WRITING ASSESSMENT

Asao B. Inoue
California State University, Fresno

As writing teachers, all of us want our students to be able to assess their own writing in order to respond effectively to future contexts and form reflective and critical practices. Many of us have also heard a familiar refrain from students, often after we have evaluated or responded to their writing: "Just tell me what you want me to do," they beg us. These are assessment problems that Peter Elbow attempts to solve by arguing that we do "*less* ranking and *more* evaluation," (1999, 176); however, too much evaluation "harms the climate for learning and teaching," so he suggests "evaluation-free zones" in a course (186). These zones are meant to allow students to explore and take risks. They act in a formative manner and attempt to dislodge writing from evaluation and grading that the institutional gaze of a teacher often creates. Elbow explains that if done right, evaluation-free zones can release students from having to ask the teacher, "How am I doing, did I do OK?" (186). Elbow's solution seems quite conventional now. Almost ten years later, most writing teachers I know try to grade as little as possible and incorporate lots of writing in their classes that does not get evaluated. So it appears many have listened to Elbow's good advice.

But Elbow's solution does not allow students to learn how to self-assess, something that Richard Larson says *is* revision (1999, 98) and that Deb Martin and Diane Penrod argue can be the topic for a writing course (2006, 71-72). Additionally, exploring and taking risks are productive writing practices, but only if they are accepted by teachers as such—that is, only if they are seen as the kinds of explorations and risks we value. Using evaluation-free zones simply avoids the problem Elbow initially identifies, which is a problem of students not being able (or allowed) to assess writing and reflect upon their practices, or not being able (or allowed) to explore or take risks in productive ways. In this chapter, I question conventional technologies of writing assessment and argue that students themselves need to engage in and reflect upon rhetorics of assessment. In short, I ask, "What can students learn by engaging meaningfully and reflecting upon rhetorics of assessment?" First, I briefly discuss three aspects of any technology of writing assessment: power, parts, and purposes. And second, I offer examples of students' rhetorics of assessment and their reflections on those rhetorics. Since each classroom context is different, I do not provide an activity to imitate; instead, I discuss a few students' assessment rhetorics as generative examples from my classrooms that suggest a range of pedagogical applications and the possibilities for learning and development.

Since I must confine myself to discussing primarily the parts of assessment technologies (i.e., the codes and artifacts produced by assessment), or the rhetoric of assessment, in this chapter, perhaps it is enough to say that it is important to construct together with students the purposes of any assessment used in the classroom, and to consider carefully how power moves, is constructed through assessment processes, and constructs authority and value in writing practices. Additionally, power typically rests where judgments on writing that count for something in the course are made (Huot 2002; Straub 1996; Trimbur 1996) and grades are produced (Bleich 1997; Howard 2000). The power arrangement set up by any writing assessment technology in a conventional writing class may look something like this: teachers assign writing. Students write drafts. Teachers respond to drafts. Students revise those drafts. Teachers grade the revised drafts. Thus, conventional writing assessment constructs writing as a demonstration of students' mastery and constructs writing assessment primarily as a process for measuring their mastery. Thus, writing demonstrates learning by students, and assessment and grading by teachers measure student learning. One linchpin that holds together the power arrangement in this traditional assessment technology, yet ironically keeps students from being able to self-assess, is the rhetoric of assessment owned and practiced by the teacher. But letting students engage in their own rhetorics of assessment is not the only thing I am suggesting. Many of us do this already in the typical writing workshop scenario, but usually a student's peers have very different expectations than the teacher, so why would a savvy student listen carefully to her peers when the teacher is still going to grade her work?

At the heart of developing effective writing practices, then, is getting students to develop effective writing assessment rhetorics that exercise a high degree of power in the assessment technology. In short, their rhetorics should mean something more than "getting feedback" from peers. Elsewhere I offer a full cycle of student-driven assessment, called Community-Based Assessment Pedagogy (Inoue 2004). This cycle is a student-driven technology of writing assessment, one that moves students through five rhetorical practices: creating assessment expectations (typically a rubric); writing assessment documents for colleagues about their drafts; dialoguing about the assessment drafts (not just the essays that are assessed); revising assessment drafts after dialogues (again, not simply revising the essays); and reflecting upon the assessment processes and documents. The central element, however, in each practice is the rhetoric of assessment. When students create, use, and reflect upon their texts, like essays and other conventional writing assignments, they must develop, engage in, and theorize rhetorics of assessment. At the highest level of abstraction, students develop and practice assessment rhetorics in order to develop flexible, effective, and meaningful writing practices.

One way to begin engaging students in assessment rhetorics is to ask them to read published discussions about assessing writing, such as Erika Lindemann's "Responding to Student Writing" in *A Rhetoric for Writing Teachers* (2001); Brian Huot's "Reading Like a Teacher" in *(Re)Articulating Writing Assessment* (2002); William Irmscher's chapter 13 of *Teaching Expository Writing* (1979); Richard Straub's *College Composition and Communication* article "The Concept of Control in Teacher Response" (1996); or Richard Straub and Ronald Lunsford's chapter 5 in *Twelve Readers Reading* (1995). Each of these discussions, while written for teachers, provides examples, terminology, and commenting practices (not simply evaluation criteria) that students can use and reflect upon. Mostly, they treat the rhetoric of assessment as a rhetoric, as a dialogical and contextual meaning-making activity. While none of the discussions above refer to judgments on writing as a rhetoric, Huot comes close when he argues for a "pedagogy of assessment" (2002, 67–71, 78–9).

THE RHETORIC OF WRITING ASSESSMENT

In my courses, regardless of their experience, students engage in rhetorics of assessment through guided dialogues, reflective activities, and the actual writing of assessment documents. I am not talking about asking students to merely dialogue with teachers about teachers' assessments of their work (Malone and Tindall 1997), or to merely generate assessment rubrics and criteria (Anson, Davis, Vilhotti in this volume; Strickland and Strickland 1997). While these are worthwhile practices, I am suggesting students benefit when they articulate judgments on their colleagues' writing and pay extended attention to those articulations of judgment.

First, of course, students must assess writing in a course, and teachers must let those assessments have direct significance in grading and the valuing of essays. Almost half of my first-year writing (FYW) course's time is spent on assessment activities. My students and I craft assessment documents carefully and reconsider them. They are central to the course's activities and discussions, not an afterthought or a short departure from the "normal" routines—they are the routines. When students write an essay or a paper of some kind, they know I will not be assessing it. Their colleagues will. While I do read everything, select examples, design class activities around those examples, and read portfolios at the course's midpoint and end, I do not want students trying to compare my judgments to their colleagues' judgments, so I stay out of most of the assessing during the semester. Like Elbow (1999) and Stephen Tchudi (1997), I want them to see and understand a distinction between the assessment and grading of their work. And like Elbow, I am attempting to get students to dislodge grading from the evaluation of performance: the first ranks but provides little developmental feedback, while the second describes and supports judgments. Additionally, I am attempting to separate responding from assessment—that is, the practices of reading and having a human response to a text as opposed to reading a text to judge it along particular dimensions (or expectations) for particular purposes and within a particular context. Grading contracts help facilitate some of these separations, as do portfolios, to a lesser extent (see Elbow 2006; Spidell and Thelin 2006).

I also have found that providing a structure or form for all assessment rhetorics helps. For example, once we have created our assessment rubric, the list of expectations for "proficient" essays, we then use it to read and assess essays. The judgments we make are simple: the essay meets or does not meet the expectations articulated in each rubric dimension. The explanations of those judgments, however, are carefully articulated, dialogued over, revised, and reflected upon. This is similar in spirit to Elbow's evaluation, Huot's "instructive evaluation" (2002, 67–8), and David Bleich's "descriptive evaluation" (1997, 30) in that our attention is on *how* the rhetoric of assessment makes the judgments it does, not what those judgments are. So if there are four rubric dimensions, then assessment documents have four sections, each offering a judgment and an explanation of that judgment in narrative form, always pitched to the writer in formative ways. We look at a few assessment documents with their accompanying essays in class each time, discuss them, and revise assessment documents for final submission to the writers.

Students often do not fully figure out assessment rhetorics until they talk to the writer and other assessors and discuss real assessment rhetorics as purposeful documents themselves. This is why revising their assessment documents is so important. Like any other rhetoric, revising helps a student improve his or her practice over time, and the class should pay attention to the way assessments improve. For instance, the following is the complete first draft of an assessment rhetoric written by Cynthia, a FYW student of mine in the middle of a semester. ("Cynthia" is a pseudonym, as all student names are in this chapter, in order to preserve anonymity, which was the agreement in both classes from which all student work in this chapter comes. Additionally, I have modified for readability most student texts, altering typos, but leaving grammar and other textual features alone.)

> First off, your essay is very good. You stayed on topic throughout your whole paper. I never not once got confused on what you were talking about. It seemed like you agreed with the author, so that showed your point right away. Your examples were perfect for this paper and they fit in well. You also had very good quotes in your paper. I didn't see any grammar mistakes that were noticeable. I think your length of your paper is good because it's not too short and not too long. You did a very good job on this paper!!

Cynthia used our assessment rubric as a guide to write this. The rubric had six dimensions, and she makes judgments about each dimension in the order they appear on our rubric. Notice, however, she never really explains how she has come to any of these conclusions about her colleague's essay. This is a typical first draft, and a good start since it addresses each rubric item and makes clear judgments. At least her colleague knows how Cynthia thinks the essay performs along each dimension.

After their groups discussed their assessments with each other, and we discussed as a class two examples I chose from everyone's assessments, Cynthia revised her assessment rhetoric and gave it to her colleague.

Her new version, a typical kind of revision, offered the following for just one of our six rubric dimensions:

> *Be clear, interesting, and organized*
>   I think this means that the person reading the paper should understand what the writer is talking about at all times. The reader should never get lost when reading the paper. The paper should never be boring either and should get right to the point. It should also always keep my attention and not make me want to not read it. I like how you put examples from your life in your paper. It makes your paper more interesting and want to read more of it. I think your paper is really interesting and I never got bored reading it. You were very clear with your ideas also. You met criteria.

Cynthia's other judgments were equally developed and similar in their structures. In class we had discussed the importance of making sure the writer understood "where the assessor is coming from" when she makes her judgments. We found that the more informative and helpful assessment rhetorics tended to offer the assessor's translation or understanding of the rubric dimension in question. In the more helpful documents, the assessor talks about what the rubric dimension means apart from her judgment. So we asked everyone to make sure they made this same rhetorical move when they revised their assessments after class.

While Cynthia's assessment rhetoric arguably doesn't offer much in terms of revision advice, she does allow the writer enough information to compare her judgment to others that may conflict. Cynthia is practicing a typical academic move: identify an assumption, discuss an example or a present case in which the assumption has bearing, and make contextualized conclusions. While Cynthia's example of including the personal in the essay doesn't point to particular language in the essay, it is a place for her and her colleague to begin their dialogue, and it is an improvement upon her initial assessment rhetoric. To help students continue developing their assessment rhetorics by theorizing their own moves, I ask each student to reflect upon her or his assessment rhetorics and dialogues, again in structured ways.

REFLECTIONS ON ASSESSMENT RHETORICS

Just as Cynthia reflected on the assessments she wrote for her colleagues, students can also reflect on the assessments written to them by their colleagues. This is similar to Chris M. Anson's practice of asking students to record their spoken reflections on essay drafts, only I am asking students to reflect not on colleagues' essays but on colleagues' assessment documents. Anson found that "students who lack control of their own writing seldom comment projectively, because there is little room for their own decision-making process in revision. Instead, they measure their texts against . . . [an] image of the teacher's 'standards'" (1999, 70). Reflecting on assessment documents encourages students to consider both the present judgments on a text and the nature of those judgments as future-looking projections that do not (or cannot) defer to a higher authority figure. For instance, I may ask students to find two specific comments or judgments, quote them, and then reflect upon what their language communicates and assumes. How do they interpret their colleagues' judgments, and how do they interpret their colleagues' interpretations of the rubric criterion to which that judgment refers? What assumptions about the rubric criterion in question can the writer find in her assessor's words? How is the assessor translating, adding to, or changing the way the writer has understood the rubric dimension?

In week eight of a FYW course, Matt reflects on two different colleagues' conflicting assessments of his paper:

> One assessor thought that I did a good job of conveying information in a constructively opinionated manner, so as to compile a substantial and well explained opinion in my paper. The other thought that the main point of my paper was in the way I worded my conclusion . . . I think the first assessor was judging the rubric elements in my paper much the same as I was. Both of us thought that I did a good job of explaining myself and using support to do so. I will take in their beliefs only if I can look at the rubric and at their suggestions and say wow! that's a good idea.

In this midsemester reflection on the rhetoric of assessment in peers' assessment documents, Matt begins to think about the discourse of assessment and how he might make decisions for revision. Specifically, he explains that in order for the assessment to be effective and allow him to hear it, it needs to connect to what he has already said, sympathize with his perspective, make a coherent argument; then he would "say wow!" Although Matt ignores the problem of seeing alternatives, complications, and disagreements, this is his initial thinking on assessment. His reflection is a tentative strategy and embryonic theory. While much thinking stills needs to be done, Matt is comparing judgments on his writing and finding practices for making decisions in revision. He is not deferring those decisions to a teacher by asking her, "How well am I doing?" or "What will work well?" He is trying to ask these kinds of questions for and of himself.

Matt returns to this theory in his end-of-semester portfolio's letter of reflection, a self-assessment rhetoric itself. He describes an assessment document he wrote for a colleague and what he tried to do there by illustrating what he needs in an assessment generally:

> I am pretty impressed when an assessor is able to explain their view on a point in my paper which they think needs changing clearly enough for me to fully understand, and more so accept . . . I am more likely to change my writing if the assessor reiterates the point I am trying to make, which to me shows that they understand what I am trying to say before suggesting an *example* of a way to *improve* upon it [Matt's emphasis]. Note those key words, because when the assessor does this, they are not directly challenging my point of view but at least appear to be using an objectively constructional approach to changes in my paper.

Six weeks later, Matt has more thoroughly theorized assessment and has articulated a workable revision strategy. This reflection on the rhetoric of assessment is fleshed out, justified, and theoretical—Matt is even conscious of the language he uses. Additionally, he goes on to discuss how his strategy allows for "credibility" and addresses each person's "bias." Matt becomes more conscious of his own discourse, calling attention to it. When students are asked to create assessment documents for each others' work, dialogue about those assessment documents, revise them, and then reflect upon them, they can explain their assessment decisions and create reflective practices that will transfer to other situations. Matt, for instance, discusses behavior, good practices, what an "assessor does," and what a writer does (the first page of his portfolio's letter describes these strategies). Matt does not simply react to a teacher's comments on particular papers, but he also becomes a writer discussing his practices as practices.

The rhetoric of assessment is effective for building practices like Matt's because it becomes a habitual aspect in the course. It is done every week, sometimes daily. More assessment documents are written and revised than papers, and even more reflections on the assessment documents and processes are written, typically weekly. The rhetoric of assessment, and our discussions of it, are habitual, chronic.

Some may say we have models already that incorporate reflections on assessment— portfolio pedagogies, for instance. While portfolios can move drafts along, even talk about them in profitable ways, they do not move writers to call attention to or reflect upon the rhetoric of assessment, nor interrogate it as a public rhetoric that leads to effective practices. Typically, self-assessment in portfolios is personal reflection, which can seem to be significant only for a singular student and her particular drafts. The discourses of assessment I promote ask for *public theorizing of personal practices*. This pedagogy embraces what many have already acknowledged: that an individual's rhetoric and the judgments it enacts are consubstantial with the rhetoric of the social world and the judgments that are socially sanctioned and perhaps determined (Faigley 1992; Ohmann 1996). Rhetorics of assessment are quintessentially public and social rhetorics, not private ones.

This postmodern account of the rhetoric of assessment explains another important outcome: engaging in these practices can make the material classroom itself a topic for classroom discussions and for assessment rhetorics. Through reflective practice, students come to see that texts are not produced or read in vacuums. For instance, for our midterm conference, I asked Betty, a student from a different FYW course, to bring a reflection on her essay and her revisions, as well as one assessment she had done and revised for her colleague. Betty offered this reflection:

> In my essay, I saw adding a personal experience as support as the biggest issue. By removing it I add a certain abstract objective to my point. With it in, there is an element of my personality and something that will help people to understand my views on the subject. I am still deliberating about whether or not to leave the personal story in my essay. I would rather . . . not put it in my essay, mainly because it is personal and is not anybody else's business.

The tension Betty reveals in revising her essay is not simply about making her assessors happy, or fixing her text. She wants to honor both her colleagues' values and her own needs to keep some things private. The social and public nature of assessment reveals this dilemma. In fact, this issue of including the personal in her writing was discussed in class, and she is continuing that discussion. Thinking about revision for Betty is not about finding *the answer* to "How am I doing?" but seeing the available options—what each colleague offers in his or her rhetorics of assessment— and weighing her audience's needs and her own in reflections. She focuses also on making a rhetorical decision, not simply fixing a text. Furthermore, revision is not just a textual matter, but one connected to material bodies and discussions in the classroom. There are no easy answers for Betty, and she can see this.

Later in her follow-up reflection to the conference, Betty discussed the importance and relevance that her practices of assessing have on her own writing:

> Assessing is important because it helps me to learn how to critique writing in general, whether it's mine or Edgar Allen Poe's. In my formal assessment for Elsie's essay I confused her with my challenge to find additional arguments. So I clarified it by saying, "This second draft definitely meets our rubric requirements. However, after the discussion of the paper in class, I don't believe it goes above and beyond the call. One more revision and a look at the origin of winners and losers in society might make a big leap forward for the paper. Also, maybe if you compare our society with winners and losers to a society that does not promote that sort of thing it would fire up your argument." I felt that this was a good suggestion and showed that I believe she has the potential to impress everyone and go way above and beyond the call of duty.

Not only does Betty demonstrate sound advice in a conversational way, but she theorizes the act of assessing as a reflective practice for her own writing—something we did not talk about in our conference. Betty realizes that assessing is theoretically a way to practice analyzing all texts—Poe's as well as her own—for meaning and insight.

Betty examines her own discourse of assessment and theorizes from it, not just for future assessments, but for her writing and colleagues' benefit. The public nature of her reflection allows her colleagues to theorize with her in meaningful ways. For example, Ursula replies to Betty's above-posted reflection on our Internet discussion board:

> I'm not sure on how I feel about adding personal experiences to a paper. Like you said, there are things that you will gain and lose by putting in it or not. I think that it really depends on the audience you are writing to. If you are writing to a room full of scientist they might like statistics or something more definite. On the other hand, if you are writing to a room full of moms, personal experiences will most likely be more understandable for them.

Ursula expands Betty's theorizing to incorporate the diverse needs of different audiences, and she reveals her own ambivalence in using personal experience. Their public discussion, which I as the teacher might call attention to in class, illustrates a theorizing of writing that developed from looking carefully at the rhetoric of assessment, then responding to each others' reflections publicly. Our classroom discussion about this exchange would focus on the assessment issues raised and possible practices of writers, both of which are rhetorical issues framed as questions revealed to us by the rhetoric of assessment: How does a writer make decisions contextually and textually? When does a writer use the personal and why? How do we make sense of and value writing in different rhetorical contexts? How do writers behave in "a room full of moms" or "scientists"?

Since we rarely get things right the first time when assessing (much like writing essays), my classes incorporate revision into our assessment rhetorics. This also gives us a chance to reflect upon those changes, rethink practices, and theorize our developing ways of judging, valuing, and articulating judgments. Jim explains in his portfolio's reflection letter how he revised his assessment of a colleague's paper, which happened to be Matt's from above:

> In the first assessment I told Matt he communicated meaning well [a rubric element]. That's a nice comment, but what he needed [to know] was how to enhance that aspect . . . so I offered him a way to focus the paper. . . . Instead of saying to use more quotes, I asked him this time to critically analyze something on top of those quotes.

Jim focuses on process and change. By paying attention to how and why he revises his assessments, or the changes in his assessment rhetoric, he learns a lesson similar to Betty's. For Jim it is not enough to "use more quotes." Now he understands that to "focus the paper" the writer should "critically analyze" the quoted material. This insight happens only as Jim consciously tries to trace his progress of making and revising his assessments. Assessing is not enough. To gain these insights, Jim needed to dialogue, revise, and reflect on his own assessment rhetoric.

Focusing on the rhetoric of writing assessment will change not just the goals of a writing class, but also its values and what counts as measurable learning. Some might worry that little improvement occurs in essays when so much time is spent on assessment documents, leaving less time for the essays. This critique assumes that a writing class should be about improving those essays, or perhaps that students' comments on peers' papers mainly serve to improve the essays; however, I do not share either of these assumptions. They set up a false binary in a writing class: essays are legitimate writing while assessment documents are not. The goal of my writing classes is not to produce strong essays, but to produce reflective writing practices and behaviors, which makes the rhetoric of assessment the goal of the course since it is a rhetoric about reading and writing practices.

Finally, the public and dialogical nature of the rhetorics of assessment in all of the above examples illustrates an important pedagogical point I am trying to rethink and enact pedagogically: the rhetoric of assessment is not just a discourse that displays judgments of writing by an authority figure (e.g., a teacher) but a set of processes and practices that themselves produce authority and power and that are woven into the fabric of classroom writing processes in ways that encourage students to engage in and reflect upon them meaningfully. Considering this, I conclude with an abbreviated, and hopefully generative, list of considerations for rethinking the rhetoric of assessment within the technology of classroom writing assessment:

- incorporate students' written assessments into the grading mechanisms of the class, and reduce (as much as possible) the role of teacher-centered assessment and grading

- choose fewer times for you (the teacher) to assess or comment on work

- create (collaboratively) common rhetorical structures for students to use when assessing each other's work

- ask students to dialogue about their written assessments

- allow students to revise their assessment documents after dialogues so that deeper insights and rethinking can occur

- focus discussions of assessments on the rhetorics of those assessments, the ways in which those rhetorics articulate and support judgments and their changes in revisions

- ask students to reflect frequently upon the assessments they write and those they receive from their peers

- and structure reflections carefully so that students have opportunities to both consider how they've assessed and how they might improve those practices.

PART TWO
Circulating Student Texts

The essays in the second section of our book discuss the ways student texts circulate in classrooms, in publications, and in textbooks. In the first piece in this section, "Ethics, Student Writers, and the Use of Student Texts," Paul Anderson and Heidi McKee investigate the ethical dimensions of teaching with student texts and offer advice to teachers on how to ethically and responsibly circulate those texts in the classroom.

Following these ethical concerns, in "Reframing Student Writing in Writing Studies Composition Classes," Patrick Bruch and Thomas Reynolds discuss how ideas about student texts and student writing circulate in their department, sharing the results of a survey to highlight the various roles student writing plays in first-year-courses in their program and how teachers perceive the value of student writing as a teaching text.

The next two chapters explore different approaches to circulating student texts in writing classrooms. In "Students Writing to Students about Writing," Laurie McMillan describes an assignment in first-year composition that asks end-of-semester students to write to the following term's start-of-semester students about what they've learned. This circulation of student texts across classess and semesters, she argues, offers a unique way students can share their knowledge about writing. This type of assignment is not confined to across semester, as McMillan identifies the benefit of asking experienced students to communicate learning to a less-informed audience.

In "The Low-Stakes, Risk-Friendly Message Board Text," Scott Warnock identifies the power of circulating low-stakes assignments via the message board in writing classrooms. To do so, he describes several specific examples of how teachers might use message boards to promote metawriting assignments that ask students to reflect on their own writing. He ends by arguing that the message board is an efficient way to facilitate a number of low-stakes, risk-friendly writing pedagogies.

The next two chapters discuss ways student texts circulate outside our classrooms, on our campus, and beyond. In "Product as Process: Teaching

Publication to Students," Karen McDonnell and Kevin Jefferson discuss a course they teach that produces *e-Vision*, their university's FYW journal. Their pedagogy centers on the process of editing and publication, with student editors responsible for the behind-the-scenes negotiations that most publications of first-year writing reserve for faculty.

Following this local context, Doug Downs, Heidi Estrem, and Susan Thomas discuss the pedagogical implications of using published student texts in the classroom. In "Students' Texts beyond the Classroom: *Young Scholars in Writing*'s Challenges to College Writing Instruction," they suggest that published student texts and the experiences they represent can offer students perspectives on writing they may not have otherwise experienced. Coupled with these pedagogical insights, they argue that composition courses might benefit from the extended revision processes that contributors to *Young Scholars in Writing* go through.

In the final essay of this section, "The Figure of the Student in Composition Textbooks," Mariolina Rizzi Salvatori and Patricia Donahue discuss possibly the most visible way student texts are circulated in our field. They examine the ways in which students and student writing are represented and positioned within composition textbooks. They survey textbooks, both old and new, and conclude by urging us, as a field, to grow more mindful of how we represent and comment on students and their texts.

5

ETHICS, STUDENT WRITERS, AND THE USE OF STUDENT TEXTS TO TEACH

Paul V. Anderson
Miami University

Heidi A. McKee
Miami University

While their contexts, pedagogies, and theoretical approaches differ widely, most instructors who use student texts in their teaching share an acute awareness that the benefits of this practice are accompanied by potential harms. By sharing student texts inside or outside the classroom, these instructors recognize students as authors whose work is worthy of study and vest authority in their words and expertise. But this practice also exposes students (and the persons whom they may represent in their writing) to potential, albeit unintended, embarrassment, ridicule, and hurt. For example,

- a student sits uncomfortably while his biology teacher projects his lab report on a large screen, pointing out the kinds of errors she wants the class to find and correct before turning in future reports

- a student in a political science course swallows her anger and humiliation as she responds to a classmate's draft that portrays people from her community in stereotyped and demeaning ways

- an education major is required to keep a blog that is accessible to anyone on the Internet, and he is distraught because several anonymous commentators belittle his ideas and writing

- a senior is upset after learning that the instructor for her first-year English class is asking his current students to read and critique an essay she wrote three years ago

- a professional writing student submits his service-learning project to the community organization's board of trustees, who complain that he has misrepresented the organization. Having received earlier praise from his instructor and his contact in the organization, he feels somewhat betrayed.

Could the instructors in these scenarios have prevented the distress of their students? Should they have? It is difficult to say without knowing more details about each situation, such as whether the students gave permission for the specific use and distribution of their texts, or whether instructors anticipated possible difficulties that might arise for students and were prepared to address them. Despite the potential problems of using student texts for teaching, we both firmly believe in the practice. But in our roles as instructors and program administrators, we have often struggled with the complex, highly contextualized and nuanced ethical questions that arise. From talking with colleagues; reading listservs for digital rhetoricians and writing program administrators such as TECHRHET and WPA-L; and studying publications such as *Public Works: Student Writing as Public Text* (Isaacs and Jackson 2001), *Authorship in Composition Studies* (Carrick and Howard 2006), *Across Property Lines: Textual Ownership in Writing Groups* (Spigelman 2000), and the work of authors in this volume, we know that many other instructors have encountered similar uncertainties.

Our goal in this chapter is to sketch a framework for addressing the ethical questions that arise when teaching with student texts. We set out to write this chapter, not because we claim to have *the* answers, but in order to help ourselves and others think through the ethical concerns we all share.

In our exploration, we want to develop ways of addressing these concerns that might be useful throughout the broad range of contexts in which instructors teach with student texts. These contexts include not only the most obvious sites—composition courses and undergraduate and graduate courses at all levels in English and writing studies departments—but also courses in every field from aeronautical engineering to zoology. In fact, one notable result of the writing-across-the-curriculum movement, which is undergoing a significant resurgence and growth, is the introduction of teaching methods, such as peer review, that involve sharing student texts in areas of the curriculum where they had previously been rare.

We also aim in this chapter to develop ways of thinking that would apply to the many means by which student texts are circulated for the sake of teaching. These include not only the very familiar peer-review sessions, but also in-class or program-specific publications, presentations in class conferences, and presentations to audiences outside the course. Sharing of student texts also occurs through course-management systems such as Blackboard and on the Web in blogs, Web sites, wikis, social networks, and so forth, that make students' texts available to classmates and, in some cases, the entire wired world. In addition, student texts are also shared in seminars and workshops for new graduate teaching assistants, writing-center consultants, and faculty.

We hope in this chapter to develop ways of thinking ethically that would be useful in working with a wide variety of student texts, not only assignments printed on paper, but also PowerPoint presentations, digital movies, Web sites, interactive media, podcasts, and multimedia communications, among others. Networked, digital technologies have greatly increased not only the means of sharing student texts but also the kinds of texts students create for their courses.

With these goals in mind, we have settled on the following definitions of the use of student texts for teaching. A *text* is any creation by which someone expresses his or her ideas, attitudes, feelings, and experiences in a way that can be perceived by someone else, regardless of medium. It is a *student text* if the writer created it in his or her role as a student; student texts include course assignments, placement exams, and documents created for service/community/corporate learning. Student texts do not include the writing students do on their own initiative outside of classroom/teaching contexts. The uses of student texts for teaching that we consider in this chapter include only those uses by an instructor or program administrator in situations where there is a clear teacher-student relationship. We are not addressing instructors' use of student texts in publications and conference papers. These uses are research, an entirely different topic. Nor are we discussing situations in which an instructor shows a text to department colleagues in an informal manner to solicit advice about how to respond, share student accomplishments, or achieve some similar purpose. We focus exclusively on the ethical considerations involved in the sharing of student texts for the purpose of teaching the student author or others, whether those others are undergraduates, graduates, faculty, or even members of the public.

GUIDING PRINCIPLES

In our view, all uses of student texts in teaching—regardless of the medium and mode of the texts and regardless of the teaching contexts—involve the same ethical concern: the impact on the student writer as a *person*. Thus, we focus not on the ethical *use* of the texts but on the ethical *treatment* of the students who wrote the texts. Our approach is built on the following principles. In formulating them, we have been influenced by the three principles of the Belmont Report (National Commission 1979), which have shaped ethical understandings of person-based research in the United States: respect for persons, beneficence, and justice.

Students Should Control What They Disclose about Themselves and to Whom

In many college writing assignments, students are asked to write about themselves, their experiences, beliefs, interests, responses, and so on. Sometimes, they are asked to argue on behalf of their opinions concerning controversial social, political, or religious topics. In many ways, and for many good pedagogical reasons, they are asked to expose themselves in writing, but they need to know to whom they are writing when completing such assignments, and they need the autonomy to choose what they do and do not feel comfortable sharing. Even texts that contain no explicitly personal content still represent the student writers, revealing the ideas, writing abilities, and knowledge of persons who are still developing in all of these areas.

Students Should Control the Circulation and Distribution of What They Create

While U.S. copyright law gives students ownership of what they write, instructors should also see that their teaching strategies do not result in distributing student texts beyond the readers that students expect to see their work.

Students Should Be Respected and Protected from Harm

Whenever students share their writing—whether with instructors, fellow students, or community members—or whenever students' writing is shared by others— the student writers are vulnerable to potential harms, including emotional harms and academic harms. Even when the students are not present for the sharing of their texts, they should be protected as thoroughly as possible from harm.

If we were to stop with these three principles, a teacher's job of examining the ethical dimensions of his or her pedagogy would be fairly simple. Any teaching strategy using students' texts that might possibly violate any of the principles could be avoided, thereby eliminating the risks of treating students unethically. However, one other principle governs the treatment of students.

Students Should Experience the Best Learning Environments Their Instructors Are Able to Provide

Given this last principle, instructors who believe, as we do, in the value of teaching with student texts often face a difficult challenge. We must determine the risk to students of using their texts in our teaching and then weigh the risk against the potential benefits. Risks, alas, are difficult to estimate. First, teaching practices that cause discomfort, even resistance, from students are not necessarily bad. As educators, we routinely engage students with unfamiliar topics and ways of knowing. This dynamic is especially noticeable in first-year college classes regardless of pedagogical approaches. In *Collision Course*, an account of a two-year ethnographic study, Russel Durst (1999) concluded that new college students enter first-year writing courses "with an idea of writing and an understanding of what they need to learn about writing that are dramatically at odds with the views and approaches of the teacher" (2). In any class, students' encounters with the new ideas that lead to intellectual and personal growth can be initially very disquieting (see Herrington and Curtis 2000). As students develop during their formal education, teaching strategies that upset students in their first college year—by challenging unexamined biases, for example—may not be as upsetting in later years when students are more familiar with critical inquiry. On the other hand, students may later feel violated by teaching practices they once embraced unquestioningly. Ruth Shalit (1998) reported on the firing of a sociology professor who asked students to write essays about dynamics in their families from the perspective of social theories. Students who first praised his teaching later complained vigorously that he had coerced them to disclose highly personal and private information they wished they had not shared.

The variability and invisibility of students' understanding of the line between public and private, combined with the disparity between students' and teachers' understanding of that line (Stover 2001), are but two of the many factors that make it difficult for faculty to accurately judge the impact on students of any teaching method. Given the highly variable nature of student responses, which can differ from year to year, course to course, and even student to student, we need to evaluate each possible use of student texts contextually. The ethical sharing of student texts requires negotiation among the instructor (and his or her pedagogical practices); the student (and his or her expectations for learning); the norms that have developed around the use of student texts at particular institutions; and the specific contexts (local and global) shaping the composing, collection, delivery, and distribution of writing.

KEY QUESTIONS

In the next sections of this chapter, we apply the principles named above in relation to key questions many instructors ask when deciding whether and how to use student texts ethically.

Should Permission Be Obtained from Student Writers to Share Their Texts?

We believe the answer to this question depends partly on how student writing is shared. Sharing texts among students is integral to the pedagogy of many courses. In most composition courses and increasingly in undergraduate and graduate courses in many fields, students share drafts of their work with one another. Provided the instructor has made clear that such in-class sharing will occur, students may then choose to remain enrolled in the class knowing their writing will be read by classmates as well as the instructor. With this expectation in mind, they are able to respond to assignments with texts they are willing to share with classmates, which also means they are able to choose not to write texts they are unwilling to share.

The same line of reasoning applies to courses where, as part of the course pedagogy, students share their texts with persons outside their class. For example, instructors in various disciplines have students in a lower-level class respond to texts written by students in an upper-level class—or vice versa. With the increased connectivity of digital communications, an increasing number of faculty have their students share texts with students at other institutions. For instance, for several years the Intercollegiate E-Democracy Project provided a means for thousands of students from across the country to write to each other in online discussion forums, often sharing drafts of essays and Web sites for peer response. As a way of learning cross-cultural communication, students, particularly those in business and professional writing courses, often conduct peer reviews or write collaboratively online with students in other countries (e.g., see Shamoon 1998; Starke-Meyerring and Wilson 2008). Students share texts in public forums as well. Public sharing occurs through university-community partnerships, such as service courses where students prepare texts for organizations outside the university. In other courses, students' texts are reviewed by clients or by panels of alumni, professionals, or instructors other than their own teacher (Graves 2001). Increasingly, public sharing occurs at Web 2.0 sites where students are asked by instructors to post to blogs, submit videos to YouTube, or edit a Wikipedia entry. In all of these cases, students give permission for sharing their texts by creating and turning in (or posting online) the texts they know will be shared.

Of course, students can only freely choose to share their work only if they know in advance that sharing is part of the course or project plan. Heidi remembers her first semester teaching composition in college when for the initial draft of the first assignment a student wrote a personal reflection on his parents' recent divorce. He thought the draft was to be read only by Heidi, and, as he told Heidi after class, he was upset that something so personal was shared in peer response sessions with classmates, explaining how he would have written on a different topic had he known. By not making clear at the outset the audiences for and uses of the student work, Heidi feels she proceeded unethically as a teacher. Students need to know who will be reading their writing so they can make rhetorical choices appropriate to the contexts of sharing. Since that first semester, Heidi has made clear at the outset of the course the audiences with whom students will share their writing. If a student is not comfortable, say, with composing a Web site for publishing to the Internet, he can discuss other possible arrangements (creating a password-protected site, uploading to a local server only, posting the site for a few days and then taking it down, etc.). If students know the first day of class the audiences for their writing, they have the option of discussing and developing alternatives or dropping the course.

But what about permission for the instructor to share student texts with readers outside the immediate and known contexts for which the students are writing the texts? These contexts might include next year's section of the same course, an entirely different course, a program for writing- center consultants, a writing-across-the-curriculum workshop for faculty, or faculty- development programs. Here, it seems to us, explicit written or oral permission is needed from the writer or, if the text is collaborative, the writers. We believe explicit permission is needed because when the students compose the text initially, it is unlikely that they envision that their texts will be shared outside of the class.

Instructors often ask permission from students currently enrolled in their classes, particularly when students have completed exemplary projects that could serve as models for future students. But asking one's current students, even when planning to share their project as exemplars, raises concerns about coercion and free will. Are students really able to say no to their instructors if they are asked while still students in the instructors' courses? No matter how collegial the classroom environment and no matter how celebratory the intended use of the student text, there is still a power imbalance inherent in a student-teacher relationship, especially when grading is involved. One approach might be to contact students after the semester is over and grades have been turned in.

Sometimes an instructor may ask a colleague to share student texts that were written in the colleague's class and that the colleague has the students' permission to share. But is such a sharing between instructors and courses appropriate and ethical? The key determination is the scope of the student writer's original permissions. Did the student give permission for her text to be used only by her instructor in his particular classes, or did she give permission for her text to be shared with other classes taught by other teachers as well? Just as informed consent forms for research must spell out the usage of particular data collected from research participants, permission to share work—whether given orally or in writing (we recommend writing)—should spell out, among other things, the person(s) with whom and contexts in which the text may be shared. Context is important because sharing in one course environment is obviously different from sharing in another. Sharing a research project written for first-year composition in another section of the same course is quite different from sharing that first-year project in a graduate seminar, especially in terms of audience reception and expectations. Similarly, an instructor who obtains permission from students at one institution to share their texts does not necessarily have their permission to share those texts when she moves to another institution. The question would be whether the students who gave their original permission envisioned that their writing would be read by students at different institutions in potentially different sociocultural and pedagogical contexts.

Instructors may wish to share student texts found online. Because of the increased integration of digital technologies in the classroom, students are often being required, or at least strongly encouraged, to write on the Internet. Student texts located in password-protected venues, accessible only by the class or only by the instructor (e.g., Blackboard or other institutional course-management systems) or accessible only by those to whom the student gives permission (e.g., WordPress, Facebook, and other public-use sites that allow users to set privacy settings), seem analogous to paper-based texts students create for use strictly within the confines of a classroom. The students wrote the original texts for a bounded, limited audience; thus, the texts are evidentially *not* public. Student permission would be required.

Non-password-protected online writing is potentially a different matter and would seem to be available for use in the classroom. But as many researchers of online writing have noted, people often view their online writing as private, particularly when writing in online discussion forums or blogging communities where a sense of community develops (Hudson and Bruckman 2004; McKee and Porter 2009). If we instructors ask students to create Web sites or blogs, or ask them to post to media-sharing sites, we have a responsibility to ensure students know of the potential full use of their online work, an issue we discuss in more detail below. We should also inform students about the archival nature of the Internet— that digital communications do not necessarily disappear when deleted. A Web site hosted on a university server, for example, exists in the backup files made daily (or weekly) by the institution. If the site has been online long enough, it has probably been archived at the Internet Archive's Way Back Machine (http://www.archive.org), where it can be viewed by anyone years after it has been "taken down" from the Web.

Regardless of how permissions are obtained from students for sharing their work—orally or in writing—instructors should view all permission as potentially temporary. Students may change their minds and request that their texts no longer be shared. For example, a first-year student who wrote an essay arguing for the legalization of a particular drug might give permission to share his essay with students in subsequent semesters. But then when he is a senior and looking ahead to future career plans, he may decide he does not want that essay, written when he was eighteen and making an argument he no longer supports, to be shared with others.

If as instructors we accept the ethical obligation to seek permission for sharing a particular text (versus using the text without permission), one consequence is that we may sometimes be unable to use a student text for teaching even if there are very compelling reasons for doing so. Perhaps the instructor cannot locate the student author. Perhaps the student, for whatever reason, does not want the text shared. Toward the end of this essay, we suggest some ways instructors can achieve their teaching objectives while also observing the ethical principles that underwrite the need to obtain permission.

What Do Students Need to Know When Asked for Permission for the Use of Their Texts?

Student permission is meaningful only if the student understands what he or she is authorizing. Students need to know, and thus instructors need to have considered, the following: who the readers of the text will be (or could be); in general, how the text will be used (e.g., for peer response in class, as a model, for critique); how the text will be distributed (e.g., shown on an overhead or document camera, handed out as printed copies, reproduced digitally); and, if the text may be shared after the current class, how the student might contact the instructor in the future to withdraw permission.

When asking students to write in publically available online environments, instructors need to make clear to students that their work is out there for others to read and use. Although students know of the Web as *world wide*, it is important to discuss the implications of its global reach, how it is impossible to predict all of a public text's audiences and the uses they may make of it. Many instructors who ask students to write on the Web develop safeguards to protect students, such as using privacy settings or filtering comments (e.g., see Mauriello and Pagnucci 2001). Others ask students to write for local area networks (LANs) rather than the Internet, thus giving students the experience of creating and responding to digital, networked texts without the risks of going entirely public (e.g., see Moran, 2001; Wall and Peltier, 1996).

But it is not just Web publication that may lead to the sharing of texts with audiences that students (and instructors) may not have considered. In some courses, instructors ask students to prepare paper-based class publications. While each student may receive only one copy, every student may pass his or her copy to friends and family members or make copies for others to read. Similarly, texts loaded at a course class-management site that can be accessed only by class members can often still be downloaded and shared outside class by any of the students enrolled. Even printed drafts circulated for peer-review sessions can be circulated if they are not returned to the writer or collected by the instructor. We are not arguing that the practice of circulating student work (whether electronically or on paper) should be avoided, but rather that when instructors consider using texts, they reflect on the means of circulation and the types of writing they ask students to share in these ways. And, as we have each found in our own teaching, it can be helpful to engage students in a discussion of what the ethics of use should be for each other's texts, making the expectations explicit for what may or may not be shared with whom. A student may feel comfortable sharing a text with classmates she has come to know well by the end of semester, but she may not feel as open to having it shared with a classmate's roommate, friends, or parents. When class publications or other types of other sharing texts are course requirements, students should be told at the outset of the course with whom their texts will be—or could be—shared.

As indicated above, in addition to knowing the potential audiences for their texts, students also need to know the means of distribution and circulation when they give permission for their work to be used in future contexts. Distributing texts electronically—for example, via a course management system, email, a class blog, or social networking site—is very different from handing out and then collecting paper copies of a text in class, particularly in terms of potential redistribution and copying. Some students may be comfortable with the digital distribution of their work, but others may feel more comfortable with a paper-based approach with more limited distribution.

When instructors seek permission from students (whether in writing or orally) to use their texts in other contexts, they should also make clear what those contexts will be and how the texts might be used. Will the text be used to teach students how to conduct peer response, for example, or will it be shared with undergraduates as an exemplar? Will it be read with an eye toward critique and criticism, and if so, what might some of those criticisms be? Will the future readers of the text access the text electronically or in print, and, if in print, will they have copies to keep? And, importantly, will student texts be shared anonymously or with students' real names attached? Students need to know the answers to these and similar questions so they have a clear sense of how their writing will be used.

What Should We Do to Facilitate the Presentation and Reception of a Student's Text?

Our responsibility to student writers does not end when we have their implicit or explicit permission to use their texts in our teaching. As instructors, we should see that students are treated as respectfully after we have their permission as when we requested it. The complication is that when we cause a text to be shared, we are not the only ones who respond to it. At times, both students and instructors (in, for example, writing-across-the-curriculum programs) can sometimes be harsh, sarcastic, and dismissive. Does this mean that critique of student texts cannot occur? Certainly not. But it does mean that the discussions and any potential critique need to be managed with care.

It is easiest for instructors to see that students' texts (and thus the student writers) are treated appropriately when the texts are shared in class with the writers present. Before asking students to read, watch, or listen to and then comment on one another's texts, we can teach them the importance of finding ways to praise and support the writer as well as how to make suggestions in a constructive way. If the need arises during a discussion, we should be ready to refocus the discussion, redirect it, or otherwise intervene. Sometimes, especially in peer-response situations, a student may disparage his or her own text, perhaps out of nervousness. Just because such critique comes from the writer does not mean it should slide by. Even in the weakest of writing, some strengths can be found. Discussions have a different dynamic when the writer is not present. Yet we feel instructors should strive for discussion and analysis of a text to take place as if the student writer were there. Sometimes, we need to plan what we will say in order to set the stage for a productive discussion that stays focused on our teaching goals by concentrating our own comments and those of the audience on the lessons we want to convey. Special care may be needed when sharing texts with nonacademic audiences, such as with service-learning or client-based projects because these audiences may work with different paradigms for textual response.

Instructors who share students' visual multimodal texts might want to be extra attentive to the reception and reaction to these works. As Jon Prosser (2000) writes in "The Moral Maze of Image Ethics," audiovisual representations are more open to (mis)interpretation and critique than text-based verbal representations. In this digital age, many instructors ask their students to post their audiovisual representations on Web sites, blogs, wikis, or other publicly accessible locations. Although it may be a violation of copyright, someone can still easily download and save image and audio files for remixing. Instructors and students need to consider carefully the digital distribution of texts when representations of third parties are involved.

What about the Third Parties Students Represent in Their Papers?

When they write, students often represent not only themselves but also other people. We believe these persons and groups should be given the same consideration as the student authors (Goodburn 2001; McKee 2008). Admittedly, acting on this commitment may lead us into frustrating dilemmas. For example, if a student interviewed a family member, the family member may only have felt comfortable having her interview shared with the students in that one specific class. If the student gave permission to the instructor to share the text in other teaching contexts with other audiences, should the instructor do so? In another instance, Amy Goodburn (2001) describes her experience as her class discussed a student's literacy report about an African American community center. How, she wondered, could she affirm the student's work while also challenging his unexamined biases, which, unfortunately, his white classmates received as "unmediated 'truth'" (29). In circumstances such as these, instructors, we think, should be prepared to offer counterinterpretations or more contextualized perspectives.

Another possible consideration is the likelihood that the information presented about another person in a student text is something the person would consider to be private and would not want to be shared broadly. The Conference on College Composition and Communication Guidelines for the Ethical Treatment of Students and Student Writing in Composition Studies (2000) addresses this point for researchers, suggesting that "[t]hey always obtain permission to use a statement they believe the student made in confidence with the expectation that it would remain private." Perhaps such a suggestion would be good for us to make with students in the drafting stages of their text as they represent third parties.

When planning assignments for which students may interview and/or include audiovisual materials that involve the voices or images of others (e.g., photos, audio recordings, videos), it can be helpful to have students obtain written permissions from the persons they are representing, either in the form of a signed release for use of audiovisual likeness or in the form of a signed research consent form. The latter may be needed if students' representations of third parties involve person-based research and dissemination beyond the immediate classroom because such work could fall under policies governing person-based research. When faced with the potential overlap of teaching and research, instructors should check with their institutions about how to proceed.

Can Ethical Problems Be Avoided by Using Pseudonyms and Removing or Changing Personal Information?

Deleting or changing the student writer's name (or blurring photographic images of the writer in multimedia projects) would address some—but not all—of the principles that undergird the ethical framework we present. Removing identifiable information may protect the student from harm. Because others may not be able to associate the text with its author, pseudonyms may also satisfy a student's desire not to disclose certain things about himself or herself or others. For these reasons, some instructors feel justified using anonymous or pseudonymous student texts without permission. However, removing or changing the name does not erase ethical considerations. Pseudonymizing a text is not a free pass for unfettered use. Whether or not their names (or images and voices for multimedia projects) are attached, the texts are still theirs (and under U.S. law they still hold the copyright to those texts). Permission should be obtained for sharing in any way the student has not authorized.

Although removing or changing identifiable information usually protects from harm, it may also inflict harm. Some students may want their names (or images and voices) to be used. To them, identification as a writer is as important as it is to published authors. Many instructors use student texts in the classroom to validate students as persons whose writing is worthy of study and publication. Assigning pseudonyms, deleting student names, or modifying multimedia undermines this affirmation and recognition. One possibility is to let students choose whether they want identifying information attached to their texts that are to be shared.

Even when identifying information is changed or removed, readers familiar with the writer (classmates, friends, colleagues, family members) may still be able to identify the writer. This is especially true for audiovisual texts that include identifiable images and voices. Although these elements can be deleted or masked using image and audio editors, doing so can be time consuming. It may also alter the original text so it is no longer a text the student wishes to share or no longer fits the instructor's teaching goal.

Should There Be Exceptions?

Instructors teaching with student texts sometimes wonder whether there should be exceptions. This question comes in two varieties. The first asks, "In this special circumstance, should I make an exception to my usual practice of seeking permissions?" Instructors might ask the first question when they believe the benefit to the students they are teaching would be much greater than the possible harm or unfair treatment of the student writer, particularly if the writer will almost certainly never learn that the text has been used without his or her permission.

This case for making an exception may seem especially compelling if the instructor plans only to praise the student text. In the abstract, this question about the balance between the good for many versus the (possibly) much smaller harm to one resonates with debates between proponents of consequentialist ethics (including utilitarianism) and deontological ethics. Rather than attempt to settle a controversy whose history extends at least as far back as Plato's time, we suggest that instructors consider whether they can teach their lesson without using a student's text they do not have permission to use. We imagine that whenever instructors want to use a student's text to teach, they want to teach a general lesson, something that has relevance to many texts. If that is the case, there will probably be more than one text that can be used to teach it. Perhaps the instructor can teach the lesson with a different student's text, one the instructor does have permission to share. Alternatively, the instructor may be able to fabricate a student text, a common practice for the authors of student textbooks who sometimes feel they can better illustrate a point or create a better exercise with a fabricated student text. Of course, substitution will not work for pedagogies that require the student to receive responses from readers other than the instructor, for instance through peer review, all-class responses, publication at a public Web site or blog, or sharing service learning with members of a community organization.

The second question about exceptions concerns the possibly detrimental impact, for whatever reason, of asking some students to participate in text sharing. Is it more ethical to require all students to participate in the same activities, or to allow exemptions in exceptional cases? The choices can seem less extreme if instructors consider offering alternatives rather than exemptions. For example, if a student does not want peers reviewing his highly personal essay, perhaps the instructor can serve in this one instance as the reviewer of this one student. However, this solution, too, will not work in all cases and it may be that the student can be encouraged to write on another topic, one that would lead to writing he or she is comfortable sharing.

HOW TO MAXIMIZE OPPORTUNITIES FOR THE ETHICAL TREATMENT OF STUDENT WRITERS AND THE ETHICAL USE OF STUDENT TEXTS TO TEACH

We can sum up our entire discussion so far by saying that it can be very difficult to assure we are always treating student writers ethically when teaching with their texts. Difficulties would arise, we believe, even if the ethical use of texts were defined using principles very different from the ones we have chosen. Difficulties arise because judgments about ethical action depend so much on context—the course goals, students' expectations, likely impact on the student, instructor's ability to accurately predict that impact, technologies used for distribution and circulation, and so on.

So, in lieu of a summary set of ethical practices, we offer the following list of steps instructors might take to at least reduce the risk of stumbling into an ethical dilemma or an unethical action.

Tell Students Clearly at the Beginning of the Course about Any Sharing of Their Texts That Will Occur

Explain orally and in the course syallabus (and in compliance with institutional policies) with whom student texts will be shared, with what audiences, and in what contexts. Students need to know who besides us, as instructors, will see the texts, at what stages of the composing process the text will be shared, what learning purposes the sharing will achieve, and whether students may request exemption or an alternative to any of the planned sharing. Based on this information, students can prepare texts that reflect their own sense of what they want to share with the persons who will read their writing, and they can talk with us well in advance about a possible alternate assignment.

Ask Permission In The Least Coercive Environment Possible

The most convenient time to request permission is when the student writer is in our class. We can contact the student easily, and our thoughts about the ways we would use the student's text are immediately in mind. But even if students give permission during the time they are our students, we might consider asking a second time after course grades are turned in. This way we can be sure the student gives permission freely rather than because of a perceived advantage in pleasing us.

Get Permission in Writing

A year later, it can be difficult to remember the details of permission given to us orally. With written permission (which includes such communications as texting and email), we can easily answer the question of whether the student granted permission for the particular use we now have in mind.

Give Students the Choice between Using Their Real Names or Pseudonyms

In this way, we enable students to receive recognition for their work or to let us use it without others knowing they wrote it.

Ask Students How They Would Like Third Parties in Their Texts Represented

Some students may wish for pseudonyms to be applied, they may give permission for selective digital editing to preserve anonymity such as blurring photos, or they may, upon considering the issue, decide they do not want their texts shared after all because of the possible impact on third parties.

Let Students Know They Can Withdraw Permission Later by Contacting You

As students develop and mature academically, professionally, and personally, they may rethink the consequences of sharing their texts, thus letting students know they can withdraw is important since they may change their minds about our use of their texts.

Even with Permission, Consider Possible Negative Impacts on the Student Writer

Some students do not realize that their classmates or other possible readers will respond negatively to texts they have given permission to share. As instructors, we might consider not sharing a student text we do have permission to share because of the potentially problematic responses the text may elicit. Or, if we do decide to share a text that may elicit negative responses, we should be prepared to facilitate the discussion in ways that respect the student writer.

Plan the Way You Will Present a Student's Text

Even if we will ask others to critique a student's text, we can present the text in a positive light, such as by explaining the circumstances under which it was written or stating that the difficulties the student had are shared by many others. If we will present the text for discussion, we can prepare in advance the ways we will handle potentially hurtful or disrespectful comments and approaches.

If in Doubt about Sharing a Student's Text, Find or Make a Substitute

Even if our unease is very mild, we need to trust our own judgment. Whatever its source, even if it is only about the maturity of the audience with whom we plan to share, it is better to opt not to use the text rather than risk treating the student in a way we will later decide is unethical.

We do not imagine every reader will agree with the principles and actions we have identified. We are fully aware that our ethical vision is no sharper than any other instructor's, and that our views are products of a particular moment in time. Ethical understandings continually change, as has happened, for example, in deliberations on ethical ways to treat students and student texts in research (Conference 2000; Conference 2003; J. Harris 1994). We hope the discussions of ethics and the use of student texts to teach will similarly continue and develop. If there is one point from this chapter we hope will endure, this is it: ethics about teaching with student texts is not about the way to treat texts but the way to treat the persons who wrote and who are represented in the texts.

6

REFRAMING STUDENT WRITING IN WRITING STUDIES COMPOSITION CLASSES

Patrick Bruch
University of Minnesota

Thomas Reynolds
University of Minnesota

In this chapter, we hope to extend and develop the discussion, initiated in part by Douglas Downs and Elizabeth Wardle, of a writing studies approach to first-year writing (FYW). As Downs and Wardle suggest in their 2007 article, "Teaching about Writing, Righting Misconceptions: (Re)Envisioning 'First-Year Composition' as 'Introduction to Writing Studies,'" the term *writing studies* signals the grounding of FYW classes in the scholarly knowledge of the field of composition studies. As such, *writing studies* names approaches that seek to transform the current situation in which the goals of learning *about* writing as a cultural practice and learning *how to* write more effectively too often operate as mutually exclusive emphases within writing programs. Extending this work, our chapter seeks to help readers think about the ways student writing can play a central role in writing classes that are consistent with current composition theory and that also prioritize improved student writing.

For Downs and Wardle, and for us as members of a new department of writing studies, writing studies pedagogies define "becoming a better writer" as, in part, developing what Wardle has called "meta-awareness"—awareness of the sociohistorical contextuality of all writing (2007, 82). Thus, we agree with Downs and Wardle's explanation that writing studies FYW classes are classes in which students practice writing and, as part of that practice, learn about "how to think about writing in school and society" (2007, 558). One pedagogical strategy for teaching students "how to think about writing" is Downs and Wardle's "Intro to Writing Studies" strategy in which students read composition scholarship. But this introduction-to-the-field strategy is just one of many for helping students attain what we see as the core outcome for all writing studies FYW classes: developing a "meta-awareness" and growing as a writer by learning about writing. For us, that outcome can be effectively pursued by other strategies, several of which are described in this chapter by the teachers in our writing program at the University of Minnesota.

In the discussion that follows, we reframe some familiar practices for teaching with student texts (TWiSTing) in ways that close the gap between theory and practice by sharing results of a survey of teachers in the large FYW program situated within the department of writing studies at the University of Minnesota. In our survey we asked teachers how they used student writing in their classrooms, what they hoped to accomplish through their uses of student writing, what they believed they actually accomplished, and their overall sense of the value of student writing in a writing studies pedagogy. Our aim for this survey was not to gain a precise measure of the teaching practices and attitudes of our writing teachers, but rather to gather a variety of insights. (We invited all of our teachers to complete the survey but gave them the choice to remain anonymous. We received responses from 75% of the teachers.) Our descriptions of the results are not meant to summarize the responses but to provide a sense of the most revealing and insightful comments. By capturing a snapshot of the practices of teachers in a single writing program, we hoped to tap into the collective wisdom of our large and diverse teaching staff regarding the how and why of TWiSTing in a writing studies pedagogy that does not pursue the intro-to-the-field strategy. This practitioner-based approach to the ongoing development of writing studies can complement more theoretical work found in field-authored texts. Our discussion is organized around the TWiSTing strategies respondents reported and described—from peer review of entire essays to sharing texts drawn from outside the classroom. We will highlight both the practices for using student writing and the ways in which those practices contribute to writing studies pedagogies that contend productively with the still-dominant notions that see writing instruction as promoting an unproblematic single, stable academic discourse. We examine how teachers and students perceive the value of student writing as a teaching text, and the understandings of improved writing that are consistent with the pedagogies and perceptions we discuss.

Though we try to be rather direct and even directive in the following discussions of particular teaching practices, perhaps the key consistency in our respondents' views of TWiSTing in a writing studies pedagogy is that they encourage students to develop their own sense of purpose and strategies, methods, and understandings of writing. For them, and us, an important part of improving student writing is helping students contextualize and begin to question their typical misconception that there is one "right" way to write. TWiSTing is thus a means of helping student writers develop abilities to analyze contexts and strategies and to weigh the potential effectiveness of options for how to compose texts. Importantly, from this perspective, becoming a good writer is not so much about aligning one's texts with particular conventions, or refusing conventions, but about improving one's ability to generate and apply strategies for creating texts that navigate conventions and expectations in ways that fulfill students' own goals and objectives. In what follows we explain the teaching strategies our survey uncovered.

USE PEER REVIEW TO HELP REVIEWERS LEARN

Of all the uses of student writing, none was discussed more frequently by our survey respondents than peer review of student essays. The practical details of how peer review functions in each class vary, but the teachers in our survey represented the writing studies approach as focused on what student *reviewers* learn from the process of reading and responding to their peers' texts. As many respondents told us, the content of student feedback had far less instructive power for students than having their peer reviewers (who were working on their own similar texts) treat them as writers whose texts were worthy of serious investigation. More important than the content of the feedback students receive from peers, respondents talked about the instructive power of being treated like a writer and of treating others as writers. Indeed many of our teachers echoed one respondent's comment that "students seem to learn more about writing from analyzing and discussing their peers' drafts than from having their own essays workshopped." In this sense, the improvement teachers valued wasn't so much focused on a particular paper, but on enrichment of students' appreciation for writing as a practice of interacting. One teacher explained that peer review "is done partly to allow students to receive suggestions for improvement from their peers, but it also gives them an opportunity to see what other students have done with the same assignment." Another echoed this sentiment, saying that peer review "exposes students to all types of writing, from developed, challenging ideas to undeveloped, banal ideas (and everything in between). This also helps the class to

continue the discussion of writing strategies and patterns of organization—what does or doesn't work and why." Interestingly, none of the
respondents explicitly prioritized the instructive value of the direct
feedback given to student authors. To us, this unanimous emphasis
reflects a shift from a view of improvement built around approximat-
ing an unchanging standard (what in this paper can be "fixed"?) to a
view of improvement that values sensitivity to writing as a practice of
thoughtfully navigating the wide range of possibilities for communicating in a given context.

One of our survey responses included a detailed process for peer
review designed explicitly to "help the reviewers learn by using the
knowledge they have about writing and also learning about what writing can be from their classmates' papers." In the practice described,
students work in pairs to collaboratively review other students' essays
and then coauthor a piece of feedback explaining to the author what
they think are important strengths in the piece, what they like about its
approach to the topic, and suggestions for further development of these
strengths. In addition to the student paper being reviewed here, the collaboratively written response to the draft can be thought of as a piece of
writing from which the students can learn. The teacher's comment highlights this collaborative peer-to-peer writing as important:

> A lot of times when students are working on their responses together, I see
> them teaching each other about writing. They say things like "let's just get
> a version down on paper and then we can adjust it" or "I like the idea of
> what we're trying to say, but maybe we could say it a little more gently or
> more encouraging." At times like that, I feel the richness of the peer review
> process. The students see other ways of trying to do the assignment and they
> get to practice *using* their writing carefully and with others as they respond
> to their peers.

To us, this approach to peer review exemplifies how a writing studies pedagogy can work to close the gap between theory and practice
through activities other than reading composition scholarship. The student reviewers, working as a team, are able to help each other appreciate aspects of the text they are reviewing that, as individuals, they might
not have noticed. In addition, this process can be used to unseat student
attitudes that imagine a single, stable academic discourse as the normative standard and thus view any piece of writing as something that is
either "right" or "wrong." In contrast, this process exemplifies another

of our respondent's explanations of peer review as challenging the ideal of the perfect paper written alone:

> By sharing work throughout the term, people use communication and edit-ing skills to work cooperatively and get ideas through this interactive experi-ence. Rather than come into the class with the perfectionist model of paper writing, we work from free-write to completed paper as a team. This allows people to suspend their perception of some innate writing abilities for which they possess either a deficit or a gift.

Attempting to discern the most effective characteristics of a piece involves developing the sensibilities necessary to better assess one's own writing—seeing writing as a dynamic activity of responding to and shap-ing an audience's expectations. Thus, in addition to having practical value as an activity that can help students improve their writing in terms of its surface features, peer review can help improve student writing in the sense of helping students better understand writing as a social activ-ity of negotiation both in terms of content and style.

SHARE AND DISCUSS PARTIAL DRAFTS AND MICRO-TEXTS TO HEIGHTEN AWARENESS OF ALTERNATIVE STRATEGIES

In addition to assignments involving more or less whole drafts of papers, almost all respondents to our survey worked with shorter, partial papers written by students. These texts, including introductions to papers, the-sis statements, single paragraphs or pages of papers, conclusions, single sentences, and citations, were treated in two ways, both aimed at increas-ing awareness of alternative writing strategies.

First, teachers made use of these texts as isolated examples of prose features that worked toward helping the whole class write successful papers. Typically, this kind of exercise involved sharing with the entire class smaller pieces of student-authored drafts by means of overhead projectors or through computer projection. Teachers asked questions and facilitated class discussion in order to connect the particular stu-dent text to the assignment. Typical discussion points included as a primary goal how the text contributed to meeting the basic assignment goals. Teachers sometimes made use of the occasion to further clarify the range of possible responses to the assignment. Concerns included questions such as the following: How did this opening lead to a thesis that responded to the assignment? How might the student build on what's here to approach this particular microtask differently or more thoroughly to more fully engage the assignment? What were other approaches that might have been taken, or that were actually taken, with this unit of prose? Although treatment of isolated parts and features of student texts might lead some writers to focus too much on one or another aspect of writing, students usually benefit through participation in an open discussion that focuses on multiplying language possibilities and seeing approaches beyond their own. In fact, creating a forum around student partial texts that are treated in draft form introduces students to, and enacts, the notion that writing remains malleable, and that their drafts are in fact unfinished and open to revision.

Second, treatment of parts and features of texts also allowed teachers to direct attention beyond the immediate assignment by emphasizing more general writing issues. Student texts, in other words, were treated as examples of rhetoric in action. Discussions offered the opportunity to introduce the notion that texts of all sorts hold power by employing certain rhetorical strategies that act on audiences. Sometimes students read aloud classmates' thesis statements that had been written on an overhead, for example, and *heard* the power of ideas inflected by actual voices. Other times, students discussed the difficulties of writing conclusions to essays and offered tips to each other based on audiences they knew. Although discussion usually highlighted different approaches taken by students in that particular class, other referents also became part of the discussion. Typical questions included these: How did this approach emulate or differ from the same isolated unit of prose in assigned readings? Did students know of any examples from their own reading or writing that worked differently from the highlighted student approach? How do advertisements, Web sites, letters, and other familiar texts employ strategies in similar ways, or do they? Directing discussion so that the particular assignment becomes an instance of a larger world of texts can help students broaden their understanding for how textuality operates in the world, and it helps them develop an awareness of the broader contexts that have shaped their writing and are shaped by their writing. Explaining this point, one teacher commented,

> By making their own writing a main text of the course, I hope for my students to be producers of knowledge and not mere consumers of knowledge. I also hope to establish a community that models the larger social sphere in that the way in which knowledge comes to be results from a transaction of individuals with other individuals as well as an environment that includes histories,

traditions, power, and the like (a transaction as opposed to an interaction . . . transaction indicating that all involved change as a result of action).

SHARE PERIPHERAL TEXTS AND PROCESS REFLECTIONS TO HEIGHTEN AWARENESS OF ALTERNATIVE METHODS

Our respondents also described ways they used other kinds of student texts, those that lie at the periphery of the essay. Typically, low-stakes but required writing includes outlines for papers, written responses to assigned readings, and in-class freewrites. These assignments, of course, are designed to help students learn methods for developing their ideas, but they can also lead students toward a richer understanding of writing methodologies.

Early in an assignment sequence, teachers typically ask students to write in order to come to another piece of writing. In-class freewriting, for instance, usually asks students to react to a piece of writing or an idea the class has considered together through a reading, advertisement, film, or other prompt. Students are asked to highlight some aspect of the assigned text in order to then share thoughts and writings with other students. This writing is not expected to be highly refined or even complete, just thoughtful. Many times students share some aspect of the process of assigned reading and writing in these moments. Teachers make use of such moments in order to address difficult ideas, but teachers also listen for students' readings that suggest they are having trouble seeing the complexities in writing that at first glance seems to students all too straightforward. For example, most students might read a text such as *Narrative of the Life of Frederick Douglass* without many difficulties in comprehension, but how to work with such a text in a paper might be a task best addressed through peripheral student-authored texts exploring the complexities of human bondage and familial relations. In this way, these peripheral texts help students re-vision their ideas as they revise their texts.

Process-oriented reflective student texts also work at the periphery of essays, but they work toward improving student writing by enhancing self-knowledge about writing. Students are usually assigned to think back on, or project forward, what they have done, or plan to do, with a particular sequence of writings. One assignment asks students to explain what a particular assignment asks them to accomplish in terms of learning about and practicing aspects of writing. Teachers also ask for judgment statements about how well the student thinks he or she has approximated the goals for that sequence. Sometimes, this space also provides an opportunity to establish continuity among assignments in the course: "In Paper 1, I didn't do such a good job of laying out my main ideas in the opening, but I feel that I did a better job in Paper 2." For some students, this space is sometimes an opportunity to express what they experimented with in their writing in order to improve, whether this is a particular rhetorical skill, an extension of an idea that might have been left alone, or a revised process such as an additional round of revision aimed at a particular side of their prose. In carrying out these pieces of writing, students make explicit their own literacy processes, often gaining a vocabulary for talking about writing in ways that help them move beyond the misconception that there is one "right" way to write. Students generally share these texts only with the teacher who assigns them, unless they occur during an early stage of drafting. In the latter case, students sometimes share plans for proceeding with a particular piece of writing, and in the process try out associations and logics that others might confirm or challenge. For students who are less sure about steps and thoughts in their drafting process, this kind of sharing of writing can result in students trying on a new or revised process of their own, or simply reinforcing their own process as being in the same ballpark as others in the class.

Assigning process-oriented texts communicates that the class values and expects a layer of learning beyond the merely utilitarian task of finishing assigned papers. Becoming a better writer involves not only giving the teacher "what she wants" but also creating an internal dialogue about oneself as writer. Writing about one's writing experience can be a powerful tool to demystify authorial processes and build confidence in what one does as a writer. One teacher describes this process in this way:

> To give students the opportunity to share their research findings, ideas, and experiences with their classmates, thus validating all the time and work they had put into arriving at these findings and ideas; to make the research and writing "real," not just an assignment for their teacher but something they could actually learn from and share with others.

This comment reflects a writing studies pedagogy that narrows the frequent gap between composition theory and classroom practice. Whereas the introduction-to-the-field strategy might rely on professional literature to convey insights on process, this approach to learning is more experiential. For this teacher, student writing experiences become a foundation for the creation of knowledge about process.

MAKE CONNECTIONS FROM CLASSROOM TEXTS TO EXTRACURRICULAR STUDENT TEXTS

So far the TWiSTing strategies we have noted have made use of student texts authored by members of individual classes. Some texts, however, are owned, in a cultural sense, by students but not necessarily authored by them. Web sites, Facebook pages, music lyrics, assignments written for other classes—the texts students spend time getting to know outside our classes, and sometimes have a hand in creating, are important for many of our teachers' classes. Teachers create spaces for these texts by asking students to combine what they already know coming into the class with what they are learning in school. In a writing studies approach, teachers see this as a crucial act of connecting what is learned through the practice of formal composition tasks with a world of literacy experienced outside our classes. Aiming at teaching an understanding of writing extending beyond immediate class assignments, teachers strive to affirm student reading and writing experiences from a wider angle, asking students to think of how texts both inside and outside the class relate to each other and how literacy itself is shaped by circumstances in which it occurs. Most often outside texts that are close to students are brought into the class when a class has discussed the significance of literacy itself, perhaps through literacy narratives they have read and/ or written. Students are asked to locate meaningful texts for their own experiences and discuss them in small groups or as an entire class. In some instances students are asked to insert these texts into an additional text created either collectively (as in a group-authored Web page) or in individual writing assignments. Students gain a sense of how diverse the experience of literacy is for different students, and at the same time they experience the sense of how literate texts can draw people together, whether through similar interests, experiences of culture, or aspirations.

A WRITING STUDIES APPROACH TO TWISTING ENCOURAGES STUDENT INVESTMENT

After discussing ways they use student writing in their classes, the writing studies teachers we surveyed were asked about their perceptions of the outcomes of using student writing in their classes (both hoped-for and actual) and for their sense of the value of student writing as a teaching tool. Many of these teachers reported that bringing student writing to the table supports the learning goals of writing studies in two ways: it challenges students' notion that there exists a single, stable entity called academic discourse, and it also helps them improve their writing. In addition, many reported that they value student writing as teaching texts because these texts can enhance student investment in and commitment to peers and the classroom community, and they can help to connect classroom-based work to the broader social context of writing.

As we have suggested above, many of the teacher respondents explicitly valued the ways that exposure to student writing can complicate and diversify students' sense of what it means to write well. As students come to see that a variety of approaches to an assignment can have important strengths, they begin to challenge the notion that there is one "right" way to write. Making this critical insight productive demands that students are invested in working to produce their best work and the best feedback they can offer to their peers. Many teachers value TWiSTing because they feel it encourages this kind of investment and commitment. Many also reported that regular use of student texts discourages procrastination and encourages effort. Here, teachers offered comments such as "students take their drafts seriously since they will be read by others," "when students must share with the entire class, the level of writing is often improved simply because they must share with the entire class," and "when your words are splayed onto a big screen, you get serious pretty quickly." But the motivation for this investment, according to teachers, was that student texts came into the classroom not as assignments to be corrected but as examples of good writing in development. One respondent explained this approach led to students' pursuing "more inquiry, less judgment" because student writing comes into the classroom not to be judged but to be treated as an object that can help students learn about writing and how to write. The take-home message of our survey responses, then, is that important insights from the field of composition studies can be introduced into the classroom through thoughtful activities focused on student texts.

7

STUDENTS WRITE TO STUDENTS ABOUT WRITING

Laurie McMillan
Marywood University

Writing tends to improve when students internalize effective habits, and such internalization is more likely to happen when students are positioned as student-scholars or "experts" who can teach others about writing. At the same time, students are often likely to trust ideas about writing when these ideas come from their peers, especially when peer writing instruction avoids didacticism in favor of a friendly, somewhat informal tone. One way to simultaneously take advantage of both these principles is to have students write to other students about their writing practices. Such a strategy creates a strong sense of community and conversation among writing students, all of whom benefit, whether positioned as expert student writers or student audience. Indeed, often students can occupy both these positions at various times within a single course. Having students address other students helps students' writing attain the status that Bruce Horner argues, in this volume, it should have: it is no longer a commodity to be exchanged, but it becomes truly useful. This approach also helps students achieve many of the goals described by other authors in this volume, such as gaining a "meta-awareness" about writing (e.g., Anson, Davis, and Vilhotti; Bruch and Reynolds; Inoue; Downs, Estrem, and Thomas; Warnick).

While there are many strategies for creating student conversations about composition across classrooms, here I will focus on one easily applicable approach and will gesture briefly to other possibilities at the end of the chapter. In my first-year composition course, I ask students to communicate to other students what they have learned in the class, thus positioning these student writers as experts. Rather than present a faux rhetorical situation, I actually do use these student texts in the following year's first-year composition class. Future students thus also profit from this assignment: they learn about writing from the content, which focuses on composition; they learn about rhetorical strategies, which are enacted (to varying degrees of success) by their peers; and they learn implicitly that they can engage in conversations about writing, both as listeners/readers and as speakers/writers. The situation thus helps all students involved to take part in a composition community from which they can benefit and to which they can contribute.

END-OF-SEMESTER STUDENTS WRITE TO START-OF-SEMESTER STUDENTS

Near the end of the semester, first-year composition students write a letter to future students who will be enrolled in the same course—an assignment that reinforces course concepts while providing closure. The letter both *tells* future students what might be important to know about writing and *enacts* these priorities. Student writers thus reflect on and assess their learning, attend to connections between writing ideas and writing practices, and use a strong voice. This metadiscursive activity helps students transfer what they have learned about composition to new situations since they are asked to explicitly articulate writing principles.

As I explain at the end of this chapter, the goals of this assignment can be realized in many ways, but I ask students to complete their letters as an in-class essay so they can practice essay exam strategies with an engaging topic. Still, in order for maximum learning to take place, it helps to (1) teach students how to prepare for and complete essay exams; (2) assign homework that serves as a prewriting activity; (3) use a strong prompt; and (4) reinforce learning with a follow-up conversation.

These first two elements create an initial framework for the assignment. Students can learn approaches to essay exams through a class discussion that both draws on student experience and offers supplementary advice and practice through an online resource such as Purdue University's Online Writing Lab. For many students, this class will be the first time they have heard strategies for essay exams explicitly articulated. Once students are prepared to write in-class essays as a genre, a homework assignment helps them think about the specific issues that will be relevant to the assigned in-class essay. I typically ask students to review learning outcomes and write a reflection pinpointing what they learned during the semester, with their answers serving as a reference during the in-class essay.

The prompt defines the writing situation as fully as possible. The prompt itself includes a concise explanation of the assignment as well as guidelines for the end product and the writing process. One version reads, "Please write a letter to students who will be taking first-year composition next year. Explain to the students what good academic writing is and what they might do to improve their own writing during the course." Students are asked not only to describe but also to implement strong writing. I also specify the types of evidence students can use to develop their ideas, such as personal experience or information from class texts and class discussions. Finally, writing process guidelines encourage students to plan, write, and review their work.

The letters the students produce vary somewhat in their focus and are only rarely model pieces of writing, but they offer reassurance and basic strategies for succeeding in a writing class. For example, one letter reads,

> To whom it may concern,
>
> As you are sitting reading this there are probably a thousand thoughts running through your head. Last fall, I was where you are, wondering how I was going to be able to handle writing all the time and the work. The main piece of advice I can give you is to not put off your work. If you are given a certain number of days use them. It is one way to not fall behind. Another thing is for the reading/writing/thinking assignments, read them one day and the next day re-read the assignment and then do the assignment.
>
> Good academic writing is made up of numerous aspects. These aspects are that you write what is expected, you make more than one draft, you revise all your work and ask for help. Go to the writing center, meet with your friends and revise each other's papers, and ask Dr. McMillan for help. I can honestly say that whenever I met with her, she was able to help me. Dr. McMillan never made me feel like my paper was hopeless although I did sometimes, the advice she would give on my papers always made me surprised to be able to hand them in and say, "I wrote that."
>
> To improve your writing during English 160 look at the feedback written on your papers. Pay attention to your errors that you repeat and work on identifying them and also fixing those errors. Many times our reading/writing/thinking journals launched topics for our papers, so do not take those assignments lightly.
>
> I wish you the best of luck as you begin English 160. Although at times it may seem difficult to get through the work load you will be able to in the end. (Draghi 2008)

Although this letter is somewhat disorganized and does not offer a coherent definition of "good academic writing," the student writer empathizes with the student reader and offers some wise advice about keeping up with the work, asking for feedback on writing, and taking responsibility for reviewing, revising, and editing one's own writing. Teachers may find her advice to write "what is expected" trite, but the writer is probably referring to something more sophisticated—the importance of considering rhetorical situation. While this letter is problematic in some ways, then, it does include positive elements, and it ultimately acts as a snapshot of the student writer who is in the process of learning how to communicate clearly to others (a process in which I imagine we are all continuously engaged).

In order to reinforce ideas from the course that student writers can transfer to other situations, I offer a brief follow-up to the in-class essay. I extract pithy quotes and summarize some of the repeating themes from the letters to share at the final class meeting. Through this feedback, students' ability to communicate useful ideas about writing is recognized and praised, and the class ends on a high note with students becoming very aware of their own learning while continuing to learn from the wisdom of their classmates.

START-OF-SEMESTER STUDENTS LEARN FROM END-SEMESTER STUDENTS

The bonus to this activity occurs the next year when I distribute the letters to a group of new students in the first week of school. The letters both jumpstart thinking about writing and help guide first-year students' expectations for the class. Perhaps surprisingly, student authors are able to communicate central ideas about the course to new students far better than I, the teacher, can, simply because students are predisposed to listen to other students for practical information about a course. The letters my students write do not disappoint. As in the above sample, students often offer information not only about what was learned about writing but also about course workload, level of enjoyment, and level of difficulty. These latter elements are not mandated by the assignment; instead, students include these comments probably because such factors seem like a way to both hook the reader and help the reader with the upcoming semester.

To help new students engage with the letters, I create a strong contextual framework. For the third class meeting of the semester, students complete a homework assignment asking them to review learning outcomes and grading standards in order to form personal goals for the

course. During that third class, I distribute the letters written the previous year, with each student receiving a letter to keep (if I have more
students than letters, I make extra copies of a few letters). Students
read the letters, note what is most useful and most surprising, and share
their answers with the class. During this whole-class discussion, I keep
track of major points on the chalkboard, being careful to arrange these
points into four categories that I ask students to inductively identify at
the end of the discussion: 1) elements of "good writing"; 2) the writing process; 3) rhetorical strategies; and 4) the tone of the class. By the
end of that period, then, students have a fairly strong sense of where
the course is heading.

For the "good writing" category, student writers tend to provide general principles since writing expectations vary widely from situation to
situation. For example, students often remind their peers to "make
sure your ideas are organized in a sensible order" or "use appropriate
examples or your argument will fall apart" (Edwards 2008). However,
other concepts are less familiar to first-year students. One experienced
student explains, "Good writing is easy to read and easy to understand"
(Strakhov 2008), a point that bears elaboration because many students
believe that unnecessarily complicated sentences signal intelligence.
Another student recently advised his peers to "break the rules a little"
(McDonnell 2008), and new students were puzzled and wanted to know
more about "breaking the rules." This student-generated advice then
became an opportunity to begin introducing ideas about style and rhetorical choice because *students wanted to know*—not simply because *I*
wanted to tell them.

First-year students gain similar insights when they share quotes from
the letters that focus on the writing process. Certainly, the usual ideas
about drafting, revising, visiting the writing center, and editing are often
articulated to great effect. More strikingly, such ideas are often expressed
in terms of "conversion," as in this recent example: "I know that in
high school you probably did not turn in a paper that you wrote many
drafts of because I know I did not. But I learned that it is truly needed"
(Martell 2008). Here, the new students are more likely to become con-
verts themselves because their predecessors have undergone change,
and the importance of composing strategies seems less abstract because
a student who identifies with them has spoken about it. Furthermore,
one part of the writing process that many of my former students point
out as essential is surprising both to me and to new students: homework.

In a rather typical statement, one student asserts, "The best part about the class is the assignments every night. It sounds crazy, I know!" The student then explains: "It kept me learning and always thinking about the class since I had work all of the time" (McDonnell 2008). When students are encouraging other students to do the homework not because the teacher said so or because it will improve the grade but instead because it is useful for "learning" and "thinking," I am happy to sit back and let such students do the teaching.

With my guidance, students also begin to develop an awareness of the rhetorical situation and credibility. I can usually introduce this topic when a humorous line is shared with the class. One student warns his peers, "Do not cut any corners. Because Dr. McMillan will catch you. Such as 12.5 font. She will recognize it right away. Believe me—I know" (Strakhov 2008). When a new student reads a line like this aloud, the entire class laughs, and I ask why this writer is being silly and what the effect is on his audience. Some students believe the humor destroys his credibility, while others say they are more likely to believe him because he seems like someone they can relate to. At this point, I have the class identify the purpose of the letters, the audience, and the techniques that are likely to work well.

Not surprisingly, student readers also quickly notice elements that keep them from taking student writers seriously, such as poor grammar and spelling, sloppy penmanship, and disorganized writing. Through guided discussion, students are able to explain that when writers' credibility is damaged, readers are less likely to believe the message. Still, I explain that the letters were composed within a class period, and the student readers understand that such a writing situation offers less opportunity for revision and proofreading than an out-of-class assignment. Even the weaker letters, then, offer a source of learning for the first-year students.

Students also recognize that in order to read a text critically, they must understand the contexts in which authors are writing. For instance, savvier student readers often wonder how seriously they should take the positive comments about the class since they note that the teacher is a secondary audience for the letters and, after all, the grades of the student writers are at stake. I encourage such questions. Rather than use the observation to dismiss positive comments, I challenge student readers to decide which advice is useful regardless of whether the student writer might potentially benefit from offering the advice. For example, one student writes, "Dr. McMillan puts you in groups and makes writing more fun and active. She will always help you on big papers or small homework. You would think writing skills would be boring, but it's not. Just keep an open mind" (Strakhov 2008). In class conversation, some students resist the idea that groups might make writing more fun and active, but almost everyone agrees that asking for help and keeping "an open mind" are smart strategies. My former students thus reassure my new students and make the transition into college easier.

Once the major ideas from the letters have been unpacked, students take a few minutes to return to their personal goals for the course and review them. Students are encouraged to either add to their goals, revise them, or simply comment on whether the goals seem achievable in light of the conversation. With this framework, first-year students move into the semester already predisposed to learn about writing and to work hard with a good attitude; after all, their more-experienced peers have spoken, and the new students have actively listened.

The reading activity comes full circle at the end of the semester when these students have the opportunity to compose letters to the next group of students. Indeed, the in-class essay assignment becomes a sign that they have made it: they have successfully moved from the role of mentee to the role of mentor. In other words, they have learned how to participate in a conversation about writing by not only listening to other experts but also by synthesizing and applying ideas from throughout the semester, ultimately offering these ideas as their own gift to future participants in the conversation.

BEYOND FIRST-YEAR COMPOSITION: EXTENDING THE STRATEGY TO OTHER CLASSES

The approach to using student texts across classrooms I have outlined here can be adapted to many other situations. For example, in addition to having first-year students work individually at the end of the semester to communicate with students who will be enrolled in the same class, I have asked upper-level students in a composition theory course to work together to write and produce a film that will translate class expertise into a widely available teaching tool. The process of making the film itself stimulates learning in the class, of course, as students become invested in understanding material thoroughly and practicing a sophisticated kind of composition (that is, creating a film that includes not only spoken and written text but also visual and sound elements).

Furthermore, like the first-year composition essay, the project has meta-discursive elements, especially because the collaborative nature of the assignment makes writing, production, and editing processes more visible than they might otherwise be.

Of course, the video, like the first-year composition letter, is not only useful for student producers but also for student consumers in other classes—and, indeed, even useful for faculty in workshop settings. For example, one composition theory class created a video on peer review; I use this video as a springboard to help both students and teachers think about what approaches tend to help or hinder peer review. Interestingly, students and faculty alike respond to the ideas precisely because they are being vocalized and enacted by *students*. Just as the first-year composition letter positions the teacher as a facilitator of a cross-classroom conversation, the film assignment likewise encourages communication between parties interested in speaking to and hearing from one another.

In addition to letter writing and video production, I also regularly have students create Web sites that include both collaborative class texts and individual writing. Such Web sites can be used to teach future students about particular kinds of writing in terms of both content and form. I imagine other kinds of compositions could similarly reach across classrooms as teachers design assignments by considering who is writing, who is reading, and what students will learn through the activity. (For instance, Scott Rogers, Julia E. Kiernan, and Ryan Trauman model some possible approaches in their discussion of multimodal student texts in this volume.) While the particular ways of having students communicate their learning to other students can vary widely, then, they are united in their ability to benefit both the student writers and the student readers (or viewers). Chances are, a great amount of learning will take place. Indeed, finding ways for students to learn from other students is key when building a community focused on collaborative critical thinking about composition.

ACKNOWLEDGMENTS

Thank you to the Marywood University students in my composition course (Fall 2008) who have generously granted me permission to use their writing here: Nicole Draghi, Heather Edwards, James Martell, Matthew McDonnell, and Dmitri Strakhov.

8

THE LOW-STAKES, RISK-FRIENDLY MESSAGE-BOARD TEXT

Scott Warnock
Drexel University

In this chapter I focus on using one digital learning tool, message boards, to help us reconceive how students create and disseminate texts in our courses. We can use message-board texts as a significant component of our courses, building them into our syllabi as many low-stakes, informal opportunities for students to take intellectual risks and develop their writing. The message board is a versatile, easy-to-use technology—all learning-management systems (LMS) have some type of message-board application—that requires little training for teachers or students. Basically, a message board is a Web-based discussion forum in which participants post written (although they can include other media) messages that can be read by everyone with access to the forum; in a course, in many cases, this access is restricted to class members. Message boards are asynchronous, meaning participants are not logged in at the same time but instead contribute to the conversations on their own time (in contrast to, for example, a synchronous tool such as chat, which requires participants to be present at the same time).

Message boards can streamline our ability to use student texts, providing easy ways of making these texts available and distributing them. When we commit to making student texts central to our courses, we are confronted with a range of logistical issues: How do we choose the texts to feature? How do we (conveniently) distribute them to the class? As sustainability becomes a bigger issue on college campuses, how do we justify the sometimes considerable use of paper? How do we distribute and use the texts in a time-efficient manner? If the texts are relatively high-stakes gradewise, does that affect students' willingness to share and critique them? Message boards provide elegant solutions to these questions. Logistically, as Rolf Norgaard mentions later in this book, new technologies are "making it easier to get student texts into the undergraduate writing classroom" (229). Exchanging student texts once involved a literal paper shuffle; we do not have to worry about such things when the texts are digital.

More importantly, message boards offer intriguing teaching and learning opportunities. By leveraging this technology, we can make the class experience focused on student texts. Indeed, because boards streamline the reproduction and sharing of texts, they allow us to put into practice theoretical ideas about writing instruction. S. Joseph Levine says message boards don't just connect learners; instead, they go beyond the potential of onsite conversations because they "support higher-order constructivist learning and the development of a learning community." Students build course knowledge with their writing on message boards, he continues: "The discussion board has the potential to provide the basis for creating a climate whereby the learning process is not limited by the traditions of face-to-face instruction" (2007, 68). Pedagogically, boards open up fascinating ways to make student texts central to our courses. Whether we are teaching online, hybrid, or onsite, we can build a substantial portion of our courses around low-stakes, informal assignments.

WHY THE MESSAGEBOARD TEXT?

Facilitated by digital tools, these asynchronous student texts have several traits that allow them to fall somewhere between personalized informal writing students might do (journals, minute papers, etc.) and the formal material in larger course writing projects. These traits help facilitate the use of low-stakes assignments, creating the possibility of a classroom culture of productive intellectual risk taking. Toby Fulwiler, discussing the use of journals in writing across the curriculum (WAC), says they can be rigorous while allowing for speculative and imaginative thinking (1982, 15). Message boards have that trait as well, helping students invest time in smaller assignments that can serve as the foundation for formal writing projects. Initial posts by students may seem disjointed, but they can "be viewed as essential experiments" with course design, interface, or how their voices will "sound" online (Collison et al. 2000, 18). In his influential writing guide, *Style: Ten Lessons in Clarity and Grace,* Joseph Williams (2005) points out that writers need written raw material to diagnose their own writing. Message boards provide this material for diagnostic writing approaches because lots of text is available. Also, since posts are low stakes, we can have open conversations about mechanics that might not be as easy to have when we are dealing with high-stakes work.

At their core, message-board texts are a conversational exchange of writing that help us "clarify and extend the thinking" of our students (Collison et al. 2000, 104–5). The well-structured use of boards allows us to make a simple but profound change in a course, converting course dialogue into an exchange of student writing, with students in a constant written feedback loop with both us *and* colleagues. The class becomes about having the students "learn through dialogue" (Hanna, Glowacki-Dudki, and Conceicao-Runlee 2000, 14).

Message-board texts are usually semiformal. Writers pay more attention to detail—such as the grammar and mechanics of Standard Written English—than they would in a chat or text-message environment, but the occasional informal grammar or even Internet-based shorthand is acceptable, as those types of writerly moves sustain the board's dialogic liveliness. And indeed, the writers must constantly think of such writerly moves because these texts are sensitive to, and to be successful must account for, multiple audiences. Students are no longer just writing to the teacher, a writing situation that many writing scholars have criticized (e.g., see Crowley 1998). Instead, students have readers with multiple perspectives and motivations. This, as the introduction points out, can transform the writer from one who is "fulfilling an assignment" to a "public writer," a coinvestigator in the class's intellectual mission.

Message-board texts are topic focused. Students typically write a message-board text in response to a specific topic or question. Thus students can, through writing, delve deeply into the topics of discussion at hand, often exemplifying WAC writing-to-learn pedagogies. Message-board texts are also rhetorically focused. The writer has not only a clear purpose but a clear occasion for writing. The class culture that develops with message-board texts is written, and as posts multiply, this environment enables discussion of written discourse communities and levels of rhetorical appropriateness. This becomes a "medium is the message"-type environment in which students investigate their communicative practices, reflecting on rhetorical decisions while creating an extensive written archive. Despite this focus, another advantage to message boards is that they can allow the conversation to take unexpected turns. Joseph Ugoretz (2007) describes how onsite class digressions run against the clock. With message boards, he finds "that the different structuring of time in asynchronous discussions can alter the way that digression functions, transforming supposedly problematic diversions into engaging and productive learning tools." Simply put, he says, teachers can let discussions wander, perhaps helping students "make new and original connections arising from their own thinking and discovery processes."

Message-board texts allow a course to become a process of peer review, as it is easy to facilitate students' ability to read and evaluate each other's work. These texts allow us to establish revision groups and allow students to post document attachments. Students respond to each other in a textually-based, ongoing conversation. Sandy Hayes (2006) notes that teacher comments on message-board texts can model constructive response for students. She points out that this is akin to how we as teachers work on hard copies, but on the message board all of our comments can be seen by all students. We can continually model constructive response.

Finally, students communicating asynchronously have, of course, resources available to them. One of my requirements is that students use evidence in their posts, whether material from other posts or Web research. This constant practice is designed to refine their ability to develop an evidence-based mind-set when they write. Also, many message-board forums have built-in html editors, and most allow attachments. Students can use the tools to broaden their concept of *text*, regularly using images, sound, and video in creating multimodal expressions of their ideas.

SOME SPECIFIC ASSIGNMENTS AND PRACTICES

I attempt to manifest the various aspects of message-board texts I describe above into the following specific assignments and practices. I include, when possible, the actual assignment instructions. Each week I create several message-board topics, usually between three and eight, and I ask students to contribute three to five posts to these topics. Students are thus not required to post on every topic, although I expect them to read all posts. A significant part of using message boards effectively involves creating good prompts. "Questions should be clear, specific, and open-ended," Peter Albion and Peggy Ertmer (2005) say. "In addition, questions that are somewhat controversial and are likely to produce different opinions can provide a powerful tool for initiating and sustaining meaningful dialogue." We shouldn't be too clever and elaborate with prompts; I think we should keep things simple initially, as we can ratchet up the complexity of the conversation with our own contributions during the week. At midweek, I ask students to post a specific number of longer posts that I call *primary posts*, and then by a second deadline later in the week I ask them to post shorter *secondary posts.* More about the specifics of assigning and grading posts can be found at my blog, Online Writing Teacher (Warnock, nd).

Posts as Evidence

I have long been interested in students' drawing from each other's ideas as sources and evidence in their writing. In onsite teaching I have required students to include in their written projects colleague quotes from our in-class conversations. Of course, this method is not ideal, as students need to be sharp journalists/transcribers to record those comments. I employ this practice more productively with message boards. In formal writing projects, I require students to use their classmates' posts as sources. This seems to enhance participation, encouraging students to read and post more carefully. They may even work to write message-board posts that help steer conversation in a way relevant to their projects, perhaps almost taking on the role of interviewer.

Weaving posts into their own writing provides subtler advantages too. They must juxtapose these comments productively against other evidence. Perhaps even more interesting are authority issues that may emerge during peer review, as students and reviewers must think about the validity of student evidence. (I like how reviewers can encounter their own quoted material when reviewing a colleague's project.)

Finally, using posts in this way can contribute to the authenticity of student writing. If we are seeking obstacles to student plagiarism, using texts in this way can help. Some evidence in students' written work must be embedded in the class culture; a student could still purchase a paper, but that student would have some work ahead in creating contexts for evidence from the class boards.

Post Proofs

Peter Elbow says that as writers we need to be tolerant of our own mistakes (1981, 38). While we always want students to revise and rethink their texts, we often use as the vehicle for that revision work high-stakes papers and projects. With the post proofs assignment, I ask students to review several of their own posts and proof them, writing an accompanying metacommentary:

Subj: Post proofs
Hi all,

Note that everyone must post a primary post here.

Go back over your own Discussions posts. Pick two longish ones (probably primary posts) and cut and paste them into a separate document.

Now, go through them carefully, seeking out writing errors. Correct those errors or comment on them in ALL CAPS. At the bottom of the document, write a sentence or two about what you think about the posts after reading them again.

Cut and paste the whole thing into a post here on this thread (don't attach a separate file).

Let me know if you have questions,

Prof. Warnock

With message boards, they can write thousands of low-stakes words, and perhaps that low-stakes environment is more conducive to their learning what we really want when we ask them to see a piece of writing again, removing their fear of finding mistakes in projects that are worth a significant part of their final grade.

My Favorite Post(er)

This assignment asks students to review all class posts up to a certain point and then either identify one especially strong post or a collection of posts written by another student. I typically assign this at midterm for individual posts and at the term's end for a particular poster. Here is the midterm assignment:

Subj: My favorite post

Hi everyone,

Please look back/think about our message boards and pick one stellar post by one of your colleagues.

Clearly identify the post so the rest of us can find it, and then describe why it was your favorite.

Looking forward to some well-earned compliments,

Prof. Warnock

Here is the way I alter this at the end of the term to focus on another student, not just a post:

Subj: My favorite poster

Hi all,

Everyone must post at least one primary post to this topic.

As we did a few weeks ago, I want you to look back through the archives of our message-board threads this term. However, this time, I want you to identify someone whose posts stood out for you all term. Identify a few examples by this person, and use actual quotes to demonstrate the talent of this writer and to provide evidence for your choice.

Give out some compliments,

Prof. Warnock

These assignments ask students to take a close, critical look at each other's writing, reflecting on what about writing appeals to them: clarity? diction? humor? evidence? The answers to these questions perhaps lead to a better question: do these same traits apply to *my* writing? Assignments like this also build assessment into the course, as Katrina Meyer (2007) points out, bringing "a form of useful feedback into earlier stages of the course." Students, by "voting" for favorite posts and posters, determine class excellence. Finally, this assignment helps build a constructive class environment: these compliments appear to build camaraderie, which is especially useful in online courses.

Writing Puzzles

Because message boards provide us with lots of informal student texts, I believe they can help us with the instruction of grammar and mechanics. I use writing puzzles for this: I cut and paste grammar and style issues from posts, including my own, and I have a separate thread during the term for this material. I call them "writing puzzles" so students can approach them as playful examples to help them work on mechanical issues specific to their own writing, not as oppressive "problems." For instance, I posted this snippet as a writing puzzle:

> Many whom argue to legalize drugs are only doing so for marijuana, making him guilty of over-exaggerating and over-stating the issue, and those who support legalization of cocaine and heroin should be quoted directly on the topic.

Students often respond with surprising interest to these puzzles, sometimes commenting in multiple-screen posts that elicit multiple responses. The author or other members of the class can work on the writing issue without worrying about grades. Elaine Maimon says, "Too often talking about commas becomes a safe substitute for teaching and demonstrating how writers behave" (1979, 365); by putting the puzzles in their own thread, I use the LMS space itself to indicate that while grammar is not always the focus of instruction, we are still learning about the nuances of correctness.

Metawriting

As the written conversation in the class develops, we can use message boards for metawriting assignments that help students investigate their own writing processes and practices. Here is one, about research:

Subj: Share your secrets

Hi folks,

I always lament that we rarely talk about writing in college. If you have some trouble with writing, it's like a dirty secret. I don't like that, and I think it's damaging to students who are trying to develop as writers.

Let's take research, for example. Where do you start? How do you do it? What techniques do you use? How do you stay organized? How do you remember how to incorporate quotes?

For instance, when I'm looking through a source (whether electronically or on paper), I jot down the page numbers in the left margin of a notebook or to the left of my Word file. Then I write my notes—some quotes, some paraphrases—until I get to the next page of my source, and then I put that page number in the margin and keep on going. That way I never lose track of what page my notes are from, and I always know where a quote came from without having to rewrite page numbers in my notes. I find it helps me keep things organized.

I also get plenty of great (well, I think they're great) ideas when taking notes. I use the code MO in the notes to indicate that this is MY OWN idea. I don't know how that got started—it just did.

Let us know some of your research tricks,

Prof. Warnock

While it might seem that students would respond tepidly to a prompt about research process, that has not been the case. In fact, they have revealed so many interesting aspects of their research process that I have abstracted the best of these responses and provide them as a "gift" to the whole class at the term's end. I create similar threads about how they read, their writing process, plagiarism, or how they develop a topic. Students can be surprisingly honest and thoughtful when asked to write about these topics on the conversational message-board forum.

Creating a Pseudonym

Another way to incorporate constructive play into our teaching when using these texts is to write from a pseudonym. For instance, I create a persona, sometimes named "Dr. Logoetho," who makes exaggerated claims students are invited to refute. I try to bait students to see if they can remain logical and poised in the face of an unreasonable interlocutor. Here is an example:

> *Subj: Challenge Dr. Logoetho?*
> Dear students,
> We will have an occasional visitor in our class, Dr. Logoetho. Dr. Logoetho has never been defeated in an argument. He has decided to test his undefeated streak against you this week with this argument (from his own hand, of course):
> "I think the whole debate about steroids is overblown. I guess kids shouldn't be encouraged to take steroids, but I think that anyone else who wants to should be allowed to take steroids. After all, life is about finding advantages. Why should steroids be any different? If you want to take steroids to bulk up or run faster or if you are a professional athlete, then I say go to it. It's nobody's business if you want to take a substance that may harm your health down the line—and I'm not even sure that's even been proven."
> If you want to take on Dr. Logoetho, go to it—but make sure you *use your evidence.*
> Good luck,
> Prof. Warnock

These "characters" I create may argue without evidence, use logical fallacies, or debate strictly from emotion. At the end of the week, we review—using specific student texts—how students responded. Have they used evidence-based counterarguments? Have they maintained poise? Have they sought logical flaws in Dr. Logoetho's stance? Because the character is not me, this seems to avoid the problem of becoming an argument between the students and me, and the texts students create become the centerpiece of often lively debates; as Dr. Logoetho, I try not to give in easily.

Peer Review

As I mentioned, when using message boards, we make our classes an ongoing exchange and peer review of student texts. Students are constantly reading and evaluating each other's written work. After a few weeks, students come to expect feedback. We can also use message boards for conventional peer review, taking it out of the classroom and placing it in an electronic environment. I often create private subgroups of reviewers; a four-person group could work together all term in a private message-board subspace accessible only to them and me.

Because I can post documents and have students access them easily, the ease of peer review even influences assignments. For instance, I often use a process assignment. First, I ask students to submit a 1,000-word argument. I tell them that word count is the most important thing. I place them in peer review pairs, and I then reveal that the reviewer's main job is to help cut the 1,000-word piece down to 500. They resubmit on the message board, and then I ask them to submit a final version: a one-page, 250-word letter to the editor. The drafts are all easily accessible, so we can use the draft artifacts to map this work. I complement this assignment with a prompt about how they worked through the process and to provide specific examples. Sure, this involves some teacherly trickery, but many students wrote—on the message board—how they appreciated the assignment. As one said, it encourages them "not to grow too attached" to their writing.

A Brief Word about Grading

With any low-stakes assignments, my advice to teachers is straightforward: do not be the bottleneck in the system. Remember what we want the student message-board posts to achieve so we do not obsessively grade every writing aspect of every post. If we do, we will burn out, with the unfortunate yet likely result that we will pare down these informal writing opportunities for our students. Juan Flores thinks mandating grades in this environment creates a "reflexive symbiosis" (2006, 433) in which students operate just for the grade, but, conversely, I think we avoid that problem by giving lots of grades. On a 1000-point scale in my course, primary posts are worth ten points and secondary posts five. I grade every post, primary and secondary, but I have clear criteria and expectations, and I do *not* overemphasize mechanics and spelling. If, for instance, a student answered the research post above with an earnest, thoughtful description of his research process written with a reasonable attention to writing detail, that is fine. Students receive many grades from me, and the number of grades alone creates a risk-tolerant learning environment. I feel this stream of grades also allows the grades to operate in an optimum way, as a form of constructive communication between us and our students. Some of us may choose to grade each week's posts collectively, but the key is not to over-evaluate these posts: let them write!

MATCHING TECHNOLOGY WITH PEDAGOGY

Many concepts and practices we associate with good writing pedagogy are given new potential with the use of message-board texts. Susanmarie Harrington, Rebecca Rickly, and Michael Day say that "technology . . . should not be used simply because it is there, but rather because it can further existing educational goals . . . pedagogical goals should determine whether and what technologies are used, not vice versa" (2000, 5). The asynchronous message-board environment enables us to create innovative assignments that make student texts central to a course. We can build a "reflective, critical pedagogy" in a risk-friendly, textual environment. Because students can review archives of their communications, the course moves into a "metadiscursive realm" in which they continually reflect on their thinking (Harrington, Ricky, and Day 2000, 9). Because they write so much, each assignment itself is only a small piece of that end-of-term grade. In addition, as Gail Hawisher notes, this asynchronous environment may foster more equitable student participation (1992, 88), opening up dialogic opportunities for all students; George Collison, Bonnie Elbaum, Sarah Haavind, and Robert Tinker put it this way: "When the only way to participate is to comment, there's no such thing as 'sitting silently in the back of the room' and receiving credit for attending a meeting or class" (2000, 78).

Obstacles to using student texts are often logistical or even financial—passing multiple copies around a room, hoping students have taken home materials and read them, and asking students to pay for copying (or paying ourselves)—but compared with print-based course limits on exchanging documents, "online courses need not be subject to the same restrictions since files and messages can be exchanged relatively easily and quickly, allowing significant additional interaction with peers" (Albion and Ertmer 2004). This added interaction helps drive a pedagogy of low-stakes, risk-friendly writing. There is so much writing that no longer does every word pouring forth from them have to mean so much—and don't all good writers understand that? When we introduce technologies to our classes, they should be used—initially—in ways that complement our teaching. Then, almost invariably, we will begin to rethink our pedagogy. Levine says message boards do not simply reproduce onsite conversations but instead "support higher-order constructivist learning and the development of a learning community. . . . The discussion board has the potential to provide the basis for creating a climate whereby the learning process is not limited by the traditions of face-to-face instruction" (2007, 68). Message boards allow students to easily share their writing. From there, only a teacher's imagination restricts what can be done with these texts.

9

PRODUCT AS PROCESS
Teaching Publication to Students

Karen McDonnell
James Madison University

Kevin Jefferson
James Madison University

Teachers in our discipline talk a good game about publication. Painfully aware of what Peter Elbow calls the "damagingly restricted, teacher- and evaluation-haunted context" of the classroom (2002, 2), we ask our students to think beyond the grade, to define a purpose, a persona, and an audience with someone—anyone—other than us in mind. At many of our institutions, we can point our students toward accessible audiences. Here's our contest for first-year writers, we say, or our journal of first-year writing. Here's our campus newspaper, or a club newsletter, desperately in need of contributors. Even more immediately, here's how to post your essays to our class blog, or class wiki, or class whatever the latest fad may be. All of this is for the good, for our students, for our programs, and for our discipline. As Nicole B. Wallack notes in this volume, the rest of the university can and should look to us when it comes to publishing excellent student writing.

The problem is that the writing process we teach treats publication as an afterthought, and that our publishing process—where it exists—is often controlled entirely by teachers. Pull any writing handbook off your shelf and check the index for the word *publish* or *publication.* It's probably not there. Our students prepare, compose, collaborate, rewrite, collaborate some more, and edit in a dizzying circle, but they do not learn to be published. Now consider all of the first-year writing (FYW) publications sold in university bookstores or linked to on writing program Web sites. In most cases, faculty solicit submissions and thus filter students' work, faculty establish the criteria, faculty read and evaluate essays, and faculty decide what should be published. While it's difficult to interrupt the student-teacher relationship, in which students write for their teacher, this structure doesn't even try. Submissions do not have to be written for a larger audience; they merely have to be better than the other essays in the class. Students hoping to win—to be published—write to please their teacher, and beyond that teacher is another set of teachers to please. This mind-set is entrenched to the point where we don't even recognize it in our teaching, in what we tell our students, and in the journals we administer.

One solution to the problem lies in making students party to the back-room, behind-the-scenes negotiations that most FYW publications reserve for faculty. The following passage by Eileen Donovan-Kranz describes the effort Boston College faculty invest in producing *Fresh Ink*, their FYW publication:

> It's never, "OK, let's find the 25 best essays." There's always a kind of balancing—of "don't we have that kind of essay already? And, hmmm, we need a textual analysis; is there any good textual analysis in here? Is it good enough? Do we have too many research papers?" So that some . . . shaping of the book happens when the committee meets, and we start [to] think about how we would teach with it and how the essays work with each other. (quoted in Loomis 2006, 53)

The work Donovan-Kranz describes is time consuming and often exasperating—hence its usual designation as "service" for faculty—but it is also where we learn from each other, test each other, and formulate or revise our ideas. When we work collaboratively to define and apply criteria to finished student texts in order to create a publication, we engage in exactly the kind of critical reading and writing we hope to teach students in FYW. We are not peer reviewing or workshopping rough drafts under a teacher's watchful eye, nor are we editing, as our students typically understand the term, with the focus primarily on formatting and sentence-level concerns. We are instead doing the work of editors, in which publishing *is* the process. Putting this responsibility in the hands of students extends to them the larger perspective afforded by publication.

In a course dedicated to producing *e-Vision*, our university's FYW journal, we've started to develop a coherent practice for teaching publication to students. Unlike most courses—indeed, unlike any course we can think of—the *e-Vision* editorial-board course depends on other courses for both its material and its meaning. Because our student editors focus exclusively on student texts (submissions from FYW students), they have nothing to read and no target audience if writing teachers do not support the journal. While this reality makes for some anxious moments, it also makes the course a vehicle for changing the way we understand the writing process. We suggest that the editorial process our students undertake offers a model that can be implemented in any writing course seeking to deepen critical reading and writing skills.

DEFINING EXPECTATIONS

Students who enroll in our editorial course come to us well schooled in peer review and workshopping. In other words, they are good at offering and receiving feedback in the weird middle ground between the expectations their teacher has established and the grade their teacher will assign. As Asao B. Inoue recognizes in this volume, writers caught in this middle ground have little reason to accept their classmates' feedback: "Usually a student's peers have very different expectations than the teacher, so why would a savvy student listen carefully to her peers when the teacher is still going to grade her work?" (47). But the problem extends also to the reviewers tasked with commenting on their peers' drafts. What incentive do reviewers have to articulate, much less apply and argue for, their different expectations when their classmates likely won't listen and their teacher might disagree? The results are all too familiar: vagueness ("Good job!"), a narrow focus on formatting and sentence-level concerns ("I think you need to cite here"), and a crippling deference to the teacher ("I'm not sure if this is what she wants"). The sneaking suspicion here is not just that our students *don't* articulate their expectations for good writing, but that years of having had evaluation criteria either imposed upon them (best-case scenario) or (more commonly) left unexpressed have rendered them *unable* to articulate their expectations for good writing. Teaching students to define their values is therefore an important first step, whether our students are working in FYW courses on their classmates' drafts, as Inoue suggests, or in our editorial course on finished essays written by students they've never met.

The editors' initial task, then, is to create the rubric they will use to evaluate submissions. Our one contribution to this process is the rubric's basic structure. Because we want it to open up opportunities for discussion, rather than shut them down, the rubric must feature expandable boxes to invite specific written engagement. Beyond this stipulation, the rubric is our editors' creation. Instead of inheriting the language from the previous year's rubric, they read the most recent volume of the journal in order to develop their own. This retrospective approach allows the new editorial board to identify values previous editors have established, and to notice what else they *should* have valued. They then work collaboratively to arrive at a preliminary list of criteria. They discard some of the criteria, combine others, clarify their terminology, compare what they have written with the previous year's version, and then finally apply their rough draft of the rubric to a carefully selected first essay that we read and discuss in class. The question is not whether the essay is good—we try to give them a good one—but whether the rubric helps them to think about and then to articulate for their classmates exactly why and how it is good. If the rubric isn't flexible enough to cover the entire range of essays generated in the various FYW sections, if it doesn't permit editors to respect and engage essays that are effective in different ways, they can agree to revise or add to its terms.

We happily accept the inevitable fumbling that occurs in these initial stages in exchange for the conversation and sense of ownership engendered. In our editors' most recent rubric, for instance, "Clarity of purpose (may be exhibited as the point, message, thesis or intent)" replaced a line from the previous year that read "clear, focused, relevant purpose that is achieved." The shift introduced different language, but it also pointed toward our editors' recognition that the earlier version would have subtly confined them to questions of whether "it does or does not do something," instead of freeing them to think more deeply about *how* each essay works. Our editors then collapsed the twelve criteria from the previous year into seven criteria, decided that the resulting list should be hierarchical and reordered it, then ended by adding a space to comment on "potential." The final version allowed our students to consider what an essay could be as much as it helped them to engage with what it already was. At a deeper level, it helped our students to see themselves as editors entrusted with assessing potential, rather than judges tasked with assigning a grade.

COMMENTING ON STUDENT TEXTS

The student-centered approach carries over into the process of reading, evaluating, and discussing submissions. To prepare for class, every editor reads the same batch of submissions and writes comments in the rubric's expandable boxes for the top two essays. The editors are thus always literally on the same page, with an emphasis on extended close attention to each individual essay. We help our editors direct their attention by offering particularly good examples of comments written by the previous year's editors, along with the essays they commented on. These models underscore the importance of clear analysis and specific references to the text in question. In their comments, we want our editors to recognize each essay's strong points and to acknowledge its problem areas. We want them to weigh different facets of the essay against one another. And we want each editor to earn his or her "thesis"—a yes, no, or maybe vote—instead of simply justifying an initial impression.

While we do offer written feedback on our editors' comments, we find that they arrive at more meaningful insights when they exchange feedback on each other's comments. These "Comments on Comments" activities give our editors a chance to point out where their fellow board members could be more complete in their analysis and more clear in why they voted as they did. Equally important, editors gain a very immediate sense of their colleagues' different values, tactics, and insights. In some cases, the pairs of students simply remark on the contrasts. "I'm not sure if I'll change my approach," one student concluded in her response to a classmate, "but we're so different—it's interesting." If nothing else, these two student editors will have a better sense of their audience when they make their arguments on essays' publication potential. In other cases, though, the students see opportunities to revise their thinking. "I need to eliminate some extra information that may not be necessary and look on the positive side," observed one editor after reading her partner's comments. Her partner's rejoinder—"She did a good job of discussing positives and negatives without sounding wishy-washy . . . [where I] probably wasn't critical enough"—suggests that both editors benefited from the exchange. Analyzing their colleagues' comments helps to sharpen editors' metacognitive awareness of their own critical practices.

Most of our class meetings begin with the editors voting silently on the week's submissions. This preliminary vote, and the fact that each editor has commented on just two of the essays, allows us to facilitate discussion. Different editors start the debate on each essay using their written comments to introduce the piece, refer the group to specific passages, and explain their votes. They attend to possible counterarguments, develop their claims, and appeal to their audience. The other editors then weigh in to expand upon, redirect, and sometimes question what has been said. At the end of each class meeting, editors revote with essays that earn a majority of "yes" or "maybe" votes set aside for further consideration later in the year. Thus, after these exchanges, editors may revise their thinking about an essay's publication potential and may in fact change their minds about their initial votes. These practices support Inoue's ideas about assessment rhetorics: like Inoue's students, our editors have a "chance to reflect upon those changes, rethink practices, and theorize [their] developing ways of judging, valuing, and articulating judgment" (56). They are enacting what Inoue calls the "rhetoric of writing assessment" (46). And in so doing, students claim a degree of power and authority so often championed in our discipline's theory but rarely yielded in its practice.

Our role during these meetings is easier to write about than it is to carry off. Because we neither voice our own views during discussions nor take part in the voting, it is inevitable that submissions we might endorse go by the way, just as it is inevitable that submissions whose merits we question are eventually published. But we hope to be teachers, rather than editors, in this process. Our intent is not to enforce what we think, but to help our students define and communicate what they think. This is not to say we remain silent. Our students need to be drawn out, especially early on. They find it safer to occupy the middle ground of a "maybe" vote, to echo what others have already said, and to dwell on essays' faults. They are often hesitant to offer opinions and unused to explaining their positions, and they have little experience at persuading their peers in a classroom setting. In short, they are developing as editors. So we keep their rubric before them, we play devil's advocate, we ask questions, and we encourage explanations. We caution them against cherry-picking a text's flaws, we rein them in when they rush to a too quick endorsement, and we slow them down when they talk past one another. What we have found is that our students grow in confidence and skill as critical readers and writers. They articulate and support their judgments, cultivate group dynamics and learn collegiality, and weigh multiple factors such as quality, range, and the writer's ability to make further revisions.

Teachers of writing will likely notice that to an extent this work resembles the peer-commenting process that most writing classes structured as workshops already embrace. However, in important ways, the process differs from, and, we argue, can enhance and easily supplement the workshop format of any writing course. Most notably different in this model are the texts in question. Students are analyzing and commenting upon "finished"—previously drafted, revised, and graded—student texts, written by students who are not present in the class, what Doug Downs, Heidi Estrem, and Susan Thomas call "'far' texts" in the following chapter of this volume. On one hand, this distance from the writer allows the editors freedom to comment honestly and openly about the quality of the ideas and the skills of the writer; on the other hand, such freedom can lead to sneering comments and group ridicule (not unlike what can happen in interoffice banter or in programmatic writing-assessment situations). But these moments are teachable moments and indeed lead to other skills that we consciously try to develop within our students: sensitivity, maturity, and responsibility.

"WRITING" THE TEXT

Our students' work over the year comes to a head during the final voting process, when they reread all of the essays awarded "yes" and "maybe" votes and decide on the final shape of the publication. We have found that the group truly comes into its own during this intense phase. As a core of publishable essays emerges, we notice a degree of calculation and passion, with individual editors recognizing that they will have to argue for their favorite essays. They will have to persuade, to compromise, and even to concede. Moreover, they must consider other factors that may have been swept aside before. Namely, if *e-Vision* is to be useful to writing instructors as a course text, then our editors have an obligation to ensure that the publication reflects what instructors teach. Beyond this concrete consideration, students must also engage more complex philosophical questions asked by the discipline writ large: Do we have an obligation to be cutting edge? How do we assess multimodal submissions? What even counts as writing? The editors' inclination to choose the most likable essays—the ones with a riveting voice and stylistic flair, usually exhibited through personal narrative—can be difficult to overcome. However, part of maturing into the role of editor means factoring in the journal's audience and purpose, and being realistic about what's possible in the short window of time reserved for working with the writers.

The final stage of the publication arc may well be the trickiest, the most frustrating, and the most unpredictable, but also the most rewarding. After our editors decide on the essays they will publish, they sign up in teams to work with the writers. The goal is to move the pieces from writing that has potential to writing that fulfills its potential. Here again, our editors enter into a set of negotiations their experience has not prepared them for. They make discoveries they share with a mixture of surprise and delight: no such source exists, quotations are taken out of context, whole chunks of an essay have been plagiarized. And, more pleasantly, this writer's research is as comprehensive and accurate as her voice is good. They consider sentence-level revisions, adjustments necessary to make the piece available to a wider audience, and the possibility of larger shifts.

Deeply invested in the success of the essays they are working on, our editors have to motivate at least that same level of investment from the writer for a piece long ago set aside. The editors' enthusiasm for the piece and communication with the writer can facilitate or inhibit this work. Editors must also strike the difficult balance between encouraging the writer's revising and controlling it. In some ways, the work we advocate here resembles the *Young Scholars in Writing* editorial process Downs, Estrem, and Thomas detail in this volume, with one major difference. While it's true that one round of the editing process for *YSW* rests in the hands of previously published student writers and students in advanced writing classes, the faculty advising editors handle the actual work with the writers slated for publication. Our model, by contrast, reserves this responsibility for student editors, who become peer reviewers in the scholarly publication sense of the term. Recognizing that "behind each student text produced for our classes is a rich network of activity and interactions and collaborations," as Downs, Estrem, and Thomas so elegantly put it (128), we believe students should reap the benefits of these productive interactions.

PUBLISHING AS CURRICULUM

Dreaming big, we would love to see writing programs across the nation develop courses dedicated to editing and publishing student texts. Doing so would send a message to everyone involved. To students, it is the clearest way to say that their institution values student writing as something more than an academic exercise. They labor as writers and editors to create a finished journal not just for a line on a résumé or for a sound bite at some future interview, but because their institution believes that the process of publication affords a valuable learning experience, and because it believes that writing is something to be shared.

To teachers, such a course validates the claim that publishing student work is a key part of the writing process. The process of publishing is not something that happens in stolen summer moments, with a few faculty members in a room; it is not service; and it is not extracurricular. It is instead demonstrably *central* to the curriculum; it is curricular. And to outside audiences—parents and administrators at our year-end ceremony, students who stumble across the course description in the catalog, visitors to the departmental Web site, and anyone who reads the publication—a course dedicated to editing and publishing student writing helps strengthen writing's identity as a discipline committed to encouraging, publishing, and using student texts.

Even as we couldn't resist offering a plug for courses like ours, we recognize that a dedicated editorial-board course is a rarity, and likely to remain a rarity. So how do we work within existing curricular structures to include opportunities for the publication process? Last year, one of our colleagues undertook a truly innovative and experimental project in attempting to replicate the entire *e-Vision* publication arc in his FYW courses. In his two sections, his students wrote their papers about *e-Vision* texts. They analyzed the texts. They debated the texts' merits. They even questioned some of the editors' decisions. As the culminating project for the semester, these students enacted a vetting process patterned after the editorial-board course. Across his two sections, students conducted blind readings to determine which pieces were the strongest candidates for publication. They argued, they voted, and at the end of the term, they submitted the best pieces to *e-Vision*. In this way, not only was the cycle of publication sustained, but first-year students also had the opportunity to see publication as more than simply an afterthought in the writing process.

It's not necessary, though, to revamp an entire syllabus or make a journal of student writing the centerpiece of an entire FYW course, as our colleague did, to achieve valuable pedagogical results. Whether it's within one section of FYW, among one teacher's multiple sections, or part of a collaboration between two teachers' sections; and whether writers are seeking publication in the class zine, the department's journal, or the institution's writing contest; elements of the editorial process we've been sketching can be retrofitted onto preexisting workshop structures. Alternatively, elements of the process lend themselves well to stand-alone exercises: ask students to develop and apply a rubric to two texts that are differently good. Have them respond not just to the comments they receive from classmates, but to the comments their class-mates receive from other classmates. Ask them to assess the sources—their quality and how they are used and cited—in a finished student text, either from a different FYW section or from a student publication.

No matter the scale, efforts to make publication part of the writing process involve students in a conscious, collaborative democracy. And students seem to see it. "We were directly involved in the entire publishing process. . . . I felt the publication was a reflection of the process," one student remarked in her end-of-the-year evaluation. Another comment indicated that the collaborative experience is a valuable one for students: "I learned a lot, especially working together as a group towards publication." Moreover, their insights reveal that the benefits of any course that values publishing run deeper than might be expected. "The comments and discussions of the advisors and peers," according to an editor, "have helped me become a more critical writer and reader." These statements validate our belief that the process of writing is made fuller and better when publication is given its rightful place as *part of the writing process*. Publication can inform our thinking and shape our teaching in ways that promote students' growth as readers, writers, and thinkers.

10

STUDENTS' TEXTS BEYOND THE CLASSROOM
Young Scholars in Writing's *Challenges to College Writing Instruction*

Doug Downs
Montana State University

Heidi Estrem
Boise State University

Susan Thomas
University of Sydney, Australia

with Ruth Johnson, Claire O'Leary, Emily Strasser, and Anita Varma

The student texts that center a writing course should include not only those written by students in that course but also those circulated texts that other students have written in other times and places. In this volume, McDonnell and Jefferson describe using student texts from first-year composition courses in a publishing course, and here we examine "closing the loop" by bringing published, scholarly student writing into FYC. In this case, we focus on articles in *Young Scholars in Writing (YSW)*, a peer-reviewed journal of undergraduate research in composition and rhetoric. Reading published student research in comp/rhet lets writing students explore a range of rich pedagogical possibilities constituted not simply by the texts themselves, but by the activities they inspire and represent and the interactional processes that have shaped their production. While discussing a variety of pedagogical implications connected to using *YSW* texts in the classroom, we want to speculate as well about underlying issues: what we can learn from the writerly practices and exchanges that lead to publication in this and similar venues; how the presence of *YSW* unsettles easy assumptions we might have about the role of student writing not only in our classrooms but in our field; and how the reflections of writers published in *YSW* might help us rethink common teaching strategies. Pushing further, we wonder about what counts as a student text in the writing classroom: the language on the page itself, writerly accounts of the production of that text, writing students' interactions with the writers of these articles? Such speculation leads us to demonstrate in this chapter that when we start engaging students with published student texts like *YSW* articles, we as teachers come to see differently *what we're trying to teach to begin with.* Ultimately, then, we're studying how using student texts in the writing classroom teaches not just the students, but the teachers.

We begin our exploration by considering four interrelated pedagogical challenges that the field seems to face and that our work with *YSW* has unsettled. From our own teaching of (first-year) writing courses, we have noticed that:

- student texts circulate as inexpert texts on the margins of the academy and the discipline in ways not heard, recognized, or valued by us as professionals in the field

- within the classroom, student texts can quickly become ossified, classroom-only genres (see Salvatori and Donahue, this volume)

- student texts are likely to be read by peers in draft stages, but far less likely to be read, valued, or interrogated as highly polished, published texts

- context-specific writing processes can devolve into *the* writing process as a familiar pattern of draft/peer-review/instructor-feedback/revise-for-portfolio forms within the structure and constraints of a class

As writing instructors who care deeply about teaching writing in engaging, compelling ways, we have seen these patterns arise repeatedly in our own teaching. But working with *YSW* takes us beyond our classrooms, helping us see differently our discipline, our teaching, and our role in fostering an inclusive space for all writers.

After a brief background on *Young Scholars in Writing*, the bulk of this chapter unpacks the four pedagogical challenges listed above, showing how *YSW* articles and the experiences surrounding them articulate with these problematic narratives about student texts. Our discussion weaves concrete teaching strategies for writing classrooms with the reflections of four students—Ruth Johnson, Claire O'Leary, Emily Strasser, and Anita Varma—published in *YSW*. While the pedagogical implications of *YSW* are intriguing, we want to explore broader principles that shape our curricula—both how we teach and *what* we teach.

WHAT IS *YOUNG SCHOLARS IN WRITING*?

As the nation's first scholarly undergraduate journal in composition and rhetoric, *Young Scholars in Writing* provides a venue for students to publish their research. The journal was founded in 2003 by Candace Spigelman and Laurie Grobman; in 2006, Laurie Grobman expanded the editorial board to include twelve faculty advising editors (FAE), including us three authors. Writers submit their work in one of three categories: Advanced Research, First-Year Writing, or Comment and Response. Submissions are peer reviewed by students in advanced rhetoric and writing courses whose teachers are FAEs or by writers previously published in *YSW*. An FAE reads a submission and its peer reviews and makes acceptance decisions. Most accepted submissions require extensive revision, facilitated by FAEs.

As FAEs, we have learned that the principles underlying our work with *YSW* reflect/refract those that inform our teaching: that writers and researchers learn through working as legitimate, public participants in the context of cultures and classrooms; that discourses become transparent (in the paradoxical senses of both visible and naturalized) through immersion, reflection, doing. We now think any student or teacher of writing can learn extensively from the rich, complex, sometimes messy process experienced by *YSW* writers as made visible in the scholarly publication process and the writers' reflections on it.

STUDENT TEXTS AS EXPERT TEXTS

First we turn to this challenge of how student writing circulates and its invisible, marginalized status. Simply through its presence, *YSW* unsettles the classroom-specific way of circulating texts only within that same classroom. If we imagine the millions of pages written each year in general-education first-year writing courses as well as undergraduate courses in composition and rhetoric majors across the nation, we see that the overwhelming volume of student text produced remains nearly completely invisible to the field as a whole. It is structurally marginalized through no fault of the instructor, but simply because it stays right there, circulating only within a particular section of a particular course at a particular university. *YSW* moves student texts from the margins; it is a documented testament to the belief that undergraduate writers can be contributors to academic discussions, not just consumers of them— or even "inventors" of them (Bartholomae 1986).

The presence of these published student texts unsettles an easy assumption that student texts are somehow essentially different from published, expert texts. As Bruce Horner observes in this volume, student texts are too often imagined in terms of exchange value but not use value. In her 2006 *College English* article on the field's citation of student writers, Amy Robillard notes that our field often positions students as research subjects rather than contributors or researchers themselves, and this perspective can become an accepted—even an invisible—conception that we bring to the classroom. We simply don't often have the time or foresight to consider how student texts might be or evolve into "expert" texts. But like Robillard, we see how *YSW* instead opens possibilities for student writing, naming students and allowing them to interpellate the discipline that we might hear their voices.

The journal similarly subverts students' assumptions that their texts can only ever be novice. Indeed, they come into our writing classes assuming (quite reasonably, based on their experiences) that they have nothing to contribute and have no right to speak expertly. Yet *YSW* showcases students who have truly contributed, had voices, been heard— allowing other students to see themselves there too and challenging their notions of who can do original research. We relish such sabotage. As Better Erickson, Calvin Peters, and Dian Strommer (2006) report, students in their first few years of college largely encounter classes that only ask them to recite and regurgitate. *YSW*—and its underlying principles—demonstrate that we're *genuinely* asking for something else, that our request of students to attempt to contribute is with precedent and not impossible, not unreasonable, not lip service. We *really* seek their thinking, and we really do believe they can study a question or a text in a way no one else has before. We see, then, *YSW* and its student texts as a means of provoking students, and teachers, to think not just about textual production but about the *entire project* of first-year writing courses.

STUDENT TEXTS AS LEGITIMATE SCHOLARSHIP

The presence of *YSW*—and the practices of the writers published in it—give materiality to intellectual genres of writing. Instead of showing "academic writing" as a monolithic, classroom-bound genre, *YSW* helps instructors and students imagine—and write for—scholars beyond the classroom. Rather than showing static research papers, *YSW* demonstrates a public, intellectual community in dynamic conversation to which students can visualize contributing. It shows research-based genres that disseminate new research and fuel discussions and debates.

For our discipline, *YSW* (particularly the First-Year Writing feature) models what student writing of research related to writing and discourse can look like. As the field explores "writing about writing" pedagogies (see Downs and Wardle 2007), a real pedagogical challenge is that most recent research in composition and rhetoric is enmeshed in disciplinary contexts that are challenging for many writing students to use. *YSW* articles give students tangible "goal-texts" or visual targets. And unlike professional articles about writing, which help students learn about the research in the field but also risk conveying that *only* professionals can research. *YSW* articles counter that impression. Finally, first-year students often struggle to understand writing *as studyable*. For them, writing tends to be a closed question—borrowing Keith Hjortshoj's (2001) terms, a set of "'laws of writing' that every college student everywhere used to write effective papers" (40). Thus, students often draw a blank on research questions related to writing and literacy. A *YSW* table of contents, used in small-group and whole-class exploration and discussion, becomes a superb invention tool, with questions sufficient to fuel publishable research.

"REALIZED" STUDENT TEXTS IN CIRCULATION BEYOND THE CLASSROOM

Within the field of rhetoric and composition, many have pointed to the implications for and effects of having students read each other's work (Ede and Lunsford 1984, for example; see also in this volume Anson, Davis, and Vilhotti; Warnock; and McMillan). Within our own classrooms, we often encourage or require students to circulate drafts, but far less often their *finished* texts, to in turn affect and shape each other's scholarly inquiry. *YSW* articles clearly support claims that students have something to say and voices deserving to be heard; but even more we are struck—particularly on listening to *YSW* writers—by what these articles can show students and instructors about being read. Students have often in previous instruction lacked having their writing *read* rather than judged, evaluated, analyzed, diagnosed, or corrected.

The Comment and Response section of the journal highlights for students how other finished student texts have been read, discussed, and written about by yet other students. It can help students understand that, and visualize how, their work could create genuine conversations with readers and might tangibly shape those readers' thinking. For example, *YSW* author Emily Groves's (2005) analysis of AIM (instant messaging) users' roles of voyeur and narcissist is taken by writing student Jonathon Ellis (2006) as a jumping-off point to "examine three additional facets of the program to provide further evidence that the narcissist/voyeur dichotomy is used within AIM" (94). As they refer to, cite, and re-cite each other, these young scholars' words build upon each other to accessibly demonstrate the cumulative, interactional nature of academic conversations that shape both the writer and the reader.

YSW can also show a great deal of what happens after a student is "finished" with their paper for the class, and in so doing, it helps writing students see what it is to be read and cited. It reinforces the notion that teachers are not the sole audience for student work and that the creative, reflective process does not end with the last week of a writing class—or at least that it needn't.

STUDENT TEXTS IN AN EXTENDED INTERACTION

Within our classrooms, as noted previously, situated writing processes can easily reify into "the" writing process. Given the constraints of university contexts, instructors inevitably require drafts, revisions, and feedback on schedule. *YSW* writers, though, experience meaningful revision far beyond the classroom. We wonder what of such experiences might usefully be brought into the classroom, and how? Along with our own perspectives about ways that *YSW* articles can make revising and being read visible, we have found it useful to listen to some young scholars for whom we have been FAEs. In order to compare our perceptions of their evolving processes with theirs, we asked *YSW* contributors Ruth Johnson, Claire O'Leary, Emily Strasser, and Anita Varma to reflect on their processes as writers and researchers. We think their responses suggest how writing students might see writing differently with the presence of *YSW* articles in the classroom.

These writers' pieces developed from a series of interactions with themselves, peers, writing-center clients, teachers, and advisors. In 2007, Ruth Johnson published a coauthored essay with Beth Clark and Mario Burton, "Finding Harmony in Disharmony: Engineering and English

Studies." In addition to their collaborative writing process, she also points to the input of their original research participants, two writing-center directors, their writing-center staff, scholars at a writing-center conference session, peer reviewers for *YSW*, and two *YSW* editors. Ruth, Beth, and Mario's article thus embeds a long series of interactions played out in verbal conversations, e-mails, and tracked changes. Emily Strasser, whose essay, "Writing What Matters," also appeared in *YSW* in 2007, stresses the same theme, telling us,

> In my work in the writing center at Vassar, a drop-in peer writing consultation service, we always encourage student writers to consider their readers, yet it is hard to take this advice seriously when they know only their professor will ever read their papers. By revising my work for publication, I learned to take ownership and responsibility for my language, and to think about how different types of readers might respond to and challenge my argument.

We also note from Emily's response the often-forgotten point that as writers, we are always addressing invoked audiences (Ede and Lunsford 1984), writing to readers called from our imaginations. More interactional writing experiences bring this home for students, and we see here Emily's distinction between publication and classroom writing, with its implication that if writing teachers can show their students the published work of other students (especially from similar courses), their students are then looking at results of such interaction. Further, we as instructors are learning ourselves. The student "texts" of their processes now shape the ground we cover in the classroom by helping us rethink how we might accommodate, encourage, and teach for this enriched view of student writing processes.

Claire O'Leary published "It's Not What You Say but How You Say It (and to Whom)" in *YSW* in 2008. Her response also helps us think about what in her revising-for-publication process had not shown up in her writing course. She describes the interactional nature of writing-to-be-read this way:

> Collaboration with reviewers both far and near geographically, who may or may not have specific knowledge of your subject matter, is a skill that requires practice. For me, having such a positive experience with the submission and the revision process for *YSW* has given me more confidence to effectively work with the comments of others and continue polishing a piece until it is as strong as it can be.

YSW articles, by this light, contain a lot of *history* of comments received and used—something we as FAEs have long recognized and are intrigued that *YSW* contributors see too. The publication process offers writers metacommunicative channels outside their main channel (manuscript) that allow them to differently hear that main channel. This writing, reflecting, talking, and rewriting as expressed by the YSW writers here represents a rich, complex set of interactions that unsettles any formulaic writing process we might (however unintentionally) communicate, or be constrained by, in our writing classes.

Another critical aspect of this extended interaction lies right in that adjective: *extended*. Time—to revise, rethink, absorb challenging feedback, revise—was critical for these authors. While writing classes are bound by short time constraints, hearing so clearly about the long-term, intensive, engaged process these writers experienced helps unsettle our notions about what is possible—and appropriate—in any one writing course. For example, Ruth says her publication experience "proved" to her the theoretical claims about process she encountered in her training for peer tutoring in the writing center. We would like, then, ways of having more students vicariously experience such proving, by bringing *YSW*'s proving experiences into the writing classroom. And yet, though we think that is possible, one of the real challenges for writing instruction lies in the material, structural constraints of the context: can writers really experience this kind of interactional, evolving process of exchange and rewriting in a specific (ten- or sixteen-week) time frame? Both Ruth's and Anita's accounts stress the function of time. Ruth details two semesters of work just to reach the draft first submitted to *YSW* (via presentations to writing-center staff and then to the Southeastern Writing Centers Association conference), with a total writing process spanning roughly a calendar year. Her story underscores the advantages of writing and revision that *YSW*'s departure from the more constricted regular classroom environment represents. Anita Varmer published "Politics of Difference in the Writing Center" in *YSW* in 2008. Her process, which up to submission to *YSW* covered more than a calendar year, also emphasizes the time/space function:

> I was able to revise with a clear eye toward the overall argument, structure, and research backbone of the piece because . . . I read the reviews, processed my mixed feelings, and let the reviews and the article sit safely on the desktop of my computer for three weeks while I located, read, and annotated the

additional recommended research. Taking some time away from the piece while still working on the piece through active reading made applying the new material I had read far smoother.

This time issue is significant for *interactional* writing; Ruth's and Anita's experiences and accounts suggest how much more likely it is that meaningful findings and their communication happen in timeframes beyond the semester (or quarter!) clock. Of course, professionals rarely work from formation of research question to publishable research in sixteen weeks, either, even though they might have the background and experience to do so. We can hardly expect undergraduates to produce contributive work in a semester or a fraction of it. Following this reasoning, using *these* student texts in the classroom suggests that to show the meat of the writing process many of us claim to teach, we may need radically restructured writing "courses" (think dining) that take place over multiple semesters.

STUDENT TEXTS IN INTERACTIVE REVISION

When student writing circulates only within the classroom, revision often becomes a give-and-take between the writer and the instructor focused on a grade. The experiences of *YSW* writers suggest that negotiating among the responses of more readers helps students to see revision less as a sign of *failure* and more as a normal function of writing—that is, as development rather than correction. Both Claire and Anita reported an initial (and seemingly inevitable) writerly reading of "please revise" as emphasizing "not good enough." Anita's account particularly captures the shift in conceptualization from revision-as-failure to revision-as-development: "Reading the feedback, I was both pleased and (at least briefly) crestfallen. I had worked on the piece for more than a year, and I was growing weary of re-revisions. Yet at the same time, I was energized by the reviewers' fresh thoughts and perspectives." For instructors thinking specifically about using student texts in the writing classroom, *YSW* articles can helpfully feed discussion on conceptualizing revision, particularly in relation to the reality (rarely well understood by students) that "good" writing truly does vary according to the situation, meaning that even an A essay in English 101 could elicit a "revise and resubmit" response from journal reviewers. The *YSW* publication process, when rendered transparent to students, can also demonstrate distinctions between private assessment by teachers and public assessment by peer reviewers and journal editors—a greater number of readers (a minimum of four), and a different yardstick (not grades, but what a piece contributes to a public discussion). As Gert Riljaarsdam's (2008) research on use testing of texts showed, students learn a tremendous amount about writing by watching readers attempt to *use* their writing—in a way that grading can never quite show.

How these enriched experiences with revision might shape our instruction is a useful challenge to consider; it's not as if teachers can hold up an article and say breathlessly, "Look at all the revision here!" The end of the publication process explicitly veneers a text's history. (A mild exception being the practice in science publishing of differentiating submission, revision, and final acceptance dates.) Even so, there are clues for starting points. That teachers simply know of and discuss such veneers with their students is a good first step. In addition, like most publications, *YSW* articles include authors' acknowledgments that frequently reference peer reviewers, editors, and the revision process. Calling students' attention to these can make for fruitful discussion, as many writing teachers are sufficiently experienced to elaborate on what revisions a writer's reference would likely involve. What you have been reading in this chapter itself can be done with *YSW* articles in the classroom: writers' accounts of their writing experiences. While the journal does not currently publish writers' e-mail addresses with their articles, the editors would happily pass along contact requests to authors, and we have found that *YSW*'s authors are happy to answer questions about how their articles came to be. Such contact would itself be interactional, not to mention teaching students good habits of scholarship and collegiality—that is, being in communication with scholars with whom they share interests.

IMPLICATIONS OF *YSW* INCURSIONS INTO COMPOSITION CLASSROOMS

YSW texts, and the experiences of the writers behind them, raise serious challenges for our conceptions of and assumptions about writing instruction. These writers' reflections on timelines that stretched beyond the academic semester prod us to think about programmatic and institutional questions both in and beyond individual classrooms. If we mean to teach students the writing processes and interactions common to texts that circulate beyond classrooms, we must look to published writing and take, to whatever extent possible, its productive knowledge and processes into those classrooms. Our analysis suggests that these likely involve

- nontraditional process instruction which breaks the linear progression from brainstorming to portfolio and inserts discussion, conversation, and multiple readers reading toward contribution instead of grades;

- shifts in course sequencing, both of assignments within courses, and courses stretched or linked to foster the carrying of projects from one course to the next;

- more audiences, more specialized audiences, and more frequent audience involvement in writing processes;

- greater scaffolding of the projects students undertake and the genres they aim to produce.

Our analysis suggests as well the need to think about texts not just as *read* but as *used*, another innovation we imagine is too rare in first-year writing courses. In short, we suggest interested teachers ask themselves what it would take to create experiences and structures that deliberately lead students to write for destinations like *YSW* (or a new venue for publication, the *National Conversation on Writing*) and the writing processes it demands.

Ultimately, the problem is one of teaching conceptions of writing resembling those that *YSW* writers experience themselves. These young scholars' words continually remind us that, as we know but too easily forget, behind each student text produced for our classes is a rich network of activity and interactions and collaborations. Utilizing "far" student texts in writing instruction, then, helps expand and complicate all of our notions of what it means to learn to be a writer.

ACKNOWLEDGMENTS

The ideas of *YSW* contributors Ruth Johnson, Emily O'Leary, Claire Strasser, and Anita Varma permeate this chapter in ways that have made them, while not exactly authorial, more than research subjects. As active participants in online discussions about this piece, their presence and interaction in our writing challenges our usual categories. Given that this text depends so heavily on thinking about (student) writing in rich, collaborative ways, we use the writing "with" convention to acknowledge the extent of our intellectual debt to them.

11

THE FIGURE OF THE STUDENT IN COMPOSITION TEXTBOOKS

Mariolina Rizzi Salvatori
University of Pittsburgh

Patricia Donahue
Lafayette College

In this essay, we examine the ways in which students and student writing are represented and positioned within composition textbooks and consider the pedagogical, theoretical, and ethical implications of such practices. Let us state at the outset that our process of textbook selection was rather haphazard (no "canon" of textbooks exists, and perhaps that is a good thing). We looked at textbooks on our shelves and those on the shelves of our colleagues. Since we teach at different kinds of institutions—a research university and a small liberal arts college—this afforded some range. We asked colleagues for recommendations. This criterion of availability made our task simpler, as did a criterion of modernity, which justified our looking only at textbooks published after 1949. (Fortunately, a considerable amount of excellent historical work on early textbooks is available.)

Our study begins with *Modern Rhetoric*. It was written by Cleanth Brooks and Robert Penn Warren, and published in 1949, before composition emerged as a distinctive field of inquiry and before the pedagogies of writing and reading were separated through acts of disciplinary dissociation. We want to use this textbook as a baseline of sorts, to trace the continuation of its conventions for representing students and their writing in current textbooks and to raise questions about the occasional uncritical adoption of those conventions. Our project is not a history of composition textbooks, nor is it a manifesto for a particular kind of student representation. Instead, we want to raise awareness of conventions used to configure—and figure forth—the student in composition textbooks. *Modern Rhetoric* provides a point of entry.

MODERN RHETORIC: EXEMPLARITY AS AN APPROACH TO READING

The authors of *Modern Rhetoric* were already highly respected authors, literary critics, and professors when the first edition of their book was published in 1949 (our focus is on the first and second editions). Brooks was a prominent architect of the "new criticism." Warren was an influential literary critic and a Pulitzer winning novelist. It is difficult to imagine today two literary scholars/writers of such prominence taking upon themselves the challenge and the labor of writing a composition textbook (Wayne Booth, Robert Scholes, and Gerald Graff come to mind as notable exceptions).

In the letters exchanged by Brooks and Warren during the years when they were writing *Modern Rhetoric,* they jokingly refer to that project as a way to make money. They also acknowledge the existence of several "competitors." And they advise each other to seek inspiration in certain books. It's clear they were familiar with the range of composition textbooks available at the time.

Modern Rhetoric displays several important features. Most notably, it accords student writing a prominent place in the form of examples—examples *of* something worth examining and learning from. In the preface to the second edition of *Modern Rhetoric,* which relies on a much larger number of student texts than the first edition, Brooks and Warren state forthrightly that the function of such examples is "in some instances, to *illustrate* the actual process of composition and, in all instances, to *counterpoint* the literary selections to which the student's attention is constantly called" (1958, ix, our emphases). They are reaffirming and expanding here on a point made in the first edition that students learn how to write from "example . . . rather than precept, and precept constantly related to example" (xiv). When they finally provide examples, they carefully teach us how to read them. They identify what they exemplify, summarize their main ideas, and often narrate what the writer has apparently done. In other words, they construct the student example *qua* example through a process of reading that establishes and controls its significance, as it explains what the reader is to learn from it. We speculate that the care with which the example is framed suggests a certain anxiety about the use of student texts and their potential "excess"—that they always say more than a teacher can capture.

Inherent and implicit in the first feature is a second one of remarkable pedagogical weight: the presentation of student themes as examples of texts to be carefully read, and as texts that reward a careful reading (see Joseph Harris in this volume for the reading he provides of student texts). It is useful to reiterate who were Brooks and Warren. They were authors, critics, and college professors, trained in literary study, but assigned to teach both literature and writing at premier academic institutions. In their own scholarship, they turned their theoretical gaze, as Matthew Arnold would say, onto the best that had been written and thought. While such works seem obviously to be entitled to the kind of close reading that New Critics were in the process of codifying, it is remarkable that they would subject student texts to equally careful scrutiny. This is not to say that their readings of student examples are as detailed or theoretically nuanced as is Brooks's reading of Keats's odes in *The Well-Wrought Urn* (1947); nonetheless, in their textbook, student writing is accorded a position of considerable importance. This respect might derive from their own classroom experience: they taught writing, and taught it frequently; they read student texts with rigor and even pleasure; and they were very much invested in the challenge and excitement of writing pedagogy.

Brooks and Warren had an important goal in writing this textbook: they wanted to apply to the "problem" of writing instruction what they had learned about reading from the so-called new rhetoric. As advocates of that rhetoric, they were certainly conversant with the classical rhetorical tradition. But in their effort to render this tradition new, to modernize it, they privileged reading and made visible not only their own reading practices but those of their students: "The basic practice of this book and the author's best claim to possessing a method—though it is at once more and less than any 'method'—is the constant analysis of specific passages. Indeed, this book may be described as a tissue of such analyzed passages" (1949, xiv). This approach to reading (what is commonly and historically called "close reading") attends to the words on the page, views meaning as contained within language itself, makes interpretation systematic by privileging unity and organic form—which are principles, they explain, of writing as well.

This theory of reading is enacted throughout *Modern Rhetoric*, both in terms of what Brooks and Warren say specifically about reading and what they demonstrate about reading through their own interpretive performances. The most explicit and possibly insightful statement about reading occurs in the second half of the book (a collection of already-published expository essays). In this section, by way of introducing these materials, Brooks and Warren make the point that no "foolproof system" of reading exists: For one thing, different kinds of writing may call for different systems of reading. . . . a system which works for one person may not work for another. In the end, the student may have to develop his own system. (539–40)

The fact that the student is included among this group of readers, as one likewise called upon to develop "his [sic] own system," is especially important. This statement is followed by a series of questions that the student reader in particular is encouraged to ask:

1. What is the material?

2. What understanding do I already have of such material? That is, do I have any basis for comparison and criticism?

3. What is the author's motivation? Is he trying to inform me, convince me, persuade me, or make me participate in a total, imaginative experience—the experience of a novel, say, or of a poem or play?

4. What is the author's basic idea or theme?

5. How is this idea developed in the structure of the work? In other words, what is the author's method of thinking?

6. What are the tone and style of the work? Do I understand the intention and the effect of the language as used in his work?

7. What enlightenment does the work give me? New facts? New ideas? New methods of thought? New sense of character? Deeper awareness of human experience? (540)

Although these questions appear explicitly in the second half of the book, they have already been at work implicitly in the first half. Early on in the book the authors reproduce a student theme, titled "Why I Wish to be an Engineer," as an example of writing that is "not well-unified" (see question #4). It is also discussed in terms of what the language reveals about the writer's quality of mind (see question #5). At this point in the book, rather remarkably, Brooks and Warren invert the usual process of application: rather than move from expert to novice writer, they ask students to apply what they have learned about writing based on their work with student themes to that of the more accomplished writers. Elsewhere in the book, student texts are favorably compared to those by famous writers (217). The last chapter of the second edition, "Characterization," offers "a rather successful attempt to absorb the analysis into the narrative itself (1958, 847)..." The analysis is drawn from an anonymous student theme.

We should mention, however, that student texts are occasionally marked as being different from published works in a negative way, as not quite measuring up. To illustrate, let us return to the seven reading questions listed above. As we have already mentioned, Brooks and Warren argue that different types of texts require different reading approaches. In the case of a text written by a published author, readers are advised to begin with analysis (divide a text into its major components) and conclude the interpretive process with synthesis (rearrange those parts into a general statement about a text's significance). By "significance," Brooks and Warren mean the power of a text's content to "enlighten" its readers, and it is not a power they attribute to student content, at least not explicitly. Instead, they encourage readers to examine student texts atomistically, dividing them into parts that illustrate something about writing or writing pedagogy: what students actually say is of no importance.

This implicit disparagement of student context should not distract from the fact that Brooks and Warren's presentation of the student text—the effort to construct it as example, the effort to read it in terms of a protocol used for published work—is surprisingly respectful. A familiar narrative within composition studies is that the student text remained invisible until composition emerged to reclaim it; with its 1949 publication date, long before any speculation about composition's reputed "origin," this textbook challenged that claim.

Since Brooks and Warren's text does offer an early vision of student writing visibility, it is useful to explore exactly how this vision materialized on the page. In terms of font and indentation, student writing looks the same as writing by published authors. However, the system of quotation marks a difference: in the case of the writing by published authors, their first and last name, followed by the title of the piece, whose full provenance is generally given in a footnote, appear at the end of the quotations. In the case of the writing by students, writers are not identified as actual people (with one or two exceptions), and writing is not provided a context. From our current perspective, there is a telling disjunction here between how Brooks and Warren think of students and the limits of representation of students and their work inherent in the conventions of literary scholarship Brooks and Warren and/or their publisher adopted.

If we were to ask, "Is there a student in this composition textbook," the answer provided by Brooks and Warren is "yes, sort of." "The student" definitely has a presence within the text in terms of writing examples, which are read to illustrate certain pedagogical principles—principles guided by the reading list provided in the middle of the book. The student is also presented as someone who is imitable and worthy of careful consideration. But this constructed student is not always a "real" one. Many examples of student writing are written not by actual students but by the authors themselves. The book is also populated by students identified as hypothetical, ghostly figures whose purpose seems primarily to allow for the introduction of issues or problems or alternatives—a fact which from our present perspective may (and should) raise concerns about what is now being referred to as "the ethics of representation." Finally, while the authors of the expository pieces provided in the second half of the book are named, those in the first half—which are primarily students—are not. As we have already said, students are afforded considerable respect in this book, but more in terms of generic rather than individualized identity.

Before we move on, let us conclude this section with a list of positive representational strategies employed by Brooks and Warren, strategies that we believe contemporary textbook writers would be wise to consider.

- Brooks and Warren make a concerted effort, whether in the form of "real" or "hypothetical" examples, to indicate to students what they are themselves capable of achieving as writers. Students are capable of doing good work because they already possess considerable experience in language and with the guidance of their teachers can continue to build on this knowledge. The example functions, therefore, as a directive to help students determine which kind of writing is appropriate to the academic context and how a particular topic should be shaped.

- Many of their examples are not "real" examples but are instead composites of student work (constructed papers) or models (hypothetical papers) Brooks and Warren crafted themselves. Such constructions are often marked by phrases such as "Let's assume that . . . " or "a student might write." These benevolent forgeries allow Brooks and Warren to trace and highlight certain writing strategies they wouldn't otherwise be able to discuss. What Brooks and Warren present as hypotheses are actually carefully thought out moves that model ways for students to achieve comparable results.

- The most remarkable gesture of respect Brooks and Warren pay their students is that they never use their writing as bad examples. (They do not participate in the "tradition of complaint," which Bruce Horner discusses in this volume.) When examples of bad writing are presented, they are either constructed or drawn from published sources. Interestingly, two such examples include an essay published in *College English* and a long excerpt by John Dewey. The lesson here is that bad prose is not the exclusive property of student/theme writing.

- The only examples of student writing that consistently bear the name of the author are research papers (and these examples often include the title of the course and the professor's name as well). Why is the writer of a research paper entitled to *his* name (the authors of the research examples tend to be male students), while the writer of a theme is not, or less frequently so? In the context of writing the research paper, Brooks and Warren remind students that "Full credit should be given for the source of every fact or deed derived from another writer" (1958, 392). Ironically, this is advice they do not themselves consistently follow in their citation of student writing. Yet it is good advice. And if we were to follow it, our students—and our published research—would certainly benefit.

AFTER BROOKS AND WARREN

In this section we want to move beyond Brooks and Warren to identify some of the representational practices currently dominant in composition textbooks. Our investigation suggests that changes have been made in the practices of citing student work, although not as consistently as one might expect. And there is obviously a lack of agreement not only on the use of student writing, but on the citation of such work. While he was editor of *College Composition and Communication* from 1994–99, Joseph Harris outlined specific procedures, which, unfortunately, were not generally adopted (see Donahue 2007). His own practice also changed—the most recent incarnation of which we'll discuss shortly. The Spring 2003 issue of *Writing On the Edge*, guest edited by Robert Brooke and Amy Goodburn, focuses on the ethics of representation of students and student writing. In this remarkable array of essays, theories and practices of citation vary considerably: from how to represent student writing to whether student writing should be used at all. Paul V. Anderson and Heidi A. McKee also discuss the "ethics of representation" in this volume, but not in terms of scholarly publication.

Recently technological developments have further complicated the issue of citation. Now that students can google their names and bring up references to themselves and their work, teachers may feel the need to exercise more caution in referencing. The practice of anonymity, while erasing the authorship of students, nonetheless grants a certain protection (Parent 2007). The wide availability of student writing on the Internet might discourage composition textbook authors from using "negative" examples, concerned as they are about the harm that might accrue if students, unfamiliar with certain academic conventions, see their efforts represented in this way. This caution poses a problem for the field of composition studies because examples are needed of what doesn't work (and why) as well as what does work (and why). To complicate things even further, IRB boards are playing an increasingly active role in humanities research, as they try to identify—and at times even to dictate—which acts of disciplinary naming may or may not harm students (Whateley 2007).

Even after so many years—years after the publication of *Modern Rhetoric*—the issue of citation remains controversial, and no consistent system of citation has yet been established. Practices vary widely, even within a given text. For example, the fourth edition of Donald Hall's *Writing Well* (1982) refers to hypothetical students ("If the student had written," 82); generic students ("a passage from a student essay," 2); unnamed students whose work is to be criticized; and several of Hall's former students, who are mentioned by name (Jim Beck, Marian Hart, Frank Rodriguez), and whose work is tracked across several chapters (we will take a closer look at this phenomenon shortly). The second edition of *Writing Analytically* (2000), by David Rosenwasser and Jill Stephen, provides numerous examples of student texts, referring to students as "writers," but mentioning their names only if the work has been published. In *Rewriting: How to Do Things With Texts* (2006), Joseph Harris generally cites student writers in the same way as published writers: names and titles appear in shadowed "intertext" boxes, using the following format: Abhijit Mehta, "The Playful Language of Math" (1st and 2nd drafts), unpublished essay, Duke University, 2002 (Mehta's name appears in the index, next to that of published writers). Harris mentions in the text itself that he procured permission from these student writers. When he subsequently refers to student writers, he provides only their first names. This is a common approach. Recent textbooks are replete with "Emilys" and "Ethans" placed alongside "Kozol" and "Orwell." The intended effect is not to devalue student writing (although it may have that effect inadvertently), but to suggest intimacy and immediacy. In contrast with Brooks and Warren, for whom the specific pedagogical moment is remote, recent textbook authors draw attention to actual students in actual classrooms, responding to actual assignments, which have received actual evaluation (Murray 1993; Summerfield and Summerfield 1988; Bazerman 1995a; Lunsford and Connors 1999; Lunsford 2008).

Current textbooks also cast renewed attention on the issue of exemplarity. Student writing continues to be constructed primarily as evidence for a prior claim. But the nature of that claim has changed, as the emphases of writing pedagogy have changed. The "effective *writing*" paradigm is still discernible (Bazerman 1995a, Harris 2006, Lunsford and Connors 1999, Lunsford 2008, Hall 1982, Elbow 1981, Murray 1993), but it is frequently linked to, or even replaced by, the "effective *writer*" paradigm. The nature and function of the example changes dramatically as well. That is, while textbooks are still replete with examples of "good writing" and "bad writing," they also have come to transform the *writer* into an example: they construct the writer as a nexus of *writerly* behaviors which student readers are invited to imitate, such as taking notes, outlining, and summarizing. (Of course, this move brings back the specter of the author—as the figure that precedes the text and determines its interpretation.)

This brings us to a final, but for us major, concern: the approach to reading encoded within different composition textbooks. Our investigation suggests that textbooks "read" either student product, or student process, or some combination of both (what we referred to as "effective writing" or "effective writers"). When "product" rather than "process" is emphasized, a considerable amount of reading (of student texts) tends to takes place. The reading of student texts tends also to be evaluative, focusing on such matters as unity, coherence, and emphasis. It is important to point out that these are categories that have changed little from the days of Brooks and Warren. But for Brooks and Warren, these categories acquired their legitimacy within a larger framework of reading that emphasized organicism, aestheticism of reading, and the transparency of language (especially in the case of exposition). In other words, their use of these terms was deliberate and strategic, and it was a powerful way of connecting the activities and writing. Since that time, different theories of reading have emerged. One would expect that different theories would yield new categories and new strategies for the teaching of reading and writing. Yet, most textbooks (there are exceptions, such as Dombeck and Herndon 2004; Harris 2006; Salvatori and Donahue 2005; Scholes, Comley, and Peritz 2000; Summerfield and Summerfield 1988) continue to employ terms like *unity* even though the theoretical rationale for such terms has either lost its potency or has disappeared altogether. In itself this is interesting to us, because so often the claim is made that the teaching of reading is separate from the teaching of writing. But the fact that terms like *unity, coherence,* and *emphasis* remain dominant in the discourse of composition textbooks suggests that reading is there and has always been there. To invoke an old chestnut of the eighties, to read is indeed to write, and to read, and to write.

In contrast, when "process" rather than "product" is emphasized, very little reading of the student text itself takes place. Instead, the moves of student writers are narrativized so as to suggest an exemplary—and inspiring—model for imitation. The sixth edition of *St. Martin's Handbook* (2008) presents an especially engaging and powerful example of this narrative transformation. In the book's preface, Lunsford thanks the "very fine student writers" who contributed to the book, expressing particular gratitude to a single student, Emily Lesk. Emily Lesk is first referenced in the textbook in the chapter "Rhetorical Situations," which describes an assignment she was given as a first-year student at Stanford University. We are told that her process of responding to this assignment will be followed across several chapters. A carefully honed narrative of this process begins to take shape. Emily's initial response to the assignment was that she found it interesting. She then thought about her audience and its expectations. She realized that if she were to post her essay on the class Web site, it "might be read by anyone with access to the Internet" (39). So she expands her initial considerations of audience to include not only peers and teacher but unknown people interested in the topic: this audience of the unknown requires her to be as "clear as possible" (39). Next, Emily Lesk (in each new subsection of the book, she is referred to by first and last names, and thereafter as "Emily," never "Lesk") distinguished between her major and minor purposes. She thought more critically about her various audiences; she made decisions about the visuals she might pair with her words (51).

In the next chapter of the textbook, we are told that Emily Lesk experimented with various prewriting strategies, such as brainstorming, freewriting, and clustering; specific examples are provided of each. We next learn that Emily needed to narrow her thesis, organize her materials, and draft her essay. The textbook presents the first draft; embedded within it are Emily Lesk's responses to what she had written, her identification of certain trouble spots ("getting off track here?") and ways to address them ("need to cite"). Her reflections are then summarized by Lunsford. That is to say, Lunsford interprets them for us: "The major weakness (she decided) was in tone" (79). We next learn that Emily gave her drafts to peers for review (there is a moment in which Lunsford suggests how Emily might have prepared for this stage), and the textbook includes the commentary produced by these students. This commentary is followed by Emily's explanation of how she plans to address these suggestions, primarily in terms of organization, sentence structure, and tone. Finally we are given the revised and final draft in addition to a small photograph of Emily Lesk herself, the "student writer' (105). Lunsford's only recommendation, at this point, is that the readers of her textbook might want to compare the final draft to Emily's first draft and discuss the changes she made.

What can we learn from this construction of a student writer engaged in the processes of composing, drafting, reviewing, and revising? First, that such engagement makes Emily appear as real as possible. Her experience is represented in ways designed to authenticate it as something that other students, engaged in similar efforts, can relate to, and thus learn from. Second, that since Emily's final draft is not discussed explicitly, or rather is not explicitly *evaluated*, (which is what the majority of composition textbooks have conditioned us to expect over the years), it would be easy to conclude that Emily's text has not really been "read" at all. Of course, that is not the case. Emily's text has indeed been "read," but in an entirely different way: in terms of the conventions of what could be called an "inspiring" (which is not necessarily the same as "heroic") narrative. To put this complicated idea more simply, we could say that Emily is presented to us as an individual (thus the photo), but an individual who also happened to be a first-year student (after all, the primary audience for this textbook is college freshman): a first year student, furthermore, at a prestigious university who engaged in a difficult academic challenge, undertook a journey of discovery and eventual achievement recorded in the unfolding of a writing assignment. The fact that Lunsford places the photo at the end of her story of writing only strengthens its appeal: the reader is supposed to feel that he or she knows this young woman and has shared her experiences. The reader's reward for participating in her journey, even indirectly, is to finally meet her, to personalize her further—sort of. Lunsford makes an interesting move here: while most composition textbooks tend to begin with the precept, or rule, and then provide an example of it, Lunsford reverses the order by providing an example, the narrative, from which we are supposed to deduce the rule.

We stated earlier that the ways in which students and their writing are figured forth in composition textbooks depends largely on how they are "read." How they are "read" can be gleaned from the interpretive protocols encoded within the textbooks in varying degrees of specificity: these protocols reflect, either intentionally or unintentionally, the disciplinary criteria for what it takes to read a student text. Here an important—and discouraging—difference between recent composition textbooks and *Modern Rhetoric* can be observed. Whatever the limitations of a formalist reading approach, Brooks and Warren consistently applied it to both published texts and student themes; in so doing, they attributed considerable force to student writing as texts, entitled to legitimate readings (See Joseph Harris in this collection). This is not always the case in recent composition textbooks. This disjunction between implied theory and pedagogical enactment suggests to us the need to reform the use and interpretation of student writing in composition textbooks. Also in need of reform is the system of citation that bespeaks and underscores the textbook author's theoretical understanding of what the representation of students entails. This sort of "reform "(especially in the sense of "re-forming") is what this book, *Teaching with Student Texts*, promises to accomplish.

We have been for quite some time invested in fostering, in theory and practice, conventions that equalize the ways in which published authors/theorists/critics and students are referenced. We are not the only ones to be concerned about this issue (see Bloom 2003, and Robillard 2006, among others). Of particular concern to us in this present context are the reasons the discipline has never ratified a consistent system for citing student work either in its textbooks or its scholarship. The issue of ratification has been sporadically raised, quite articulately, but interestingly, it does not seem to have had much effect. It is significant, for example, that different textbook publishers follow different conventions, over which an individual writer may have little control. Brooks and Warren obviously were able to control the material representation of student texts in their textbook. In our work, *The Elements (and Pleasures) of Difficulty* (2005), a book that emphasizes student writing, we were able to insist on the use of first and last names, and we were able to include student names in the table of contents and in the index pages; we were not, however, able to persuade the publishers to place student writing in the same typeset as our own writing or that of the published writers from whom we quoted. It should also be noticed that there is no consistently recognized process for procuring student permissions, and individual IRB boards vary greatly in their requirements for informed consent.

The transformation of student writing into disciplinary exemplar carries with it theoretical and ethical responsibilities. While no one would argue that composition textbooks ignore the student text, the process by which this text is converted into an example of disciplinary possibility and constraint has received only minimal attention. As we discussed in this essay, this transformation is effected through certain practices of reading. These practices include acts of framing, whereby the readers of textbooks (which include both teachers and students) are taught how to interpret these texts. And they also include acts of citation, whereby the student text is accorded or deprived of authority depending on how its relationship to so-called expert texts or texts by published authors is defined. In other words, for a student text to become viable as an example, as a signifier interpreted and contextualized for a particular purpose, it has to be read in an already sanctioned way.

Our discipline has not yet accorded this issue the attention it deserves.

ACKNOWLEDGMENT

We want to acknowledge the dedicated efforts of our research assistant Rachel Heron, an undergraduate at Lafayette College, in compiling our information.

PART THREE
Changing Classroom Practices

The essays in this final section of our book show how bringing student texts to the table can invigorate the kinds of work that go on in writing courses. The first several pieces describe specific strategies for working with and talking about student texts. In "Workshop and Seminar," Joseph Harris distinguishes between two classroom formats. In a *workshop*, students offer each other practical advice towards revising their work in progress. In a *seminar*, a teacher leads a discussion of a student text in order to pose a more general lesson about writing for the entire class. Harris does not argue for one format over the other, but rather urges us to make reflective and strategic use of both. We need workshops to support students as they draft and revise their projects as writers; we need seminars to teach them about the moves and values of academic writing.

Maggie Debelius agrees that we need to clarify what we mean by terms like *workshop*, since we use them as shorthand for so many different activities. In "What Do We Talk about When We Talk about Workshops?" she traces her use of a variety of workshop techniques in the first five weeks of a required first-year writing course at Georgetown University. Just as students need to learn the moves that matter in academic writing, so likewise they need to learn the moves that matter in writing workshops—and this is what the first month of the class is designed to do.

In "Texts to be Worked On and Worked With," Chris Warnick discusses ways of working with student texts that encourage them to think of their ideas and their writing as *theoretical*. To approach student writing as theory, he suggests, means to ask this question: what can we as thinkers and writers *do* with the ideas in this student text? To illustrate this approach, Warnick describes how he led a classroom discussion of a student draft that not only helped its writer develop the ideas in it but also encouraged the other students in the class to see their ideas as having value in intellectual conversations within and beyond the classroom.

How do we help beginning teachers lead such discussions of student texts? Margaret J. Marshall takes on this issue in "Writing to Learn, Reading to Teach: Student Texts in the Pedagogy Seminar." Marshall describes a sequence of activities she used to help graduate students learn to identify patterns in student writing that warrant whole-class instruction and to use student writing in the lessons they design. Working with their own writing and that of undergraduates helps graduate students begin to think like teachers, makes institutional contexts for writing instruction clearer, and foregrounds the assumptions and values teachers bring to their interpretations of student writing and student learning. Marshall suggests that such a sequence can create experiences for graduate students in a pedagogy seminar that parallel those of the first-year students in the composition course they are themselves teaching.

The next several essays explore teaching formats that move beyond the conventional parameters of workshop or seminar. In "The Writer/ Text Connection," Muriel Harris argues that teachers should view the text and the writer who produced it not as separate identities—the person and the document—but as a single intertwined entity. How did that writer produce that text? What does that writer need help with? How should readers respond to that writer and her text? Drawing from her years of experience in writing-center tutorials, Harris offers strategies for working with student writers in peer-response workshops, student conferences, and classroom discussions. Through conversations with writers about their texts, she argues, teachers will gain a close knowledge of how to respond more effectively to their work.

In "Learning from Coauthoring: Composing Texts Together in the Composition Classroom," Michele Eodice and Kami Day argue that the value of collaborative work is intensified when students are asked to go beyond peer review to actually creating text together in class. They offer guidelines for forming groups of student coauthors, and show how students learn in such groups using excerpts from conversations during the coauthoring process, examples of collaboratively written student texts, and student reflections on coauthoring.

Scott L. Rogers, Ryan Trauman, and Julia E. Kiernan show how teachers can coauthor a pedagogy in their essay on "Inquiry, Collaboration, and Reflection in the Student (Text)-Centered Multimodal Writing Course." Rogers, Trauman, and Kiernan collaboratively designed a course organized around principles of multimodal composing and student-directed, sequenced inquiry projects. Their essay centers on three vignettes—one from each of their sections of the same writing course—that highlight strategies for teaching with multimodal student texts. The first describes a collaborative revision activity within a networked classroom, the second a group critique of student work in progress, and the third a collective discussion of a multimedia student presentation.

In "Workshopping to Practice Scientific Terms," Anne Ellen Geller and Frank R. Cantelmo offer another example of teacher collaboration, describing how they worked together to make more effective use of writing assignments and activities in an introductory science course for nonmajors. Geller is a writing specialist, Cantelmo a biologist. They explain how they codesigned a series of in-class workshops with student texts whose aim was less to sponsor revision than to help students identify key terms and concepts used in journalistic descriptions of scientific studies. They used their classroom work with student texts, that is, to help students think more like scientists.

In "Bringing Outside Texts In and Inside Texts Out," Jane Fife describes how, over the course of her teaching career, she has come to make increasing use of both *inside* texts (written by students in the current class) and *outside* texts (written by students in previous classes or published student work). Fife aims to expand students' sense of possibility for their work as writers. She uses outside texts to model genres, to spark invention, and to suggest possibilities for publication, and she uses inside texts to highlight effective writing strategies. Fife argues that if we hope to make student writing more visible, and thus more valued by both students and faculty, we need to look for ways to bring inside texts outside the classroom.

In the closing essay for this section, Rolf Norgaard reflects on how using student texts requires *teachers* to change how we imagine our own work as intellectuals. In "Embracing Uncertainty," Norgaard shows how working with student texts can make teaching opportune or *kairotic.* This means we need to be willing to work in the moment, to improvise, to revise our teaching strategies as students themselves shift and mature as writers. Most important, we need to continually rethink the roles we ourselves play in the classroom, and to see that through taking risks as teachers, we can help students appreciate the intellectual risks they need to take. Uncertainty can be our best ally as we refashion our pedagogies to teach and learn on the page; embracing that uncertainty can help us recognize and utilize the *kairos* of teaching with student texts.

12

WORKSHOP AND SEMINAR

Joseph Harris
Duke University

WORKSHOP

Fall 2008. Towards the middle of the semester. I am sitting with a group of four students in a coffee shop on the Duke campus. (I had cancelled our regular full class session so we could meet instead in small groups.) Each of the four students had written a first full draft of an essay and posted it to the course web site the day before. All of them had then read and commented on those drafts. Each student thus came to our meeting with four printouts—one of each of the three drafts they had read and written comments on, and a clean copy of their own piece.

My role was, in effect, to chair the meeting. I asked who wanted to go first, and after a moment or two, Katherine Thomas took a chance and said she would. I told Katherine that she would soon be handed copies of the comments her three classmates had made on her draft the evening before, but that I would like to make sure our conversation added to what they had already written. So I asked her to do two things: (1) identify a passage about two pages long in her piece that she would like us to focus on as readers (the drafts ran from five to seven pages), and (2) tell us what concerns or questions she had about that passage.

In this case, Katherine decided to read the closing pages of her essay. She was concerned that she had introduced a new idea too late in her piece and that her prose was overly formal and dull. I asked the three other students to note these issues on their copies of her draft, and to be ready to mark any words or phrases that stood out for them as they reread her closing pages. Then Katherine read those pages aloud. When she finished, I asked her to be quiet for a few minutes, and to listen and take notes on what her readers had to say.

For about the next ten minutes, each of her three readers spoke to the author from the notes they had made on her piece. I served as moderator—keeping the readers on track, sometimes asking them to say more or to point to specifics in the text, and once telling the author, when she began to answer a question that had been raised, to remain silent and instead to write down what she wanted to say.

It turned out that Katherine's prose was a little stilted at points, and her readers pointed to a number of places where she might make her writing more direct and conversational. And she had indeed introduced a new idea very late in her piece. But here the solution her readers urged was not to cut that idea, which had been her instinct, but to bring it forward, to talk about it earlier in her essay. This led some readers back to the more general comments they had written on her work the evening before—and I urged them to point to ways Katherine might now restructure her piece around this emerging idea.

After all three readers had offered their responses, I asked Katherine if she had any thoughts or questions. She did, so we chatted some more about her draft for a few minutes. I then asked the members of the group to hand Katherine their copies of her piece, with the notes they had made on it both during the prior evening and in the last few minutes, and we then moved on to another writer and another draft. Since the whole process—framing questions, reading aloud, responses, closing conversation—had taken us about twenty minutes, we were able to talk about the drafts by each of the four student writers in the group in an hour and a half.

I'm sure most readers of this book are familiar with some version of this sort of small group *workshop*. Indeed, I would argue that the workshop has been the default mode for talking about student writing since about 1973—when Peter Elbow described it with such conviction and grace in *Writing without Teachers*. We've even turned it into a verb: *to workshop*.

And there's good reason for its ubiquity. The workshop treats students seriously as writers. Its purpose, after all, is to help them revise and improve their writing. But for that to happen, students also need to learn how to read work in progress with care and generosity. So the workshop offers them practice in both critical writing and reading. And, when things go well, workshopping is fun. It's interesting to learn what other writers in the class are doing, and it's useful and rewarding to have them read your own work closely. In most of my courses, then, I schedule small-group workshops for each major writing project I assign—which usually means breaking the class into such small groups some two to four times per semester.

But there's the rub. If over the span of a fourteen-week semester, I meet with a class twenty-eight times, and four of those meetings are devoted to workshops, then what happens in the other twenty-four—especially if I want to center the course on the writing of the students in it? I've seen teachers respond to this question in a number of ways—most of which, I must admit, have not much appealed to me. Some teachers simply schedule more and more small-group workshops—which can have the effect, it seems to me, of making the class as a whole lose a sense of identity or purpose. Others spend class time talking about readings, which distracts from a focus on the work of students as writers.

Still other teachers run a series of whole-class workshops, in which twelve or fifteen or twenty students offer advice to a single writer. This has always struck me as overkill—how many responses to one draft can any of us really absorb and use? I've also wondered what the twelve or fifteen or twenty students whose work was *not* being talked about were supposed to take away from the conversation. The power of a workshop stems in large part from its intimacy and immediacy. You work hard as a reader and you are repaid at once by the responses you get to your own writing. A large group throws this discursive economy out of whack. We have, on the one hand, a writer besieged by feedback and, on the other hand, a large group of readers who must wait until next week, or next month, or until who knows when, for their own writing to be discussed.

SEMINAR

So, what then? How can you talk about student texts in class in ways that are of direct use to everyone in the room? Most of my attempts to do so take the form of a writing *seminar*. In a seminar, a teacher leads a conversation about a text written by one of the students in the room. But the point of this talk is less to offer the writer advice for revision than to frame a lesson on writing for everyone in the class.

The difference might be put this way. The question that drives a workshop is "*How can we help this writer revise?*" The question that drives a seminar is "*What can we learn as writers from this text?*"

In running a seminar, then, I try to help students see something new about writing—an insight they're not likely to come to on their own or through the process of trading responses in a workshop. Let me point to two forms this work often takes.

Multitext seminar

In one sort of seminar, I work with excerpts from the writing of several students in the class. As I read through a set of drafts, I identify a number of passages, each usually a page or less, in which students are grappling with similar issues or trying to make similar moves as writers. I assemble these excerpts into a handout I bring in as the text for our talk in seminar. What's key is that there's an idea or issue connecting the passages—a problem in writing that many or most of the students in the class are confronting right then. And, if I've chosen them well, the excerpts on the handout will show not a single correct solution to that problem but a range of responses to it.

For example. In fall 2008 I taught a first-year writing course in which I asked students to draw on George Lakoff 's *Moral Politics* (2002) in analyzing a text or figure from the Obama-McCain presidential campaign. (To reduce *Moral Politics* to a bumper sticker: Lakoff argues that our competing political views are rooted in differing metaphors of the family—that conservatives uphold a view of society centered on the image of a strict father, while liberals appeal to the idea of a nurturant parent.) But to take on Lakoff's approach as a thinker and writer, students first needed to define, in their own terms, exactly what that approach was—which was the task I set for them in one of their early writings for the course. To do so, I suggested that students think about the questions driving Lakoff's work, the ways he tends to answer them, and the kinds of materials he cites as evidence for views.

As I read through their drafts, I quickly saw that many students were struggling to identify the materials Lakoff uses for evidence. That made sense—for what really does count as convincing evidence for arguing that certain metaphors underlie how people think about politics? That was a question students would need to answer if they were to understand Lakoff as readers and to draw on his approach as writers. So I put together a handout for our next class with brief excerpts (about 150–200 words) from five separate drafts, each of which approached the question of Lakoff's materials differently.

For instance, Ryann Child had this to say about Lakoff's materials:

Lakoff will repeat a point many times through the use of several different examples. When describing the importance of moral wholeness in strict father conservatism, Lakoff quotes seven different words recognizable by the reader as commonly used by conservatives in politics. All of the words provide a direct link back to the strict father value of an untouched moral foundation (Lakoff, 90-91). As in this example, Lakoff in the first three sections of his book relies solely on words used by conservatives and liberals as evidence for his position. (Child 2008)

I actually needed to pose the question several times—"What does Ryann identify here as Lakoff's materials?"—before one student decided that maybe the answer I was looking for really was *that* obvious, and finally replied, "Words." Pleased, I forged ahead, and asked, "So was that what the rest of you said?"—which was of course met by a series of unsure glances or intense unblinking stares at the xeroxed pages on the table. So we moved to the next excerpt, by Alex Galonsky, who wrote:

> *Moral Politics* is chock full of metaphors . . . The two primary metaphors in the book are the strict father family metaphor and the nurturant parent family metaphor. Lakoff also uses a variety of less significant metaphors, such as the ones used to describe morality. For example, Lakoff uses a myriad of metaphors to qualify the mother metaphor of "moral accounting," such as retribution, restitution, and reciprocation. Lakoff also uses sub-metaphors for the primary family metaphors. (Galonsky 2008)

By then students were catching on. Alex says that Lakoff's materials are *metaphors*, they quickly asserted. But aren't metaphors made out of words, I asked? Yes, but metaphors also combine images and ideas in ways that single words don't, they explained, so Alex's point differed from Ryann's. And *that*, of course, was precisely what I'd hoped they would notice.

The rest of the seminar moved more quickly. As we read through the next few excerpts, we noted how Cydney Ross emphasized Lakoff's use of examples from ordinary life and common-sense anecdotes, and contrasted this with how Arjun Chandra highlighted Lakoff's references to the media and current events. Finally, while Steven Feister felt that Lakoff can be "a bit light when it comes to background research," he did acknowledge his use of "works by liberals and conservatives, such as *A Theory of Justice* by John Rawls and *The Bell Curve* by Charles Murray," and his citation of "previous works from his field of cognitive linguistics" (2008). By the end of our work with the handout, then, we had identified five distinct forms of evidence used by Lakoff: words, metaphors, anecdotes, current events, and scholarship.

I thought students had done strong work as readers of Lakoff and one another. But this was a course in writing, so I wanted them to reflect on how they might apply these ideas to their own essays. So I asked them to get out the drafts they had written and locate where they talked about Lakoff's materials. Jot down some notes, I told them, on how, given this conversation, you might now change or add to what you said. This applied to the five students whose writing I had excerpted, too. I then gave them some more work to do for our next class, which was to find one text from the fall presidential campaign that illustrated Lakoff's approach and one that posed some problems for it—and to be ready to talk about how these materials fit (or didn't fit) into the set of categories we had just developed.

I think that such teaching moves, which direct students back to their own work in progress, are what ground a seminar in the actual practice of writing. But I also think it's worth noting what did *not* happen in this seminar. I didn't ask students, for instance, which forms of evidence they felt were more or less important or convincing. That seemed to me a question for them to wrestle with later, in their own work extending Lakoff. My aim at the time was to illustrate a range of possibilities. And I didn't ask students to offer the writers of the passages we read advice about how to develop their ideas. This was not a class focused on revision, but one centered on the problem of evidence.

Some of the seminars I design are centered, like this one, on writing problems tied tightly to the particular texts and issues we happen to be talking about. Later in the Lakoff course, for instance, we held another seminar on ways of writing about Sarah Palin—who seemed to many students to confound his categories of strict and nurturant parents. But there are many other issues that recur in almost every course I teach: How do you begin an academic essay? How do you end one without simply restating what you've already said? How do you distinguish your own position from those of the writers you are responding to? When do you quote and when do you summarize? How do you comment on passages you've quoted? These are not questions about how to make particular pieces stronger, they are questions that anyone trying to write intellectual prose needs to think about—and thus that a group of writers can talk about usefully together.

Single-Text Seminar

There is a second characteristic form of a writing seminar that also takes on such questions, but in a somewhat different way—and that is through the close reading of a single, complete essay. (Or, in some longer classes, perhaps two or three such pieces.) In many ways, this sort of seminar discussion—with its focus on the work of one writer—might seem much like a workshop. But there are important differences in format and aim. First, the seminar is led by the teacher, who usually chooses the text to be read and has a specific set of questions to raise about it. Second, the aim of those questions is to raise an issue in writing that everyone in the room can apply to their own work in progress.

Let me offer another example from the Lakoff course. The week after we worked with the five excerpts on evidence, I brought into class the full draft of a student essay commenting on a *New York Times* article about the divided responses of Roman Catholic voters to Joe Biden's candidacy for vice president. The author of this essay, Taylor Duhe, already knew how to do a number of things comfortably and well: she began by summarizing what Lakoff says about religion and politics, outlined the article from the *Times,* showed how this article illustrated several of Lakoff's ideas, then showed how Lakoff's ideas explained the article, then explained how the article and Lakoff were connected, then . . . well, you start to see the problem: the article Taylor had chosen to write about seemed to fit Lakoff's theory so seamlessly she was left little more to say about either text than that they agreed with each other.

But was that really the case? I had also brought copies of the *Times* article into class. When I asked the group to look through it for anything that did *not* align well with Lakoff's thinking, several students noticed that several of the Catholics interviewed fitted Lakoff's description of nurturant liberals, with one exception—their opposition to abortion rights. I suggested that Taylor had the beginnings of an essay exploring this disjuncture. (And, in fact, she continued to work this one question as her main writing project for the semester.) I then asked her classmates to turn back to their own work to look for similar moments where Lakoff's ideas didn't quite explain the texts from the campaign they were reading or viewing. For those were exactly the points, I argued, where they might have something to add to his thinking.

The job of the teacher in a single-text seminar is to identify moments in an essay that can lead to more thinking and writing. What Taylor most needed to do was not to fix what she had written, but to add to it. That was also pretty much the task facing most of her classmates at that moment in the semester. The format of the seminar allowed me to point to the need for them all not merely to correct their prose but to develop their ideas.

BOTH/AND

I suspect that good seminars help set up good workshops. Recall what Katherine's readers urged her to do in the workshop I described earlier—to take the idea at the end of her piece and put it front and center. That's ambitious advice. It's also the kind of thinking about writing a teacher can encourage in a seminar—to urge students to become bolder, to say more, to point out problems with a theory, to suggest other ways of seeing.

My point here is simple enough. The workshop and seminar do different things. As writing teachers, we need to do both. The focus of a workshop is on the individual *writer*. It's a space for practical advice. The seminar, though, is more of a metaspace. Its aim is to help the *readers* of a text understand something new about the craft of writing. Of course, the writer in a seminar will no doubt hear useful advice about his piece, much as the readers in a workshop can learn from the drafts they read and respond to. But there is a difference in emphasis, in focus and aim, down to the ways the two formats tend to come to a close. In a workshop, the writer usually thanks her readers for their feedback. In a seminar, the readers usually thank the writer for sharing her work.

Several writers in this volume—Bruce Horner, Margaret Marshall, Chris Warnick—offer more insights into how to structure a writing seminar, while still others—Maggie Debelius, Anne Geller and Frank Cantelmo—explore varying forms and uses of workshops. My aim here in distinguishing between workshop and seminar has not been to argue for one format over the other, but to suggest that we need both.

This claim might seem innocuous, but I'm not sure that's the case. Our field tends to link teaching formats to intellectual and ideological positions. Over the years, I've talked with many writing teachers who refuse, on principle, ever to put students in small groups, and with many others who refuse to do nearly anything else but. I learned the value of the seminar format when, near the start of my career, I taught in a composition program at the University of Pittsburgh that, for many in the field, seemed to oppose everything Peter Elbow and workshop teaching were about. (For some, this was a good thing, for others, bad.) Indeed, the 1995 debate between Elbow and Pitt's David Bartholomae articulates a series of choices that many writing teachers still feel they must make—between a commitment to student voice or academic discourse, to freewriting or revision, to personal narrative or cultural criticism—all of which often then get mapped onto the choice between workshop or seminar. To draw on another set of Elbow's terms, the workshop tends to get cast in this debate as a version of the *believing game*—a mode of teaching that is warm, supportive, empathetic, collaborative, and student-centered. In contrast, the seminar can seem to enact the *doubting game*—cool, critical, analytic, agonistic, and teacher led.

My argument here is for both/and. We need workshops to support students as they draft and revise their projects as writers; we need seminars to teach them about the moves and values of academic writing. Once we distinguish the sorts of work with writing we can do best in each format, we can decide how and when to use both.

ACKNOWLEDGMENTS

My thanks go to the students in my fall 2008 Writing 20 course at Duke University who have graciously allowed me to reprint and discuss their work in this essay: Arjun Chandra, Ryann Child, Taylor Duhe, Steven Feister, Alex Galonsky, Cydney Ross, and Katherine Thomas.

13

WHAT DO WE TALK ABOUT WHEN WE TALK ABOUT WORKSHOPS?
Charting the First Five Weeks of a First-Year Writing Course

Maggie Debelius
Georgetown University

The writing workshop, one of the most ubiquitous techniques in college writing courses, has lately received some bad press. Lynn Freed argues against the tyranny of workshops in "Doing Time: My Years in the Creative-Writing Gulag," in the July 2005 *Harper's*. In a reprisal of the old blind-leading-the-blind argument, she claims untalented writers learn nothing from talking to each other and that trying to teach them is torturous, apparently equivalent to human rights abuses. David Sedaris sees torture for the participants, claiming that "the template for the standard writing workshop" strikes "the perfect balance between sadism and masochism" (2000, 91). Words like *gulag, masochism,* and *sadism* suggest that it's high time we writing teachers reevaluate our classroom practices.

I am interested in what happens when we vary Sedaris's "template for the standard writing workshop" to combine three major trends in writing instruction: individual, peer, and expert learning. I attempt such variation in my section of a required first-year writing class at Georgetown University in Washington, DC, entitled Nice Work. The title (besides alluding to the Gershwin tune) refers to the assigned texts that address labor in various contexts, both academic and professional, but the subtext of the course is the work of writing and writing workshops. When I ask students to reflect on their varied workshop experiences, the course itself becomes a metaworkshop. The workshops described below take many different forms, and most of them attempt to get the writers in motion (some require students to literally move across campus while others require intellectual rather than physical movement).

THE WORKSHOP AND ITS DISCONTENTS

Workshops have become staples of college writing classrooms because they perform the values many of us want to share with our classes: a sense of audience, writing as a process, and the importance of revision. It's essential, however, that we clarify what we mean by *workshop* since we use the term as shorthand for so many different activities. Although the first curricular use of the word *workshop* dates back to George Baker's 1906 Harvard dramaturgy course (Myers 2006), today the most common conception of a workshop consists of a group of peers critiquing the work of their colleagues. Sedaris describes it this way:

> Here is a system designed to eliminate pleasure for everyone involved. The idea is that a student turns in a story, which is then read and thoroughly critiqued by everyone in class. In my experience the process worked, in that stories were occasionally submitted, Xeroxed and distributed hand to hand. They were folded into purses and knapsacks, but here the system tended to break down. Come critique time, most students behaved as if the assignment had been to confine the stories in a dark enclosed area and test their reaction to sensory deprivation. (2000, 92)

While Sedaris is, of course, a humorist, we need to take his critique seriously since our students are far more likely to have read it than works by composition theorists.

Academics, however, have also objected to aspects of the workshop. Enduring complaints include that students either don't know how to offer meaningful feedback ("it's the blind leading the blind") or are reluctant to offer and accept feedback from their peers. Some, such as Carol Bly, object on emotional and psychological grounds; she echoes Sedaris in arguing that workshops amount to "low level sadism" (2001, 17). One of the most widespread objections to peer learning, of which workshops are one variety, is that they promote conformity. John Trimbur (1989) cautions that collaboration can suppress dissent, Gail Stygall (1998) examines how gendered social roles operate in a peer writing groups, and Carrie Shively Leverenz (1996) looks at the effects of consensus and dissensus in a multicultural composition classroom. Nevertheless, most critics hold out some hope. Trimbur in particular imagines the potential of collaborative learning to "release collective energies to turn the means of criticism into a means of transformation, to tap fundamental impulses toward emancipation and justice" but fails to explain how collaboration as transformation might play out in actual composition classrooms (1989, 477).

Below I describe workshop formats I use for a group of twenty students in the first five weeks of a first-year writing class. For the purposes of this paper I broadly define a workshop as a meeting that focuses on a piece of student writing and generates feedback. Early assignments include a personal essay, a summary of a critical argument, and a response to either David Brooks' "The Organization Kid," a 2001 *Atlantic Monthly* article which criticizes the superficiality of overachieving college students, or Mark Edmundson's "On the Uses of a Liberal Education," the widely reprinted 1997 *Harper's* article which argues that the consumer culture pervading American colleges has lead universities to kowtow to students. The sequence for each assignment is to draft ideas, give and receive feedback, reflect, and revise. Because few students can leap into an all-class discussion of student writing without guidance, the earliest workshops are designed to train them to respond effectively. Just as students need to learn the moves that matter in academic writing, so likewise they need to learn the moves that matter in writing workshops— and this is what the first month of workshops is designed to do. Only by letting students know that we take not only their writing, but also their responses to the writing of others, seriously, can we make student writing the central texts of our courses.

I begin by addressing criticisms of the workshop head-on: when discussing one of the first assigned readings, a Kenneth Bruffee piece (1984) on collaborative learning, students list their objections to this educational method and we consider the assumptions contained therein. While my students may not use terms like *the oppression of normative discourse* to describe their previous workshop experiences, they nonetheless understand that workshops have flaws, that good ideas can get overlooked, that writers are reluctant to give up control of their prose, and that some groups perform more effectively than others. I then explain that our class will rely on workshops and that every writer will have the opportunity to have his or her work reviewed several times during the semester. I add that I will strive to vary the format in an effort to address some of the more common pitfalls. Because there is value in consistency, however, I always schedule workshops on the same day (usually Fridays) and introduce them with the same rule, namely that the writer initiates the conversation by asking colleagues for specific kinds of feedback.

WEEK 1: SPEED CONFERENCES (OR TAKING THE TIME TO KNOW THEM)

David Foster argues that collaborative learning is based on a fundamental mistake, that Bruffee's "overeager application of the social constructionist label" causes him to overvalue social practices and thus deny the value of the individual in creating knowledge (quoted in Trimbur 1989, 462). While I disagree, I nonetheless want my students to understand that I see them first as individuals rather than members of a group. In the first week I meet one-on-one with each student for five to ten minutes. This accomplishes two goals: they learn where my office is, and I learn what matters to them. The content of the meeting is fairly simple: our central piece of writing is an informal, in-class paragraph they've written about their writing goals. More important than the answers they give me is the message I want to send them: that writing is a highly individual, idiosyncratic process and I need to know who they are in order to offer relevant feedback. This private meeting also gives them the chance to tell me about issues (medical, social, cultural, etc.) they may not want to announce in class. These meetings help me become more aware of the gender and cultural dynamics of peer writing groups that Leverenz and Stygall address.

WEEK 2: THE LISTENING WORKSHOP

As Wendy Bishop and others explain, one reason peer workshops fail is that members are afraid to share their work and offer criticism of others (1998). To encourage students to take risks, I schedule a listening workshop in the second week of the term. The goal of the workshop is to help students confront anxiety about sharing their work. They bring their first writing assignment, a draft personal essay about a moment in which they were educated, to class and read it to a group of three others. I encourage students to respond to each other in a general way by smiling, nodding, or asking for clarification but not focusing on heavy criticism. (I assure them that criticism will come later, but this draft is ungraded so the group members aren't obligated to "improve" the work.) I then ask respondents to write about what they interpret as the main point of the narrative and share these documents with the writer.

Students spend the remaining class time writing a reflection on the experience of sharing their work. Reflecting allows them to assess the workshop and express lingering anxieties and objections about collaborative learning. Although not required to cite any assigned authors, many connect their own workshop thoughts with Bruffee and their own writing with an assigned chapter from Ken Macrorie's *Telling Writing*, which, despite being dated, speaks forcefully to my first-year students with his warnings about artificially elevated prose or "Engfish." (Although writing about writing is not our primary focus, I find it useful to assign some readings about writing to give students a model of how they can effectively reflect on their own composing process). They revise the personal experience draft based on the listening workshop and receive written feedback from me. Then we put the pieces away for the rest of the semester and revise them again for a final portfolio, using the techniques and responses they glean over the semester.

WEEK 3: MODELING EFFECTIVE RESPONSE

Another longstanding objection to the workshop is that students lack the knowledge or vocabulary to critique their peers' work. After the personal essay, students tackle what initially appears to be a more straightforward summary assignment. In this workshop, however, I want them to begin offering more substantive feedback. But it can be difficult to leap from the listening workshop to the summary workshop because many students are still unprepared to offer meaningful responses to their peers. Barriers include an inadequate understanding of the argument they're summarizing, a misunderstanding of the assignment itself, or reluctance to criticize a peer. Because they have been taught to play nice, many students can't get beyond, "You have a typo in the third sentence."

My solution is to schedule the summary workshop in the writing center (because once students cross the threshold, they're more likely to return) and assign writing-center consultants (many of whom are alumni of my course) to facilitate the small-group summary workshops. Students usually respond to the summaries with varying degrees of success. Recently one group discussed this student-written summary of George Orwell's "Politics and the English Language" (1946):

> The English language has deteriorated. To fix the current trend of boring, vague modern English, individuals must change their writing styles and follow five basic rules. First, one needs to eliminate common metaphors from their writing and invent provocative, unconventional ones. Second, one must eliminate excessively complicated and ostentatious words and simplify their

vocabulary. Third, the passive voice should be avoided. Fourth, where possible, shorten a sentence; there is no point in 'fluff' cluttering one's thoughts. Fifth, one must use simple, everyday English words, rather than a foreign or scientific complement. Following these rules will prevent ambiguity in one's writing.

The initial group reaction was that this summary is concise, well written, and meets the assigned 250-word limit. Perhaps because the students were playing nice, however, they failed to point out that the writer misses half of Orwell's argument: she discusses the decline of language but fails to connect it with politics. After letting the group talk, the writing consultant asked about the missing political argument and pushed the conversation forward. With more authority than a classmate but less than a teacher, the trained consultants model and invite the students to participate in constructive peer conversations.

WEEK 4: THE RESEARCH WORKSHOP

Carol Bly argues in *Beyond the Writer's Workshop* (2001) that writing workshops dogmatically emphasize techniques and neglect ideas, preventing writers from creating their most passionate work. Although I disagree, I occasionally sense that my workshops aren't as helpful at developing new ideas as I want them to be. It's much easier for students to comment on organization and sentence structure than to challenge or interrogate a thesis.

My solution is to build a workshop around a piece of student writing that consists of ideas devoid of technique: a simple list. Students come to class with a list of Brooks's sources and evidence for "The Organization Kid. "The ultimate goal is to write a response paper in which they disagree with or build on some aspect of Brooks's argument. But even before they begin drafting an argument, they work in small groups to evaluate Brooks's sources as a step toward developing a meaningful response. Some might not even call this exercise a true workshop since the primary text amounts to little more than an excerpted bibliography, but the pared-down nature of the writing is precisely what makes the students focus on ideas. Working in a wired classroom in the university library, students look up sources ranging from William Straus and Neil Howe's *Millennials Rising*, to The National Youth Soccer Association, to the Higher Education Research Institute, and then examine and question the sources (2000).

Working as a group, students last year discovered that the authors of *Millennials Rising* gathered data from a small research sample of high-school students in Fairfax County, Virginia, a county which hardly represents the nation as a whole because of its high income, educational level, and ethnic makeup. Two years ago my students examined membership in the National Youth Soccer Association. While Brooks infers that the rising number of players over the past two decades suggests that students today are overly programmed, my students speculated that the rising numbers reflected an increase in both the number of girls playing organized sports after Title IX and an increase in immigration from countries where soccer is popular. Whatever they discover, their research and conversation help them formulate questions for their response papers.

The goal of the research workshop is to explore the connections between writing and research. Too often students segregate these activities rather than understand how they complement each other. Like writing, research is a recursive process, so this workshop is designed to help students explore how research can help them expand their thinking. Because the workshop piece is a simple list of sources, a piece of writing in which technique is irrelevant, the format forces us to focus on ideas. Before incorporating this workshop, I received response papers that relied too heavily on personal rather than analytical evidence. With the addition of the research workshop, however, students developed more sophisticated responses in which they not only found the flaws in Brooks's argument but also considered how the flaws developed. They also learned to incorporate studies like the National Survey of Student Engagement to build their own claims about student involvement beyond the level of personal anecdote.

Another clear benefit of the research workshop is that it gets students to question why *they* have to compose the source list when Brooks himself doesn't include a bibliography. This gives us a chance to talk meaningfully about the difference between scholarly and popular sources and to consider how the use and presentation of their source material builds credibility.

WEEK 5: THE EXPERT WORKSHOP (OR ACQUIRING A NEW PERSPECTIVE)

In "On the Uses of a Liberal Education," Mark Edmundson, one of the most cogent critics of collaborative learning writing today, argues:

> There's a new emphasis on group projects and on computer-generated exchanges among the students. What they seem to want most is to talk to one

another. A classroom now is frequently an "environment," a place highly conducive to the exchange of existing ideas, the students' ideas. Listening to one another, students sometimes change their opinions. But what they generally can't do is acquire a new vocabulary, a new perspective, that will cast issues in a fresh light. (1997, 48)

This critique has always nagged at me because it makes good sense. In response, I've developed a workshop format that introduces "a new perspective that will cast issues in a fresh light" into a group workshop by inviting guest experts to join us. This approach allows us to combine expert learning and peer learning in one workshop.

In the fifth week of the course, students post draft response papers to Brooks or Edmundson on our course Blackboard site (one of those "computer-generated exchanges" Edmundson loathes). Many object to Brooks's assertion that college students today are "overmedicated" and "lack any sense of alienation" (43) or Edmundson's charge that students lack "passion" (48). To challenge these claims, we meet as a group with a professional counselor at the Georgetown Office of Counseling and Psychiatric Services. I assign students to review excerpts from several student papers beforehand; as a group we offer both peer and expert feedback about how the writers might question claims about student mental health. Joseph Harris, in this volume, rightly calls such instructor-led discussions of selections from multiple papers a writing seminar, but I cling steadfastly to the term *workshop* since it reinforces the Nice Work theme of the course.

In this setting, students acquire the new vocabulary that Edmundson craves while still working within the format of a peer workshop. What distinguishes this class from being a guest speaker session is that we anchor our conversation in draft student papers. Meeting with an expert gives students the confidence, vocabulary, and evidence to take on an expert. Another workshop that keeps writers in motion, this meeting has the added benefit that students who enter the counseling center for my class may be more likely to return if they need to use its services.

Additional workshops continue throughout the semester, with student writing always anchoring our discussion, and drawing on a blend of individual, peer, and expert responses. Students meet with me in pairs for conferences (where they get the benefit of both individual and peer instruction while also seeing yet another model of response), in small groups on their own or with writing-center tutors, or for whole-class reviews. Because we've paid careful attention to training and reflection during the first month of class, I can count on the writers to avoid sadism or playing nice. The last workshop of the semester is an oral rehearsal of a final project. After completing an annotated bibliography for and a draft of a persuasive paper, every student presents a five- to ten-minute oral argument to the rest of the class. The biggest challenge of this phase of the class is to help students understand that the oral argument isn't an end in itself but rather a rehearsal of the argument they plan for their final paper. The goal is the same as the writing workshops we've had all semester: to clarify important aspects of the paper before turning it in for a grade. Peers offer feedback about the argument, use of evidence, visual components, and other elements. The absence of a written text helps the respondents focus on the argument and counterargument rather than copyediting.

The final essential element is to allow adequate time for students to reflect on which assignments and workshops they find most and least successful. Sometimes these reflections take the form of in-class writing immediately following the workshop experience, sometimes they happen as part of a conference, other times they happen as part of a writer's report turned in with a final paper. Students include selected reflections in their final course portfolios, giving them a chance to see how they've moved forward as writers and readers—and letting them know that I value these reflective pieces alongside more traditional assignments. By varying and asking students to reflect on the workshop form, effective peer response becomes a course outcome rather than just a pedagogical tool in the service of writing.

Each semester my individual, peer, and expert class workshops continue to succeed and fail in unexpected ways. My goal as a researcher in my own classroom is to redefine these failures as steps toward a more effective pedagogy—to do my best to mitigate the sadism, masochism, and gulags that haunt the margins of the writing workshop.

ACKNOWLEDGMENTS

Thanks to Virginia Bell, Norma Tilden, Joe Bizup, Lisa Sternlieb, and Mike Schiavo for providing feedback, and to the Charles Engelhard foundation for a grant to support the expert workshop idea. I am also grateful to six years' worth of students (especially Ashleigh Walker Gorowski and Alexandra Landegger), tutors, and teaching assistants in HUMW 011 at Georgetown for exploring the writing workshop with me.

14

TEXTS TO BE WORKED ON AND WORKED WITH
Encouraging Students to See Their Writing as Theoretical

Chris Warnick
College of Charleston

This essay will discuss a workshop I conduct with first-year writing students to encourage them to think of their ideas and their writing as theoretical. My impetus for getting students to appreciate the theoretical value of their work relates to my belief that first-year composition courses should provoke students to examine what it means to think like, read like, write like—to in fact *be*—an intellectual and participate in real intellectual debates, both within and beyond the classroom. In making this claim, I do not wish to suggest that all intellectual work is necessarily theoretical, nor do I wish to suggest that theory represents the pinnacle of intellectual labor. I do, however, want my students to learn how to *do theory*, so to speak, because it is a persuasive and heuristic strategy used by intellectuals and because it is an important stage of the learning process.

Let me say briefly what I mean by theory. When I encourage students to do theory, I do not ask them to write deconstructive critiques filled with obscure cultural references and esoteric language—which of course is the oversimplified version of theory popularized by critics hostile toward the rise of continental theory within the humanities and within English studies in particular. As students and I discuss, to do theory is to build an idea, a way of looking at the world, and to apply this perspective to other objects and situations. A theory, I tell students, is an analytical framework, an idea or concept that we can do work with and put to further use.

Gerald Graff describes theory in similar terms when he discusses the work of Deborah Meier, who elaborates for him the idea that first-year composition is a course in enculturation. According to him, "Meier describes a college sophomore whose education was transformed when he heard a senior classmate saying, 'I have a theory about why. . . .' Meier argues that, at its deepest level, being well educated means 'getting in the habit of developing theories that can be articulated clearly and then checked out in a thoughtful way'" (Graff 2003, 24). Even though Meier stresses theory's transformative qualities here, she also characterizes theory as a practical tool that intellectuals use to examine and engage with their subject.

To approach student writing as theory, then, means to design workshops that ultimately ask this question: what can we as thinkers and writers *do* with the ideas in this student text? The workshop I discuss in this essay concentrates on the writer's argument and encourages students to think theoretically in that it asks students to do further work with their own and with another writer's ideas. When students see that their writing presents ideas that can be worked on—that can be applied to other texts, elaborated on, even challenged—they begin to see their ideas as having value and participating in intellectual conversations within and beyond the classroom.

ANONYMITY, READING ALOUD, AND OTHER (NOT SO) PRACTICAL MATTERS

Before going into detail about this particular workshop, I want to briefly explain some of the general workshop procedures I use and my rationale for using them.

First, when it comes to selecting an essay to workshop, I tend to choose a piece that exhibits a problem I see in a number of different student essays. I use the term *problem* here in its most positive sense, meaning a question, line of argument, or stylistic feature worth thinking about with students. For instance, if I notice that a set of papers relies on a particular part of an assigned text to make their arguments, I might choose a representative example and ask students to discuss why they found this part of the text valuable and to consider what would happen if the writer chose to include other passages from the text as evidence. When conducting these kinds of workshops—which in many ways resemble the "writing seminar" that Joseph Harris describes in this volume—I preface our discussion by mentioning that an aspect of the particular essay we're examining appears in other student papers, and that we will concentrate our discussion on this topic. One reason I prefer to workshop representative essays is to make discussion relevant for all students in the class. Students sometimes complain that workshops are useful for the writer of the particular essay under discussion but have little value for other students in the class. Choosing a representative essay helps combat this attitude.

When reproducing student work, I keep the author anonymous. I am aware that erasing students' names from their work appears to contradict my project of encouraging students to think of themselves as intellectuals; however, I want to create a space where students explore what it means to be an intellectual in their own terms—something I think would be compromised if I declared the author's identity. More powerful for me, and I think for students, are moments of self-disclosure when a student announces to the class that she is the author of the piece under discussion. In my classes such occasions present powerful teaching moments, opening up conversations about authorship, persona, and authority.

Although on occasion I ask students to work in small groups with excerpts from different student texts, I prefer conducting whole-class discussions of an unabridged student essay. Organizing a workshop this way takes up more class time, but it prevents the problem of students reading an idea out of context. More importantly, focusing our sustained attention on one whole student paper suggests to students that their writing is worthy of the same consideration as the assigned course texts. To focus our attention even more, we read the entire essay aloud before discussing it. I typically select students at random to read individual paragraphs, and I ask students to keep a particular question or idea in mind as we read aloud, marking passages in the paper that relate to this question or idea. This kind of tactile work with the student text reinforces the idea that student essays, just like the published writing students are asked to read and write about, are texts to be worked on.

WORKING ON (AND WITH) ARGUMENT

The workshop I want to discuss focused on the draft of an essay, written for a literature-based composition course, which examined the relationship between the characters Kip and Hana in Michael Ondaatje's novel *The English Patient*. This draft, by Evan Rosen, was written in response to an assignment that asked students to compare these characters' relationship to that of the French diplomat Rene Gallimard and his lover Song Liling in David Henry Hwang's play *M. Butterfly*. From analyzing these two relationships, students were expected to develop a position on what they believed "the two texts [were] attempting to argue through these relationships," to quote from the assignment. By the time their first drafts were due, students would have read Ondaatje's novel; during the time they were revising their drafts, they were to have read *M. Butterfly*. I designed the assignment this way so that students were required to revise deeply; my hopes were that students would be prompted to rethink their earlier readings of Hana and Kip's relationship in light of Gallimard's Orientalist fantasy and Song's manipulation of this fantasy.

Evan's draft was among many that had difficulty making an argument that moved beyond the commonplace. "Love is complicated, plain and simple," Rosen writes at the beginning of his draft. "In Michael Ondaatje's historical fiction novel . . . this broad generalization's truth becomes apparent in many of the characters affairs, most notably the relationship between Hana and Kip." Despite its underwhelming thesis, Evan's essay struck me at the time as an ideal candidate to workshop because it makes a number of observations about Hana's attitude toward Kip's racial identity that it doesn't take the time to explain. For instance, Rosen observes how Hana seems to be attracted to Kip's skin color, "going as far as pouring milk on it to see its effect on his color." Evan explains how Kip's work as a sapper causes him to maintain some distance from Hana, even as their relationship becomes more intimate. But he comes back again to the problem of race later in the essay: "Hana is fascinated by most aspects of Kip: his skills as a Sikh, his body, most significantly his skin. She thinks greatly of him, even going as far as calling him her 'Princess.'" In this last moment especially, Evan showed that, as a critic, he could pick up on nuanced details from the text, although he experienced difficulty making meaning of these details and fitting them into a more grounded interpretation of the text.

The same could be said of the majority of drafts I received. So with that in mind, I reproduced Evan's draft for class discussion. I began the conversation by telling students that this draft, like many others, experienced difficulty posing a coherent argument about the text, although it made points that could, with further revision, be formed into an argument. In the previous class session we had discussed the first half of *M. Butterfly*, and I wanted to find a way to keep our conversation going while also showing students how they might draw connections between the two texts they had to write about. So before selecting students to read the essay aloud, I asked the class to pay attention as we read how Evan explains Kip and Hana's relationship. I asked that they consider how the essay characterizes this relationship and explains Hana's attraction to Kip. Finally, I told them to mark passages in the essay that could help them answer these questions.

In the discussion that followed, students commented on how Evan brings up Hana's continued interest in Kip's dark skin, and they pointed to places in the draft where Evan references particular scenes from the novel. Several students suggested that for revision, Evan should include quotes from these scenes to support his reading. Given these suggestions, I asked students how they responded to this interpretation of Hana and whether they supported this analysis. This prompted us to closely read some of the scenes from the novel Evan mentions, and students generally agreed that, based on these passages, Evan's essay offered a valid reading. In fact, a number of students indicated that Evan's essay opened up for them a different reading of the novel, as they had not picked up on Hana's fascination with Kip's race in their initial reading of the text. The room, however, grew silent when I asked students to explain the significance of Evan's observation that Hana at one point calls Kip her "Princess." (I should note that the exact term used in the novel is *goddess*, not *princess*.)

I took this opportunity to sum up the class discussion to this point: the general consensus among the class was that this piece presents a useful yet incomplete interpretation of Hana. I suggested that one way we might fill in this essay's gaps, while also answering the question regarding the significance of Hana's calling Kip a goddess, would be to apply Evan's analysis of Hana to Hwang's play *M. Butterfly*. How might we use Evan's analysis of Hana, I asked, to examine Gallimard and Song's relationship? How, in other words, does Evan's analysis potentially help explain Gallimard's attraction to Song—and vice versa?

One of the reasons I paired *The English Patient* with *M. Butterfly* is that both texts examine the nature and effects of Orientalism, although Hwang's play does so much more explicitly. *M. Butterfly* in some respects offers students a language they can use to examine how stereotypes about the East surface and get deconstructed in Ondaatje's novel. Thus, after I posed this question about how Evan's reading of *The English Patient* could be applied to *M. Butterfly*, several students spoke about how Gallimard similarly appears to be obsessed, although they added that Gallimard is obsessed with an idealized image of femininity based on the tragic heroine Cio-Cio-San, from Puccini's *Madama Butterfly*. We discussed Gallimard's image of the ideal woman, how it is based on stereotypes about Asian women's submissiveness, and how Song plays with this image to get into Gallimard's confidence.

I ended our discussion by coming back to the question students were unable to answer before: in light of what we have noticed about Gallimard and the fantasies he has about "Oriental" women, what is the significance of Evan's observation about Hana referring to Kip as a princess? In the few minutes remaining, students concluded that Hana's comment suggests that she views Kip as a woman, and they left the class wondering whether her obsession with Kip, like Gallimard's obsession with Song, is fueled by racist stereotypes.

From this discussion of his draft, and from our subsequent discussions of Hwang's play, Evan revised his essay significantly, recasting his argument from one about the complicated nature of love to one about how both Hwang's play and Ondaatje's novel illustrate the potential dangers of adhering to stereotypes. Here is the revised opening paragraph of Evan's essay, which now situates the literary texts within a broader cultural context:

> From the American public's fascination with pop star Michael Jackson's color changing skin…to Slim Whiteman's 1952 hit single "China Doll," in which Oriental women are portrayed as "doll[s] of clay," the human interest with differences in appearance, weather it be due cultural boundaries or genetic differences is obvious. This phenomenon is discussed thoroughly in both Michael Ondaatje's historical novel, *The English Patient*, and David Henry Hwang's work *M Butterfly*. In each piece many of the characters affairs, most notably the relationship between the two main characters, Hana and Kip and Gallimard and Song, show first hand what can result from an obsession with differences in appearance and culture. (Rosen 2008)

What strikes me about this new introduction is the way it opens by examining race—or what Evan calls "the human interest with differences in appearance"—in texts other than Ondaatje's and Hwang's. It also displays a sophisticated understanding of what constitutes a text, as Evan recognizes both Whitman's song and Michael Jackson's body as texts.

Most important to what I am discussing in this essay, though, this revised opening paragraph shows Evan to be building a theory about how racial differences are negotiated in the culture at large and applying them to *The English Patient* and *M. Butterfly*. It could be argued that, by referencing Whitman's song and Jackson's body, Evan is simply making quick connections to examples from popular culture that will draw readers into his argument about racial differences within the literature. Though this may be partially true, I think it is also the case that, based on the changes Evan made to his initial draft, which only referenced Ondaatje's novel, this statement is also the articulation of a working theory about cultural attitudes toward race. Based on his reading of a pop song and a pop artist—and possibly on our discussion of his draft—Evan constructs the theory that American culture has a problematic fascination with race, something he sees Ondaatje's and Hwang's texts participating in.

One reason I prefer to label the writing Evan does here as theoretical—as opposed to critical, analytical, or even intellectual—is that I believe theory is a more accessible concept for students, many of whom tell me they are familiar with it through their science coursework. In every writing course I teach, students and I negotiate the language we use to talk about writing, and because of this I ask students to discuss their understanding of concepts like criticism, analysis, theory, and intellectualism. (For a more thorough discussion on how to develop with students a shared language about writing, see Anson, Davis and Vilhotti's essay in this volume.) Students frequently mention to me how categories such as *critical* and *analytical* strike them as vague; they cite occasions when they asked a teacher to clarify advice like "Your writing needs to be more analytical" only to receive an unsatisfactory answer. In a first-year writing course I designed that centered on the issue of intellectualism, a number of students expressed their lack of interest in seeing themselves as intellectuals because of their assumptions about intellectuals being aloof, esoteric, and hyperacademic. Theory, as other students have explained to me, is something they see as having practical value; it is an idea or framework that can be clearly tested and evaluated, and, if supported, eventually become law, a certainty many students find assuring.

While I question this movement from theory to law, especially as far as the humanities are concerned, I believe a concept like theory, especially in the first-year writing classroom, can operate as a bridge term, one that showcases for students some of the work that intellectuals do without falling prey to the negative attitudes many students have about intellectualism in general. In other words, a concept like theory can introduce students to the intellectual demands of first-year composition in a less alienating way.

I want to end by returning to Evan's writing. His revised essay suggested to me that he both contributed to and learned from the intellectual discussion we had in class. His observations about Ondaatje's novel offered students a lens through which to read *M. Butterfly*, which they then used to reread *The English Patient*. In addition, Evan appeared to have taken away from this conversation as much as he gave, since his revised piece concentrated on Orientalist stereotypes, which was addressed in our class discussion. This underscores what I find to be one of the most beneficial aspects of encouraging students to see their writing as theoretical, as texts to be worked on and worked with: it illustrates to students that our class discussions, similar to the image of FYC Bruce Horner examines in this collection, constitute a real intellectual conversation and that their ideas can potentially change this conversation.

ACKNOWLEDGMENTS

I would like to thank Evan Rosen for granting me permission to quote from his essay "Fascination Leads to Generalization."

15

WRITING TO LEARN, READING TO TEACH
Student Texts in the Pedagogy Seminar

Margaret J. Marshall
Auburn University

As the essays in this collection make clear, there are many ways to work with student texts in a writing course. But unless the course is structured to feature each student's work in rotation, the teacher must make choices about *which* student texts should be brought into the class at any given moment. Such decisions are informed by the course objectives, requirements of current and upcoming assignments, and evidence of student learning. Choosing texts requires the ability to read a class set of papers to identify patterns and the creativity to design class work to foster learning for the entire group. Beginning teachers often find these choices difficult, shrouded in mystery or requiring pedagogical instinct that they fear comes only with years of trial and error. The pedagogy seminar, often required of entering graduate students prior to or during their first semester of teaching, is one place where practices can be made more explicit and where discussion of undergraduate student writing can, as Nicole Wallack suggests in this volume, "help us to name and analyze our assumptions." A pedagogy seminar is also a place where beginning teachers can practice producing the kinds of texts that teachers regularly produce—comments on student writing, lesson plans, and the like—and where teachers who come from another institutional context can adjust to new expectations. In this essay I describe a sequence of activities I developed at the University of Miami that helped graduate students learn to read undergraduate papers looking for patterns, to use those patterns to shape instruction, and to develop whole-class activities that make use of specific pieces of student writing chosen intentionally for their pedagogical value. The sequence I describe thus requires the use of both first-year student texts and the writing that beginning teachers produce as they reflect on their own experiences, respond to texts, craft lessons that other teachers can follow, and develop teaching materials directed toward undergraduates.

UNDERSTANDING LEARNING AND COURSE/ASSIGNMENT OBJECTIVES

Before beginning to read scholarship or institutional documents that position the courses they will teach, graduate students write their own literacy narratives to share with the rest of the class. The prompt for the literacy narrative is simple—tell us a story about how you learned to write for college—and is completed in about thirty minutes of the first class meeting. As the narratives are read, listeners identify key terms that emerge. At the end of all the stories, those key terms are listed on the board, creating clusters of issues involved in learning to read and write for academic purposes. Typical issues include the impact of teachers, development over time, tensions between thinking and correctness, the role of grammar or conventions, differences in genres, contrasts between school and personal writing, revision, responding to others' writing, and the relationship between reading and writing. Though each group of stories generates different key terms and variations in patterns, inevitably some narratives recall moments of humiliation, joy, triumph, pain, or anger that lie behind interests in and commitment to reading, writing, and learning. More than once, someone has confessed early ambivalence, even dislike, of reading or writing, and a shift in perspective created by a pivotal learning experience or influential person.

The differences in these stories help individuals see that their own experience is not necessarily the norm, and that writers can develop along any number of trajectories. Descriptions of different teachers and various classroom episodes elicit talk of teachers' impact on, or irrelevance to, learning. Because the narratives generate a number of issues, they illustrate the richness of the intellectual terrain that encompasses writing instruction. Honoring stories of experience encourages a reconsideration of what we think we know and establishes the importance of reflective teaching. The exercise also models a way of using class time to produce writing and a procedure for using individual pieces of writing to generate patterns or raise issues. Because the literacy narratives put the graduate students' own writing at the forefront, the exercise establishes the value of student (and teacher) writing for a writing course. Finally, writing these stories and telling them to each other forges a community of learners constituted by texts in much the same way first-year composition classes become communities constituted by texts.

The work assigned for subsequent class sessions involves reading and making notes on a collection of institutional documents—course descriptions and objectives, profiles of students, sample syllabi, placement procedures, evaluation standards, and introductions for the first-year textbooks used in the program. When the class reconvenes, the graduate students work in small groups to make a semantic map of three key terms reflected in the title of our pedagogy seminar: *teaching, college,* and *composition.* Large pieces of paper and colored markers are provided so that the end result is a visual representation of the issues these beginning teachers are thinking about. The groups then present these maps to the whole class, explaining the connections between issues they have identified as they understand them so far and questions for further investigation they've identified as they've worked on the semantic map. The map from one class for *teaching,* for example, identified preparation, classroom presence, standards of evaluation, motivating different kinds of students, and decision making as big issues with subsidiary concerns of writing the syllabus, managing time, dressing the part, recognizing learning styles, working with students with identified learning disabilities, working with nonnative speakers of English, being fair, handling attendance problems, and responding to student writing. The group working on *college* identified local concerns like hurricanes and the diversity of cultures in south Florida, but also more universal concerns affecting first-year students like adjusting to college life, managing finances, deciding on a major, understanding academic expectations, and moving beyond high-school assignments. In generating the lists, then, these beginning teachers recognized how much of college life for students exists outside the classroom, especially outside the classroom of a required course in writing. As the groups presented these semantic maps, they made connections to the collection of institutional documents they had been given, beginning the process of piecing together a picture of the university, its students, and the first-year course based on something other than assumptions drawn from their own experiences as undergraduates. They posed questions for further investigation ranging from local policy and practice (How much should be deducted from the final grade for missing class?) to the more theoretical (What is the relationship between the first-year composition course and subsequent courses? How do cultural differences impact students' assumptions about writing?).

Working with semantic maps helps make visible and concrete that not all composition courses are the same and not all institutions have the same kinds of students. Graduate students need practice in seeing how institutional documents can help identify the type of course they are being asked to teach and how the documents fit together, contradict, or complicate each other. These initial activities establish the context for specific assignments and the work with student writing that follows. Without setting such a context, work with student writing becomes an abstraction rather than a response that exists in a rhetorical and cultural/institutional setting. Although we could just talk about the documents they've been assigned to read, the semantic map demonstrates another way of using collaboration to generate knowledge, tests individual understandings in the safety of small groups, contributes to the building of community through a shared task, and illustrates how reading materials can be *used* and not just talked about in the writing class. Creating the map is a different kind of writing task for most graduate students, a task that makes them consider both form and content simultaneously in much the same way that Dennis Barron's description (2009) of having students write on clay tablets shifts writing away from being an invisible technology so it can be considered as a particular literate practice.

IDENTIFYING WHAT STUDENTS CAN AND CAN'T YET DO

A small set of undergraduate papers written in response to the same assignment are provided, and graduate students are asked to read the set to identify (1) what the students can do; (2) what they haven't done that would make the papers more successful; and (3) what they've started to do but haven't managed successfully. The graduate students are asked to mark the papers in any way they wish in preparation for discussion at the next class meeting. When we begin the discussion, I put the three categories on the board and we generate a list of features in each.

The list for what students already know how to do is often unexpectedly long. First-year students at our institution usually know, for example, how to write complete sentences and spell most words correctly. They structure paragraphs, introduce, develop, and conclude. They usually respond to the assignment, or at least parts of it, and often know how to take a position or develop an argument with examples and generalizations. Listing such features on the board, and pointing the graduate students back to the work they've done earlier with course objectives, typical student profiles, cognitive development, and literacy helps move the discussion away from counting errors or complaining about logical fallacies or formulaic writing.

The second category—"what students could have done to make the writing more successful"—though grounded in the common language of course expectations, usually reveals the variety of interpretations readers have of student work and generates debate about what the assignment expects. Multiple interpretations force discussion of the specifics on the page, engage participants in the question of what leads one reader to see what others had not considered or had interpreted very differently, and generates talk about why some readers are more bothered by particular moves than are others. My objective in encouraging such discussion is not to come up with a single interpretation, but rather to have these young teachers begin to take responsibility for articulating their judgments and substantiating them with the evidence on the page. I also hope they begin to recognize personal peeves and develop expectations for academic writing that are broader than what they personally like or find disagreeable. When we look at a collection of undergraduate end-of-term portfolios later in the course, graduate students are almost always better able to articulate a pedagogical judgment and support it with evidence in student texts, suggesting they have learned to think like a teacher.

The last category—what students have started to do but not really mastered—is the most important and usually requires comparison across the student papers being discussed. It is this last category that leads directly to designing whole-class instruction; we teach in the zone of proximal development (Vygotsky 1978) where careful instruction can serve to scaffold learning and foster new abilities. We also teach within a particular context and so respond to papers not in the vacuum of some abstraction like "good writing" but as more or less successful performances within the rhetorical situation delineated by the assignment and course objectives.

My aim in asking graduate students to read for patterns is to get them to see past errors or deficiencies in individual papers and to consider instead how multiple responses to the same assignment can be indicators of what a group of students needs to learn. It is precisely this ability that lets Joe Harris bring different pieces of student writing into the class to foster discussion about evidence or Chris Warnick decide which common *problem* will inform the selection of a representative essay (see their essays in this volume). And, it is the ability to see patterns that lets a teacher treat student writing as primary pedagogical texts rather than inferior products in need of improvement. Imbedded here is an assumption that student writing serves as assessment data that informs pedagogical decisions. We teach, we assess what they learned via the writing produced, and we modify our subsequent teaching accordingly.

READING FOR PATTERNS AND DESIGNING CLASS LESSONS

Working with a set of undergraduate papers, graduate students next work with a partner or in a small group to develop a class lesson based on what they determine the students represented in the class set need to learn to do better. The class activity they design must include student writing in some way and be structured to benefit the entire class. In other words, lessons cannot isolate problems better addressed in individual tutorials, and teachers must identify the evidence from the paper set that led to their chosen focus. We often work on writing individual comments before we turn to the whole-class lesson, so that prompting revision, identifying strengths and weakness of individuals, and writing to a student audience have already received considerable attention. When the groups present their lessons and their rationales to the rest of the seminar, they also field questions, receive suggestions, and consider ways to revise their plans.

With a collection of undergraduate student papers on file and permission to use their writing to help other teachers, it is relatively easy to assemble a set of five or six papers that also demonstrates different levels of writing fluency and different approaches to any given assignment. Keeping the set small allows readers to remember the entire corpus as they work on developing and critiquing class lessons. Working in groups gives beginning teachers support and a built-in challenge since different interpretations have to be negotiated to develop a lesson. Collaboration isn't always popular with graduate students who are more accustomed to working independently, but since collaborative work is so regularly used in the composition classroom, they need a recent experience to draw on when they reflect on this practice. End-of-term comments from these beginning teachers often mention their initial resistance to group work while acknowledging how much they learned from their classmates. Many note that the experience taught them to watch group interactions differently and gave them another perspective from which to evaluate directions for collaborative tasks.

Requiring that the class activities feature student writing produces interesting variations: using whole papers versus parts of papers, working with two papers in juxtaposition versus one paper in depth, dividing papers or parts of papers among different groups or keeping the whole class together, assigning specific tasks like rewriting or reorganizing versus framing questions and anticipating how to move the discussion in ways that accomplish the goals for the lesson. Such variations let us view student texts as teaching resources and consider the relationships between teaching strategies and learning objectives. Because the lessons all derive from the same set of student papers, everyone in the room knows the student texts well and can respond to the patterns identified by others. In one recent rendition of this exercise, groups presented lessons built around description, organization, coherence, interpreting data to make an argument, expanding and refocusing the argument, framing the argument, and signaling the relationship between details and the thesis all from the same set of student papers. As we discussed what patterns in the set generated these concerns, we were able to compare working on organization directly versus working on organization as a feature of building an argument or interpreting data. Because the groups chose different student papers as featured texts, we were able to consider how they made those decisions, whether other student texts could be substituted, and how the lesson would send individual students back to their own writing with a concrete strategy or a different understanding of the assignment or the requirements of academic writing.

In crafting the whole-class lesson, each group produces a written lesson outline including approximate timing for each step of the lesson; a bibliography of any resources they consulted, including suggestions or materials they gathered from other teachers in the program; an indication of how they will determine what students have learned from the activity; a list of possible follow-up steps; and any handouts or directions they would give students. Writing out a class lesson plan with accompanying handouts requires graduate students to produce writing intended for two very different audiences: other teachers who receive a script, rationale, and list of resources; and prospective undergraduates who are the audience for handouts, directions, and examples. In the discussion of these materials, questions of genre, audience, and purpose shift from being abstractions they will teach undergraduates to concrete practices they have to negotiate as teachers/writers themselves. Of course, most graduate students have had to consider genre and audience in the other kinds of writing they do, but they may have done so instinctively rather than with the overt attention necessary to make such decisions less obscure to first-year students.

Class discussion of these documents returns us to the concerns raised in the literacy narratives and semantic mapping. Is the lesson logically derived from what student writers have produced and the course or assignment objectives? Is it presented in a logical and understandable way? Is there enough time allotted for the work students are being asked to do? Are students likely to learn something useful from the activity? But there is also considerable discussion of what might be considered stylistic concerns. Are the handouts clearly written? Can teachers follow the sequence of steps in the activity? How do these written documents represent the teacher as a teacher? Like our discussions of end comments on student writing, content and style are thus considered simultaneously and the issues of teacher authority, establishing standards, or motivating students are revisited as concrete practices constituted discursively. Having these pieces of graduate student writing enter the seminar is essential to this discussion.

Because the lessons include resources, beginning teachers are forced to move beyond their own experience or imagination to consult others. Sometimes they make adaptations of practices they have seen while visiting classrooms, but just as often they discover the numerous books and articles in our field that provide suggestions and examples of classroom work. Including next steps or follow-up issues in the lesson allows discussion of how the individual class session works as part of an ongoing set of instructional moves that includes homework, sequencing of assignments, and revision. In fact, discussions often involve how the different group presentations might work together as a series of interconnected lessons and lead us to consider the arc of instruction across an entire term as we play with the variations that might be created by reordering or recombining individual lessons. Both the discussion of sequencing and the discussion of evaluating what students have learned from the lesson set up later work on designing the course sequence and evaluating student learning.

Since most graduate students enrolled in a pedagogy seminar have not had practice in writing as a teacher, or to other teachers, writing lesson plans becomes a terrain of new rhetorical moves similar to what first-year students are trying to negotiate. Likewise, writing handouts gives beginning teachers practice in writing for a student audience, an audience most graduate students have not considered. The limited scope of handouts fosters focused attention on what they are trying to accomplish. Composing documents for both teachers and students requires beginning teachers to begin creating a teaching persona or at least to play with the discursive representations of themselves as teachers. Attending to the written documents allows the seminar group to talk about how to represent teaching and when and why teachers do so, and clues graduate students to begin collecting such documents well before they get to the job search.

Typically this assignment is done twice, with two different sets of student papers written in response to two different assignments. In the first cycle, the class lessons concentrate on a global issue, and in the second on a sentence or paragraph issue, though not an issue that is a matter of simple correctness or following standard conventions. Examples of sentence- or paragraph-level lessons have included embedding quotations, varying sentence structure, incorporating fragments for rhetorical effect, and integrating visuals like graphs, charts, or illustrations.

Since our first-year students rarely have grammatical errors that are so widespread they warrant whole-class attention, setting such matters aside helps beginning teachers avoid obsessing over superficial errors or ESL issues that may be visible in only a few papers. Instead, beginning teachers learn to focus on a range of other sentence-level concerns they might otherwise ignore—such as considerations of style, rhetorical tone, authorial personae, genre constraints, and audience signals, rather than correctness, conventions, or punctuation in isolation. Cycling through twice gives the graduate students a chance to revisit the practice of reading student papers for patterns that need whole-class instruction, but creates enough variety that they can't simply repeat what they (or classmates) did previously. Such an approach also mirrors the way our sequences for first-year students require slightly different moves rather than the same moves from one assignment to the next. Separating sentence-level issues and delaying those until later in the term fits with the programmatic objectives of emphasizing critical reading and writing but expecting reasonably correct prose and increasing sophistication of expression. In either or both of these cycles, the group of beginning teachers is able to discuss how global and sentence-level issues are connected and can practice reframing an issue of correctness as an indicator of some larger rhetorical or logical feature like cohesiveness, organization, tone, or the connections between genre, audience, and purpose.

VALUING AND CIRCULATING STUDENT/TEACHER TEXTS

Because graduate students participate in teaching circles that bring together all the teachers in our program to discuss curriculum and pedagogy, the lessons they develop in the seminar are often shared with other teachers in the program. Likewise, the undergraduate student writing we read in the seminar and the discussions of that work regularly prompt revised assignments or new sequences of assignments. In some cases, graduate students have gone on to propose a theme for a second-semester course, producing lesson plans and assignments for review by a committee of teachers in the program. The other writing graduate students produce in the seminar also circulates into new contexts precisely because writing can, as Chris Warnick suggests in this volume, spawn ideas to be worked on. The literacy narratives have, on more than one occasion, been the springboard for a deeper consideration of some aspect of literacy instruction, in one case producing a panel on bilingualism for the Conference on College Composition and Communication that led to additional scholarly publications and to an experimental course where students wrote in English and Spanish. A lecturer not in the pedagogy seminar built on this work to develop a creative writing course using both languages. Likewise, the semantic maps and the discussion of context for writing courses invite graduate students to take up complex research projects and have led some to pursue advanced graduate work both in composition and in related fields like higher education administration. Collaborating with other teachers led one graduate student not only to pursue additional research into collaboration, but to propose and then teach a course collaborating with the local art museum that required students to produce collaboratively authored multimedia texts. Valuing student writing, both undergraduate and graduate, thus supports important pedagogical objectives, fosters professional and scholarly work, and promotes the shift from being a student to thinking like a teacher.

16

THE WRITER/TEXT CONNECTION
Understanding Writers' Relationships to Their Writing

Muriel Harris
Purdue University

Contributing to this collection of essays on the importance of student texts as pedagogical tools places me in an uncomfortable position. I've spent my entire teaching career as a director and tutor in a writing center, and as such, I have tried never to consider the text as a sufficient pedagogical tool in itself. In my tutorials with student writers, and when training new tutors, I've emphasized the connection, the intertwining, of student and text—the combination so tightly bound together that we can't consider one without the other. Perhaps too often, I've invoked the tired metaphor of the golf instructor whose responsibility it is to teach a novice golfer. If the pro stays in the clubhouse, waiting for the novice to come back with a scorecard, how much instruction can the pro provide by looking only at that scorecard?

Thus, for me, the instructional nexus is the relationship of the writer to her writing. Looking at a paper without understanding how *that* writer produced *that* paper or what *that* writer needs (other than fulfilling the assignment, of course) evokes yet another metaphor. That is, looking solely at the paper is akin to walking down a road and seeing that proverbial turtle sitting on the fence post. We don't know how the turtle got there, don't know what it wants, and aren't much help until we figure out what should be done. Moreover, the turtle may be just as mystified as we are. And so, tutors talk, ask questions, listen, and collaborate. Then, if all goes well, we have helped the writer resee her writing—and writing in a more general sense—and prepared her for further writing and revising. My plan here is to share some aspects of how writers are connected to their writing, what mental processes affect what is produced, how students inhabit their writing, and how they react to it. With that in mind, I offer some strategies to engage the writer and her text in ways that promote learning on the writer's part. From the vantage point of a tutor, I am encouraging all of us, in any teaching situation, to focus not just on the writer and not just on the paper, but on the inseparability of writer and text.

The text can be the starting point for instruction, the means by which we plunge into the conversation that gets students talking to us. From that entry point, we begin to learn where the student is with this text and with his writing and then go on to work with that student's perceptions, concerns, questions, and ideas. Though we want to talk with students to help them become more proficient writers, they are riveted on the particular assignment they have to complete. And so, instead of launching into minilectures about the problems in the paper, we should put aside our agenda so we can see the writer/text connection. To do this, we often begin by asking the writer what she thinks is a strong aspect of the paper or which part she especially likes. That not only starts the conversation on a positive note but also helps us learn how the student assesses her writing. Then we can ask what the writer needs help with or what is causing problems. However, many students can't easily identify what to work on in the drafts they have in hand. Some students, of course, can explain what they need help with, or where or why they got stuck, or where they want to go next with a draft in process. But absent suggestions by another skilled reader, a large percentage of students flail around in tutorials as they grope for words that tap into their concerns. They are likely to begin by asking for feedback or for help with grammar (because that's something concrete that can be worked on), or by offering vague responses such as not liking that draft, or not being sure if it makes sense, or wondering if it meets the assignment. Perhaps they don't have the metalanguage to categorize what they feel is lacking, or perhaps some don't even know exactly what is not working, other than to ask "Can you help me with this paper?"

Some students come to tutorials holding drafts with feedback from an instructor, but can't make the connection from the instructor's carefully composed comments to what they are supposed to do about those comments. I've met students who have papers so carefully annotated I can't fathom how the instructor had enough time to write all that. But too many students don't read those comments closely, or are so overwhelmed by the sheer quantity of comments that they need help interpreting the marginalia or end comments. Moreover, students rarely see the writing as an entity separate from themselves. Thus, when a paper has a marginal note that the writing lacks organization, the student takes that as a comment about her—that she is disorganized. This makes an objective interpretation even more difficult. Sometimes, in tutorials, that kind of interpretation results in a student's sitting down, putting the paper between us, and desperately intoning the verdict: "He doesn't like my writing." (Sometimes, the phrasing is a bit more colorful.) Or students know they need to work on abstract concepts, as when the teacher notes the paper lacks transitions or needs a tighter organizational structure or should have a more specific thesis or lacks convincing arguments. The student knows what those concepts mean, but can't use them in any strategic way to revise their own words. Constructive suggestions too often are expressed as broad concepts not tied to any particular part of the text. It requires conversation to learn that student writers often lack the ability to see where and how to incorporate general rhetorical qualities in text-specific ways.

Such conversation can happen in any setting where the student and text are present—in tutorials, workshops, and teacher conferences. But when tutors and teachers meet individually with writers, there are, of course, differences. The teacher knows the student and the assignment; knows what she, as the instructor, wants to talk about; has other evidence of the student's writing; is placed by the student in a position of authority because of the power of being the grader and editor; and may have more restrictive time constraints than a tutor has. The tutor usually has an hour or half hour to work with the student, works in a nonevaluative setting, exerts no authority over the student, and can continue to meet on a weekly basis. But, like the tutor, the instructor must learn what the student needs to know. In the workshop, however, the context is closer to that of the tutorial. As Joseph Harris points out in his essay in this collection, the focus in the workshop is similarly on the individual writer, on how to help that writer revise. Like the tutorial, a small-group workshop can be, as Harris puts it, "warm, supportive, empathetic, collaborative, and student-centered" (153). "The power of a workshop," Harris continues, "stems in large part from its intimacy and immediacy" (147). Like tutors and workshop respondents, teachers can also listen, ask questions, and offer feedback in conferences with student writers.

Thus, because the strategies tutors are familiar with can serve in multiple settings, I offer the following suggestions for effective ways to interact with students and their texts, to get a sense of the connection of the writer to his or her text. The student may have a draft in hand, but most of these questions and conversation starters also work well for students in the earliest planning stages. If the conference is the setting for the discussion, rather than the tutorial or workshop classroom, a word first about the seating arrangements. Sitting next to a student, rather than across a desk, sends the unspoken message that we wish to help, not be the authority who will control the conversation or the paper.

ASK THE WRITER WHAT SHE THINKS THE ASSIGNMENT IS

Of course the instructor and responders in a workshop know what the assignment is (though the tutor usually does not), but this step is a necessary check on whether the writer really understands the assignment in detail and knows the purpose, audience, and type of paper that meets the assignment's requirements. Reading assignments correctly is an analytical—and necessary—skill to start off papers successfully. But some students haven't learned this difficult part of a writing task—how to find out what kind of text they are asked to produce. The draft may seem inadequate, but it may also have been written to meet another assignment the writer had envisioned internally. Thus, it helps greatly to listen closely to the student's summary of the assignment to see if the student has a clear grasp of its essentials and the requirements that have been spelled out. Sometimes, however, assignments can themselves be the cause of less-than-acceptable texts. (For a discussion on how to compose effective assignments, see my forthcoming "Assignments from Hell: The View from the Writing Center.") When the assignment is clearly written, but the student does not grasp the goals, purpose, and audience for the assignment, the conversation has to start there, precisely because it's not likely that a paper will turn out well if the end product is muddled in a writer's mind. Students who don't have a clear picture of who the intended audience is can be perplexed by how much explanation, information, or detail should be included. They lack a set of criteria to use when deciding if such matters are integral to the effectiveness of the paper. If the writer doesn't indicate that the assigned analysis of a reading requires critical thinking and not just a summary, the paper will focus on a summary of the reading. In sum, if the student doesn't grasp the parameters of the assignment—and this is a very real and frequent source of confusion—then there's little hope that an adequate text will be produced.

ASK WRITERS WHAT THEIR PAPERS ARE ABOUT

This is an effective way to learn if the student's main point is clear in her own mind. If the writer can't succinctly summarize her draft in a sentence or two (or a few more, if the paper is long), then her text is less likely to be focused and clear. Early drafts of papers often ramble as some writers must write for a while before they clarify their thinking. Occasionally, the discussion that follows as the student works on summarizing the contents can be helpful, as the student begins to formulate more tightly thoughts that are swirling in her mind but have not yet settled into words that can be recorded on paper. This harkens back to the classic result: "I don't know what I think until I see what I wrote" (or the corollary "hear what I said"). While many experienced writers recognize this as a characteristic aspect of their writing processes, in that they know they should write and write for awhile and then sift through the writing to finally compose a focused draft, less-experienced student writers may see first drafts as final drafts (and are also prone to handing in what is really that early exploratory draft). If the student can't "nutshell" the paper's contents, then summarizing the draft is a helpful direction for conversation to focus on. We or the others in the workshop can help the student by asking questions, listening, and maybe even recording the words the writer uses as she works towards defining the paper's thesis or argument. The intent here is to help the student verbalize in her own words what she is writing about. This can be the major accomplishment because it was the initial stumbling block the student couldn't get past. Rather than revising specific parts of the paper, if the final nutshell description is different, the student can be encouraged to start over, using what fits from the previous draft and discarding (or filing away for future use) the rest that turns out to be extraneous or irrelevant to this text.

ASK WRITERS TO READ THE PAPER ALOUD

Not all students are willing to read their papers aloud, but if the assignment is clear in the student's mind, and if the student's thesis is clear, then reading the draft aloud helps many writers gain vital distance from their writing. Sitting alongside the writer in some informal way also emphasizes that listeners have moved out of the teacher role to that of helpful reader. This positioning also enables informal interaction. For reasons no one has adequately explained, many students begin self-correcting as they read aloud, adding missing words, correcting some grammatical problem or awkward sentence, or even seeing that they need more detail or need to amplify an argument in a specific part of the paper. This reading/listening to their own words gives students that needed distance from the text we all benefit from in order to assess its effectiveness. Skilled readers reread their texts and listen, either aloud or internally, but many student writers need to be introduced to this important step. ESL students, depending on their skill levels, might be able to start self-correcting when they read, but many cannot if they are more skilled in silently reading written English than in hearing it aloud, even when it's their own writing.

BEGIN THE CONVERSATION WITH A POSITIVE COMMENT AFTER HEARING THE DRAFT OR ASKING THE WRITER FOR AN ASSESSMENT

Students routinely assume the role of a teacher or other readers is to criticize the paper, to note what it's lacking or what needs revising. Thus, writers often brace themselves for negative comments, ready to assume a defensive posture or to duly make excuses for mistakes. Too often it is easy to forget how anxious and insecure most writers are about their writing. An initial positive comment about what is working well or what is interesting or what was particularly well written turns the situation into a pleasant conversation. Who doesn't respond well to compliments? In addition, the writer has a better idea of what has been achieved or what is working effectively. That knowledge is as important as learning what needs revising. With the tension reduced, the writer can relax and begin considering what she wants to talk about. Another option after hearing the writer's paper is to let the writer speak first, perhaps asking, "What do you think?" or "How did it sound to you?" That opens a space for the writer to raise her concerns.

ASK WRITERS WHAT THEY HAD DIFFICULTY WITH WHEN WRITING THAT DRAFT

The point here is to ask an open-ended question, not a closed yes/ no one such as, "Did you have any difficulty writing this paper?" With this approach, it may seem that the instructor's conference agenda or the established protocol of the workshop is being ignored, but it isn't. If there isn't a negotiation or an opportunity for the writer to surface whatever he wants to talk about or ask, the writer is less likely to listen closely to whatever others say. Many conversations go nowhere because as each person speaks, the other isn't listening but waiting for an opening to say what's on his mind. Once the writer begins to identify where in the text he struggled, that concern is part of his agenda and has to be factored in as the conversation flows forward. Now there's an entry into which direction the conversation will go. It may be time to bring up reader concerns as well as the conversation moves more specifically to that part of the text.

ASK "WHY ARE YOU TELLING ME THAT?"

When the writer reaches a place in the text that digresses into extraneous discussion, we can ask (since we are readers trying to make sense of what we're reading) why the writer is telling us that. If there is a logical connection in the writer's mind (but not in the paper), we have uncovered a missing step in the text. Less experienced writers don't realize they have omitted relevant material that connects one idea to the next until someone else asks for help in understanding the connections. But if the writer also seems stumped, then she has found a part that needs to be deleted. For a writer trying to write to a word count she hasn't reached, deleting words is a painful procedure. It helps for readers to assure the writer that we can talk about adding additional information.

USE READER RESPONSE LANGUAGE

When responding to some part of the text, we should use the language of a reader working to understand what is written. If something is unclear, instead of labeling it an "error" or "an incomplete thought," we can point out where we're confused and ask for more information. This approach can surface the need for more specifics as the writer sees that the information or details or explanations are missing. When we find some part of the paper that is working well, we can comment on it as readers, remarking that some sentence is particularly well worded or that some description offers a vivid mental picture.

LISTEN, REALLY LISTEN

Other students in workshops may assume that once the writer is through talking, they need to jump in and comment—a tendency that limits real listening. Teachers are similarly inclined to begin talking. Those of us who teach writing find it a rewarding endeavor for many reasons, but somewhere in there is a love of words—reading words, saying words, hearing words. And too many of us are uncomfortable when a silence occurs in a conversation. We find ourselves filling the silent void that seems to last six hours or more, but in reality is probably about eight to ten seconds. Study after study has confirmed the tendency of many instructors to ask a question, to wait no more than a surprisingly small number of seconds, and then if there is no student answer, to provide answers themselves. We often don't give writers enough time to think about the answer, so we should sit back, relax, try not to be uncomfortable with the silence for maybe ten or more seconds longer than we might otherwise have done. With nonnative speakers of English, this necessity to wait is especially important as some may have to hear our words, translate them into the language they are more comfortable with, consider an answer in that language, and then translate it back into English. Another important reason we may not be listening is that we are engaged in formulating our next comments and not attending to what is being said by the other person. As Jeanne Simpson advises, to be effective listeners, we must turn off the interior tape of "what I'm planning to say" (2008). On the other side of this grouping of writers and readers, writers also need to pause and listen rather than speaking immediately. Joseph Harris, in his essay in this book, describes how he asked a writer in his workshop "to be quiet for a few minutes, and to listen and take notes on what her readers had to say" (145).

BRING THE CONFERENCE OR WORKSHOP DISCUSSION TO AN END WITH PLANS FOR THE WRITER

When the conference or workshop conversation is drawing to a close, or when it's apparent the writer is either fatigued, restless, or needs to move on, it's time to bring the discussion to a productive end. One way is to summarize the conversation or to ask the writer what was talked about. Or we can help the writer formulate a plan for what he will do next with the text. Helping the student verbalize what will be worked on makes the next steps more concrete and memorable in the writer's mind. We can also help the writer compose a written plan to take along as a guide or memory jog. Somewhere in that time, it helps to ask the writer if he has any leftover questions. If in a conference a question surfaces that will take more than a short time to answer, part of the plan is to come back another time to address this unanswered question. Keeping very brief records of what was covered can help us recall and then pick up where this conference left off.

ADAPT SOME OF THESE APPROACHES TO THE CLASSROOM

While my focus here has been on strategies to use in conferences or workshops, some are adaptable to classroom use. For example, class time may be spent checking to see if students understand the assignment. After the assignment has been given, students can be asked to explain what the assignment is, what the goal is, who the audience is, how they are going to approach it, what difficulties any of them can foresee, and so on. Or they can be asked to write down their answers. Some students can then read their responses aloud. Some will be on target, some won't. But getting them all on the same page before beginning a draft is critical. For students, this has the advantage of articulating generally what they will write about, will help them redirect when they are off in the wrong direction or are unclear about the assignment, and will allow some to hear the explanations perhaps in terms they understand better, given that the responses will be in student language.

All these suggested approaches are meant to highlight the student's text as an unfinished product of a writer in the process of composing. Working on already graded texts where revision is no longer possible may be useful. But for many student writers, that's more of a postmortem. For student texts still open for discussion and revision, the text is a basis for talking about writing, but the real discussion is about that writer and her interaction with that text. The text is not a disembodied entity; it is merely the physical or visible evidence of the writer and her composing skills. As we seek an understanding of the inseparable connection of that writer to that text, we are engaged in a particularly valuable act of pedagogical inquiry.

17
LEARNING FROM COAUTHORING
Composing Texts Together in the Composition Classroom

Michele Eodice
University of Oklahoma

Kami Day
Johnson County Community College

Since our first coauthored paper in graduate school, we have written articles, chapters, a book, conference presentations, and edited a journal together. In addition, each of our dissertations studied coauthors. Collaboration is central to our pedagogies, and in a collaborative classroom, students are continuously learning from their own and their peers' texts. In fact, the most important text *is* the students' writing. One element of collaborative work is coauthoring, which can be defined in a number of ways, especially across disciplines. However, we define coauthoring in our writing courses as "face-to-face, word-by-word collaborative writing" (Day and Eodice 2001, 31). We firmly believe that coauthoring in the writing classroom is a pedagogically sound method for exploring more openly the rhetorical challenges of writing for diverse audiences and for orienting students to the realities of future workplace writing. When our students work in small groups to coauthor papers, they gain in both affective and cognitive ways; the texts they work on—from the messy drafts to the final product—are in front of all of them at all times, creating rich, authentic engagement with the kinds of rhetorical moves writers make. But more than that, this engagement is visible, necessary, and rewarding.

Elsewhere in this collection, authors discuss the learning that takes place when students hear or read, respond to, and edit each other's individual work; this chapter focuses on the learning that takes place when students read, revise, and comment on texts they collaboratively create in real time. Our contribution describes the ways Kami prepares students to write together in her community college composition courses and then facilitates that writing. We include, with the students' permission, snippets from transcripts of students talking as they coauthor, student reflections on the process, and an actual student text.

SETTING UP A COLLABORATIVE CLASSROOM

From the initial class meeting, the work of writing—and writing itself—is framed as collaborative, and students begin to internalize this message as they read the first page of the syllabus: "This will be a collaborative classroom, so most of your class work will be done in groups and you will be sharing most of your writing with your peers." On the next page, in the list of writing tasks, students find this: "a coauthored paper, written with your group (hard to tell how many drafts!) in class." After reading the syllabus, and with their often negative group work experiences in mind, students might express apprehension about the collaborative work, particularly coauthoring. However, because they have already determined that composition courses must be endured, and because changing their schedules is almost impossible, they stay in the class. Most are not sorry. By the end of the semester, a majority of students write in their portfolio reflections that even with the challenges of writing together, they enjoyed and learned and even grew from the experience.

Successful and productive coauthoring does not just happen simply because students are in groups. As Russell Garth writes in *Learning in Groups*, "There are two essential elements to successful collaborative learning: an active learning process involving peer interaction; and faculty guidance" (quoted in Ede and Lunsford 1985, 123). Students must see collaborative work as integral to their learning, so such work must be part of every class period, including the first one. Joseph Harris points out in this volume that frequent group work "can have the effect . . . of making the class as a whole lose a sense of identity or purpose" (147), and we agree, but we think the tradeoff is worth it. There is not space here to describe all the collaborative activities possible early in the semester, but, for example, students can participate in a guided interaction on the first day, and the second day they can dive into constructing knowledge together by reading and responding in writing to each other's learning log entries and discussing those entries as groups.

Coauthoring can and should begin early. During the second week of the semester, Kami writes a sentence on the board and the whole class works together to "flesh out" the images and concepts in the sentence using concrete details, powerful verbs, and vivid nouns. This activity may look like an ordinary brainstorming exercise, but it's a warm-up for upcoming collaborative work in which students will be asked to generate ideas out loud with others and then write together. Then, early in the third week, Kami puts the students into groups that will stay together for the remainder of the semester. Some instructors advocate allowing students to choose their own groups, some advocate organizing groups randomly (counting off, etc.), but Kami, after watching the students for a couple of weeks, creates the groups based mainly on combining introverts and extroverts, and also tries to create mixed-gender groups. In addition, she tries to make sure each group includes at least three students who have been coming regularly to class. Attrition creates challenges at a community college, and occasionally groups must be reconfigured when students stop attending. Some instructors ask students to change groups several times during the semester, but Kami's experience has taught her that the respect and trust students build within their groups, if they stay together, is worth preserving. This stability is conducive to a productive learning experience for everyone as they engage in the risky and intimate activity of writing. And students attest to the value of this early and consistent work with their peers. One student, Nicole Bettes (2008), wrote, "Working together in our groups this semester definitely helped with doing the coauthoring. We were able to get to know each other pretty well before having to write a piece together. That is always helpful." A majority of the students echoed her sentiments.

AN EXERCISE IN COAUTHORING

Once the permanent groups are formed, Kami gives each group a copy of the same generic paragraph about a music concert:

> A big crowd of kids had been waiting in the theater for a long time for the band to start the show. They had been restless and had started to cause some trouble. The curtain was open, and the audience could see the stage, which had a lot of equipment on it and a screen behind the equipment. Finally, the band came onto the stage. Their appearance was outrageous. The audience reacted wildly seeing them. The band started playing very loud music and their behavior on the stage got out of hand. The audience got out of hand too. The police had to come and break up the concert.

She assigns one or two sentences from the paragraph to each group, and they are charged with developing the sentences into a paragraph or two as a group. Kami does not give the groups many directions beyond asking them to choose a scribe, and the students work for the rest of that class period on their paragraphs, not knowing what other groups are developing.

Kami collects the paragraphs and then hands them back when the students come in the next time. Each group chooses a spokesperson, and those students line up at the front of the class in the order the sentences appear in the original paragraph. She asks them to read aloud the paragraphs they have developed with no break between them, creating an instant coauthored text, as the other students listen and make note of any words or phrases that strike them as memorable. The result can be hilarious—paragraphs about Kiss juxtaposed with paragraphs about Hanna Montana, or Green Day next to a church choir—and often applause spontaneously erupts at the conclusion of the reading. Kami then asks the groups to share their processes, and they talk about how they invented ideas (maps and webs, lists, freewriting), the challenge of incorporating everyone's ideas, fun, conversations about which word sounded best for what they wanted to convey, the realization that they were making assumptions about their audience. Students also point out details that jumped out at them as they listened to the paragraphs. They talk about writing and the process of writing, using the text they have created as a result of an enjoyable and low-risk coauthoring experience.

STUDENTS WRITING TOGETHER IN CLASS

The students have many more opportunities to coauthor during the semester. They collaboratively compose paragraphs; they coauthor paraphrases and summaries and works cited pages; they create a coauthored mini-researched paper using a template that helps them integrate outside texts with their own, a process most first-year composition students find quite challenging (see Graff and Birkenstein 2006). And, of course, they continue to read and respond to each other's work. In addition, they write one coauthored essay, assigned when the semester is well under way. Kami gives the students the whole class period across several meetings to work on their coauthored essays, partly because she wants to watch them work, but mainly because the lives of community college students are often complicated and getting together outside class is almost impossible. Attendance often improves during this time because students know they must write all the "major" essays to pass the class and they cannot write this particular essay if they are not in attendance. They also know Kami will consider their responsibility to their peers as part of their final grades.

Directions for this essay remind students that they already know how to coauthor and to continue to do what they have been doing so well all semester. Kami also asks them to change scribes for each writing session because scribe can be a powerful position (heads always nod when Kami brings this up), and she stresses that at the end of each coauthoring session, she will take up any writing the groups have done; if they have been working on a computer, they must her email what they wrote that day. She learned to take this precaution after, on several occasions, the student who took the writing home did not show up for the next class period. While the groups are working, Kami circulates but does not offer much direction or feedback unless a group is truly at an impasse. This essay gives students a chance to practice what they have been learning during the semester, so she wants them to rely on each other and not on her. Also, they have in each other an immediate diverse audience made up already of several perspectives, what Ede and Lunsford (1984) call the "audience addressed," so conversations about the writing are rich and feedback is constant.

Directions include the admonition to develop text together in class, creating one voice from three or four (or sometimes five) voices, rather than smooshing together sections written by individual group members. Successful coauthoring demands a great deal of talk. According to our research for our 2001 book *(First Person)*[2], about eighty percent of coauthoring is talk. If students write separate sections and then simply stitch them together, they miss out on the process of word- and sentence-level negotiation—negotiation that is key to developing what Shannon Carter calls "rhetorical dexterity" (2008).

The following is an excerpt from a coauthoring session in which the students were writing a rhetorical analysis. This group consisted of three women—Andrea Wright, Karissa Wilcox, and Megan Ellis—and two men—Taylor Maine and Chris Moguchy. They were analyzing a 2007 article by Brent Staples, "Just Walk on By," about his experiences of being feared because of his race. Megan Ellis was the scribe in session one, and Karissa Wilcox for session two. Quotation marks enclose text they were trying out for their analysis. We struggled to find a way to show the pauses, overlaps, incomplete thoughts, and messiness of the process. We've used ellipses to give a sense of it.

Session One

Andrea:	He uses humor with pathos . . . the credibility is in the example.
Megan:	Pathos uses humor . . . the ethos is his experience.
Karissa:	The logos is his stories, the book he wrote . . . .
Megan:	Would you say . . . we're working on ethos . . . is it really pathos?

[They all agree it is.]

Megan:	We could have two paragraphs . . . ethos . . . logos . . . use ethos as a transition.
Karissa:	How do we finish up pathos? Do we stick with one story? "He goes on to tell many stories . . . ."
Chris:	He also refers to other situations.
Karissa:	Pathos . . . what did we want to put in the other day? Something about making themselves less threatening?
Andrea:	That's part of ethos.
Karissa:	Let's finish it up and go on the pathos.
Megan:	"This is an example of the stories Staples uses to illustrate . . . ."
Andrea:	Are you trying to establish credibility?

By the "final" draft of the analysis, the sentence had evolved to "He went on to provide more examples from his experience in a humorous light, while maintaining the seriousness of the all too common problem of racial profiling."

Session Two

Andrea:	. . . our internalized struggle . . .
Megan:	What's the intent of this sentence? "He was feared . . .was feared . . . has been feared . . ." Do we want to go into a specific instance?
Andrea:	We should.
Chris:	The working in the intro . . .
Taylor:	It's a memoir . . .
Megan:	We'll make the sentence sound nicer later.
Andrea:	"For example, race discrimination at an early age . . ." Look up recollection . . .

Megan: "His first recollection of racial profiling . . ."
Karissa: Good word . . .

[Discussion of Staples's experience]

Andrea: ". . . happened to be walking down the street . . ."
Megan: ". . . when a white woman fled from him because of race and
             presence."

This section of their text became "For example, his first recollection
of racial profiling was at age 22, when a white woman fled from him in
fear of his presence." Also, in the final version, they combined ethos,
logos, and pathos rather than relegating them to separate paragraphs.
Here is the final draft:

Staples, a writer for the Chicago Sun Times, holds a PhD in Psychology from
the university of Chicago. In 1986 Staples wrote an essay entitled, "Just Walk
on By," which was published in Ms. Magazine. The essay aimed to educate
uninformed Americans about the struggles that young African Americans
face.

Staples did this by illustrating his own experiences with uncomfortable situations. Throughout his whole life, Staples has been feared simply
because of his race. For example, his first recollection of racial profiling was
at age 22, when a white woman fled from him in fear of his presence. As a
self-proclaimed "softy," this even shocked and distressed him, but as Staples
soon found out, events like this would become common. Staples reaffirmed
this racial profiling by referencing Norman Podhoretz's essay" My Negro
Problem And Ours". Podhortez, a white male, elaborated on his "terror of
black males" throughout his life. Based on his experiences, Staples developed strategies to appear "less threatening", to appease others, and to avoid
uncomfortable situations. Despite serious and touchy subject matter, Staples
illustrated his experiences in a rather humorous light. He referred to the
woman of his first encounter humorously as his "victim," even though he
later states that he could barely even "take a knife to a raw chicken." He went
on to provide more examples form his experience in a humorous light, while
maintaining the seriousness of the all too common problem of racial profiling. His choice to lay low and "remain a shadow" in society reflects his character and willingness to accommodate others. Despite this attempt, people still
regarded him as a menace merely based on his appearance.

In Staples' essay, "Just Walk on By" he validated the reality of racial
and profiling in our everyday American society. Drawing form his own

experiences, Staples used humor to reveal the harsh judgments of everyday Americans. Keep in mind Staples' experiences the next time you judge someone based merely on their appearance. (Ellis, Maine, Moguchy, Wilcox, and Wright 2008 [unedited])

Kami's sense as she watched this group all semester was that every group member was actively engaged—it was the most successful group in this particular class—but as we (Michele and Kami) read this excerpt, we realized that Taylor's and Chris's voices are muted. Both of these students were quite introverted, but in their end-of-semester reflections, they both spoke positively about collaboration and coauthoring. Taylor wrote, "I am definitely more confident about my writing and communication skills . . . because I was somewhat forced to give feedback to others and reply to theirs. My communication skills at the beginning of the semester were definitely worse than mine at the end. And it's not just in this class in this group. I've noticed my social skills have improved slightly outside of this class as well" (Maine 2008). Taylor went on to coauthor a highly successful research project with another member of his group. Similarly, Chris wrote, "This semester has definitely been a very enjoyable experience. . . . After working with a group for a few papers, I feel so much more confident when sharing my writings. . . . I am positive this class has made me a more secure writer and a more attentive reader" (Moguchy 2008).

THE VALUE OF COAUTHORING

Exactly how group talk contributes directly to learning is difficult to discern, but when we (Michele and Kami) describe to each other what we think learning looks like and what we see in our classes, our images match. In his 2003 *Learning Paradigm College*, John Tagg draws extensively on research to support his assertion that effective learning involves students' attempting "tasks that are visible and meaningful to others" (155). In our experience, when students coauthor, their thinking is made visible in their conversations and in their written products—products in which they all have a stake. Tagg goes on to say that "through performance . . . we learn to integrate knowledge . . . so it can be transferred" (162). In our classes, students perform writing in zones of proximal development (Vygotsky 1978), actively teaching and learning from each other; even if instructors are driven only by a list of outcomes, they could not find a more visible manifestation of student learning. When students coauthor, they discuss meaning, word choice, placement of words, sentences and sections of text, punctuation and spelling, and so forth. They use the shared text they are creating to explore what makes writing clear, engaging, and effective for the audience they have in mind. Yes, students can do the same thing with their individual texts as they draft alone, but when they write with peers, they inevitably encounter several perspectives for each choice they must make, and often students say they would never have thought of the most workable solution to a writing problem, or they would not have thought of a salient point, on their own. In his reflection on this process, student Noah Quinn (2008) wrote, "It was a good learning experience for me when my group members took their turns writing and ended up contributing things that I never would have thought of to the paper. All in all, I'd say that it was a positive experience, and a good assignment. Because writing in a group forces everyone to grow in some area that they are not good at. It's a different area for different people, but everyone grows somehow."

By the end of the semester, Kami's role is mainly supportive as her students engage in conversations about how to get a reader's attention, what points they want to focus on, where to best place paragraphs, whether a one-sentence paragraph is effective, how to conclude their papers in a way that the readers take away something to think about, and so on. She admits she finds the editing discussions particularly fascinating because the students approach punctuation rhetorically, talking sometimes at length about why a semicolon is better than a colon, or whether a comma is necessary to convey the meaning of the sentence clearly.

Because coauthoring is so time consuming, Kami's students understand that she considers the process to be more important than the product. Some of the more diligent groups, those who have worked the most smoothly all semester, come close to feeling they are finished with their coauthored essay, but Kami calls the products "early drafts," and students almost always complain that they would have liked to have more time to work on their essays. And, of course, coauthoring does not always go smoothly and coauthored texts are sometimes pretty rough, but that is true of individually written texts as well. We cannot claim that coauthored writing is better than singly authored work (although it often is), but it is certainly as good, and in addition, successful coauthoring can result in affective as well as cognitive gains. Students are given an opportunity to practice negotiating difference, listening carefully, recognizing and valuing the strengths of others. They often become friends and develop a supportive cohort.

Teachers of student writers take varied pedagogical stances. We happen to value coauthoring. We guide our students to coauthor because we believe the process itself scaffolds students as they acquire and practice the rhetorical dexterity necessary to reach their audiences and accomplish their purposes. Our overarching goal is not simply to teach coauthoring, but to leverage coauthoring as a way to help students make sense of the challenges of writing any text, at any time, with anyone. What we find most rewarding about our way of teaching writing is seeing students, their heads bent over a text, using "language about language . . . . the vernacular to be internalized for each member's future use" (Gere 1987, 92).

ACKNOWLEDGMENTS

Our thanks go to the students in Kami's composition courses at Johnson County Community College, who gave us permission to use their written and spoken words.

18

INQUIRY, COLLABORATION, AND REFLECTION IN THE STUDENT (TEXT)-CENTERED MULTIMODAL WRITING COURSE

Scott L. Rogers
University of Louisville

Ryan Trauman
University of Louisville

Julia E. Kiernan
University of Louisville

To teach with student texts is to acknowledge that students are savvy and experienced enough to collaboratively shape and enact productive classrooms. It seems only natural that these same students recognize what scholars in our field have been arguing for more than a decade: that "what counts as a text and what constitutes reading and writing are changing" (Hull and Nelson 2005, 224). If we're going to ask our students to work closely with their classmates' texts, it is important to remain sensitive to their perceptions about what count as texts.

Students are often skeptical about genres and modes of composing with which they are unfamiliar or that they suspect are out of date. This is not to say that our traditional prose-centric genres and typographic modes of composing are becoming obsolete. Rather, we argue, along with the New London Group, that "literacy pedagogy now must account for the burgeoning variety of text forms associated with information and multimedia technologies" (1996, 61). These new texts include Facebook pages, streaming videos on YouTube and CNN, and media-rich blog and wiki entries. What's important about these emerging genres is not just that they are multimodal (employing sound, image, typography, video, etc.). Students have long encountered such complexities in popular media. Instead, students are increasingly taking advantage of emerging technologies to produce texts employing strategies with which they are familiar. Kathleen Blake Yancey characterizes this phenomenon as a "tectonic change" in the ways students are encountering, producing, and distributing texts (2004, 298). In other words, students are taking a more active role in defining which texts count.

In this chapter, we offer snapshots of work with student texts at three different stages of a multimodal composition course. Each moment, derived from a different instructor's interpretation of the same basic course design, reveals the collaborative, rhetorical, and reflective potential of placing student work at the center of the multimodal classroom. Our goal for the course was to encourage students to produce nontraditional (multimodal) as well as traditional (print-based) texts, thereby extending their literacy practices into varying modes of communication. We hope to show how nontraditional, multimodal student texts can function at the heart of a composition class, how these texts diverge and converge with traditional student work, and the extent to which these design strategies extend student engagement beyond the walls of the classroom.

To manage the diverse goals of this course, we built our pedagogy around strategies suggested by David Jolliffe in his 1998 textbook *Inquiry and Genre: Writing to Learn in College*. Jolliffe's inquiry-based approach emphasizes traditional forms of academic work—exploratory essays, research reports, and so forth—as well as less traditional, more public iterations of that work. We see the slow process of learning through questioning, responding, writing, and rewriting as the glue that binds together the disparate reading and writing strategies we organized for the class. Students engaged difficult theoretical readings about multimodal design (Hull and Nelson 2005; Sirc 2004; Yancey 2004) as well as multimodal texts spanning genres and communities of interest (including Web pages, Cornell boxes, and episodes of *This American Life*). The struggle to critically comprehend new discursive strategies and to complicate more familiar ones gave all of us the opportunity to challenge our own preconceived ideas about what constitutes classroom work and what effect this work could have on an audience.

Assignments for the course consisted of weekly reflections and an inquiry-based portfolio, which culminated in a final multimodal text. The weekly writing assignments were designed to focus on how individuals encounter, read, and produce texts composed using a variety of modes, including print, image, sound, and space. The portfolio emphasized more traditional writing subjects like researching and drafting, but concluded with a multimodal assignment meant to bring the two clusters of classroom discussion together. At several stages of portfolio development, using what Jolliffe calls the "Inquiry Contract" (1998), students were required to revise, discuss, and reevaluate this work. In our classrooms, this strategy lent itself to the highly communal nature of multimodal design. Student texts, or "inside" texts, were approached in the same manner as "outside" or published texts. Students were asked to react to the work of their peers as they would the chapters in a composition reader, Web pages on the Internet, or short movies on YouTube. This strategy emphasizes not only the value of student texts, but also how their own readings of text are important to how their peers choose to revise future drafts.

As with more traditional print essays, multimodal design challenges students to produce final texts that stand on their own as readers experience them; however, multimodal *drafts* often evolve in much more unpredictable and responsive directions. Students might explore the opportunities available in one mode of composition, only to discover that another mode might offer richer opportunities. These sorts of changes sometimes result from an individual student reckoning with their own texts, but more often students engage one another in ongoing discussions throughout the process. In order to facilitate this sort of collaboration, we formalize this aspect of the process as we ask students to present their work in progress, both sharing discoveries about their own processes, as well as eliciting feedback from their peers.

Ultimately, our courses required students to use multiple design strategies in semester-long investigations of one area of interest. The classroom became a space where students explored their subjects together, layering their knowledge through assignments designed to expand their critical and modal resources. Working collaboratively, they heightened their sense of audience as different modal opportunities offered a dialogue between designer and reader, and they complicated their awareness of the dynamic conversations at work in any given subject area.

NETWORKED COLLABORATION

Julia's multimodal writing section resisted traditional hierarchies of skill separating teachers and students by cultivating a cooperative, student-centered space. In terms of multimodal composition, Julia and the students in her class were all experts and novices in overlapping ways. As such, bringing students' "inside" texts into the classroom emphasized the fact that everyone could learn something from the person sitting next to them. Also contributing to student-centered instruction was the location of class meetings, as each week the class met once in a traditional classroom and once in a Computer Assisted Instruction (CAI) classroom. Working with computers transformed the classroom into a gallery space where traditional and multimodal compositions could be easily shared. Each computer station became a place for students to exhibit their evolving work; a central screen was useful for visually amplifying specific texts. Because of their networking capabilities, the computers encouraged student contact, reciprocity, cooperation, active learning, and feedback—important tenets of collaboration not always achieved when students peer review paper texts.

Moving toward the completion of their working documents, the class spent a lot of time developing individual student texts within the sequence of assignments. A particularly useful revision exercise, dependent upon the CAI classroom, was the distribution of digital student documents for community revision. Rather than just making suggestions verbally or through marginal notes, computer screens enabled students to become invested in the work of their peers because they could see their role in the revision of an actual working document. Julia designed a process for motivating this movement from individual to group revision by first posting student texts to a discussion board and then assigning individuals particular sections of a peer's text to read. In class, students opened these documents on personal computers and made suggestions or changes to the text (tracking changes via MS Word). Next, all students working on a particular section of the document formed into groups in order to work together with the original draft of the document, negotiating suggestions from each member of the group. At the end of this stage, each group posted their revisions to the same discussion board as the original draft. Finally, everyone came together to discuss their strategies and suggestions with the class. Each group took a turn using the central computer, which was projected onto a central screen, moving through revision suggestions and explaining their reasoning. Upon completion of this mini-presentation, the class discussed the group's suggestions, accepting or rejecting what was presented.

This revision exercise takes advantage of the networked classroom by allowing students to view revisions instantly, often leading to animated discussions. Students appeared more enthusiastic because they could *see* their role in the writing processes of their peers. While this process became a community activity, final choices were—of course—made by the individual student author. Being able not only to see, but also to hear through discussion, how revisions altered the meaning and function of the text was beneficial for students developing their work. Moreover, the ability to assess immediately the suggestions of others, using computers to observe how revisions affect a text's purpose, made revision a dynamic and tangible process.

MULTIPLE EXPERTS AND DESIGN SOLUTIONS

Ryan's version of the course was designed to get students working together and drawing on each other's various sets of expertise. The culminating assignment for the course was structured as a three-stage process. For the first stage, each student wrote a Document Proposal describing a possible multimodal text he or she wanted to produce. Students met in small groups to offer suggestions and explanations of their projects. The second stage of the process involved the production of a multimodal working draft of that text, as well as a classroom presentation explaining it. Here, too, students offered each other substantial feedback and ideas for revision. It was during the third stage that students responded to those revisions in producing final versions of their multimodal texts. In order to provide a specific, material sense of how these assignments were enacted, we discuss our impressions of one student's experience in the course.

Duane had been a long-time fan of hip-hop radio stations on the internet. He loved the music, and the DJs' commentary between songs often revealed meaningful connections for him. Ongoing class discussions investigated ways different texts operate in various discourse communities. Duane recognized that DJs helped construct and identify different conversations within the hip-hop community. As the students researched and talked about their chosen communities, they helped each other identify specific topic areas and genre conventions. Within the context of the course goals, Duane quickly recognized parallels between the rhetorical practices of hip-hop culture and the rhetorical practices of more traditionally academic discourses.

In their Document Proposals, students had described their chosen discourse community, an ongoing discussion within it, a genre of multimodal text operating in that community, and a research question they planned to pursue. Although Duane was a bit vague about his chosen discourse community, he proposed a talk radio show looking at public discussions about interracial dating. At his first peer-review session, he played a few potential songs for his workshop group and listed potential questions. As he had hoped, his group offered suggestions about his proposal and their own alternatives. They drew heavily on their own experiences listening to talk radio and their own music catalogs. What Duane hadn't expected, though, was that his group also offered some technical strategies for producing his show. He had been at a loss as to how he might record the phone calls he was planning. He was also relatively unfamiliar with audio-editing software and with ways of capturing and preparing files for production. In this way, Duane used his proposal to facilitate collaboration with his peer-review group towards the presentation of his final multimodal text. For the next two weeks, the project's second stage, Duane continued to experiment and seek feedback about capturing audio, directing actors, and editing sound files.

As Duane played his text for the second workshop session, this time in front of the whole class, it was hard not to recognize his investment in his project. The music faded in and he introduced his show (complete with fictional station call letters) in the voice of a seasoned professional. After a brief introduction, he proceeded to interview several "callers." However, while technically polished and generically representative, the shortcomings of Duane's text quickly emerged. He asked each of his guests the same simple question without follow-up or clarification. As the unrehearsed responses piled up, it was clear that what Duane had produced was an audio survey offering little insight into the questions he had hoped to pursue.

At this point in the term, students had only a week to make any final adjustments to their texts, and Ryan had challenged them to revise their projects in the third and final stage of the production process. During the feedback session following Duane's presentation, his classmates suggested a wider variety of callers and shorter musical transitions. Ryan asked Duane how, with his radio show, he might incorporate or respond to some of the texts he had researched for the project. The ensuing discussion was fruitful for both Duane and his classmates. He formulated possibilities for more engaging questions. He also wanted to frame a discussion about his topic to open the show, so that his callers could place themselves within it.

But revision is always a demanding process, and working with multimodal texts only exacerbates those challenges. With so little time left in the term, Duane wasn't able to interview new subjects, re-edit the overall document, and export it again. Instead, he re-recorded his concluding remarks, quickly noting the difficulty of public discussion on his topic. He did, however, still manage to sign off with those slick station call letters and his smooth radio voice.

REFLECTING (ON) MULTIMODALITY

The final project, the multimodal project, was also very difficult to complete . . . eventually I chose to make a movie/documentary about women and graffiti. It was hard to make my point clear and convey the right things. I knew what I wanted to say, but not how I wanted to say them. I knew what I wanted people to think, but not how to make them think that way. Another problem, was making sure my movie was not too long and that I only included essential information, I did not want to be boring, but I felt I should give a lot of information because not many people know about the women in graffiti . . . I am trying to make people more aware, so I want to include all this information, but I do not want them to be uninterested in all that I have to say, so I include less information. (Student author's reflection on *Women in Graffiti*)

Framing a multimodal composition course around published and student work encourages students to exercise critical/composition skills on a more familiar level. Instead of imagining a product their instructor might desire, students assume a social use from communication as well as material value from a culturally favored discourse. *Women in Graffiti*—a student documentary that uses still images, audio narration, and video to draw attention to the underrecognized role women play in the graffiti subculture—exemplifies these potential benefits. Despite its technical flaws—poorly mixed audio, awkward gaps in the accompanying voiceover—it resonates as an MTV-esque documentary geared to an audience that is specifically marked in terms of age, interest, and, arguably, politics.

Near the end of the semester, students in Scott's class took turns presenting working drafts of their multimodal documents and leading response discussions. While he often introduced student texts anonymously in order to give individuals the opportunity to opt out of the public eye, the nature of the course and the community-oriented development of the Inquiry Contract required students to stand (literally) by their work. Work done prior to actualizing the project made this public exhibition easier as peers were already familiar with each author's topic and approach. Experiencing the text in the classroom together, as we had experienced "professional" texts throughout the semester, at once lent validation to the work as something worth sharing, and mimicked the public manner in which multimodal texts are often experienced—on television, in advertisements, and on the Internet.

The presentations occupied several weeks (five fifty-minute classes). Five student texts were discussed per session. Each student was thus allotted five minutes for an introduction and presentation (video or audio productions were restricted to five minutes by the assignment prompt), with at least five minutes for discussion to follow. Every effort was made to prepare the necessary technology in advance, but this is an important caveat to introducing student texts into the MM classroom: technology is inconsistent, or rather, human use of technology is inconsistent.

Student authors led discussion by outlining the goals of their project, an "ideal" audience, and their rationale for selecting specific modes. After presentations, peers responded as this "ideal" audience, though they could discuss anything they found compelling, problematic, and so on. The author of *Women in Graffiti*, a quiet student with a lot of traditional writing ability, suggested that it would not be difficult to imagine her ideal audience: most people, including those in the graffiti subculture, don't value the participation of women artists. The class was expected to draw on preconceived notions about graffiti, and hip-hop culture more generally, being a "man's world." In fact, the original cut of the documentary opens with James Brown singing "It's a Man's World." The author said little about the modes she had selected for her video, but in discussion she explained that she wanted to lend a sort of credibility to women's work in graffiti. As such, her choices of very traditional documentary style make sense. Images cut together with video explained by a voice-over narrator are documentary commonplace, something even only casually interested viewers would expect to see.

The ensuing discussion—evident in the reflection cited above—focused on accessibility and value. The author is at once aware of the repercussions for doing a project like this "wrong," expressed by her fears of coming across as unclear or "boring." She wrestles with how her audience receives the text because she experienced her audience receiving it. For example, peers questioned the lack of voice given to women; no interviews were conducted or appropriated for the piece. One respondent went so far as to suggest that James Brown has the most prominent speaking role, despite the intended irony of his inclusion. As a result, the song was removed, a change the author admits undermined the character of the project.

This intersection of content and materiality brought about an interesting discussion—from the students themselves—regarding choices about what to include and how to integrate it into the larger project. What we would highlight as unique about this scenario is the immediate accessibility of both the creative and technical discourses of multimodal composition. Placing the student texts at the center of the course, then, validates their work as something familiar and exciting, something "marketable" in the cultural capital of the day.

CHALLENGES IN THE MULTIMODAL CLASSROOM

Like any strategy, placing student texts at the center of multimodal writing comes with unique uses and limitations. For students, multimodal texts are often more dynamic and approachable than traditional texts and therefore garner increased attention and engagement. Further, when resources are available, situating students in a computer-equipped classroom encourages a level of community difficult to attain with more "conventional" group or peer work as students are able to interact physically and electronically, working on mediums that many of them are quite familiar with. We do, however, feel that a word of caution is necessary here. While we believe these practices are becoming increasingly popular, they are still inconsistent and uneven. To assume that all of our students engage in these practices is to assume easy access to the required technologies. It further assumes that all of our students operate in a culture that values these practices enough for them to dedicate significant social energy and time. In other words, instructors need to be sensitive to students who don't embrace these practices with the same fervor as others. While teaching with multimodal student texts often fosters collaborative writing environments, it also has the potential to intensify student differences. It is important that assignments within these contexts are flexible enough to allow for low-tech modes, such as collage or live performance, as well as digital technologies.

Other issues arise as well. Students publicly encounter boundaries brought on by their attempts to compose in nontraditional forms; student-led discussions might compel changes that are problematic; material limitations imposed by course length or design may inhibit student work. We feel, however, that these issues can be productive sites of conflict. A major benefit of using student work in a multimodal course is in reducing the likelihood that surface dominates substance. Problems of materiality and the choices required to realize a vision are the very difficulties inherent in any composition practice. For instance, talking about revising audio tracks can be an opportunity to talk about revision in multiple discursive modes. Our students were compelled by social context and productive discussion to move beyond an easy appreciation for multimodal forms to the hard task of designing text, engaging critical discussion, and reflecting for productive revision. Ultimately, multimodal texts complicate ideas about what "text" and writing processes should look like in the university. Situating them at the center of a composition course offers teachers the challenge of publicly engaging student work in modes and mediums that many of us were perhaps not trained to value.

19

WORKSHOPPING TO PRACTICE SCIENTIFIC TERMS

Anne Ellen Geller
St. John's University

Frank R. Cantelmo
St. John's University

Over the years, it became apparent that our students in Scientific Inquiry: Environmental Sciences-Honors 2700C (for nonscience majors) were having a great deal of difficulty critiquing the content of popular scientific articles in various magazines and newspapers. Scientific Inquiry is a required core class at St. John's University, a private Catholic university with approximately 14,000 undergraduate students. Students were generally not able to identify scientific concepts and terminology within a wide range of articles. Our initial approach to address this concern involved traditional lectures on scientific terminology using Jeffrey Lee's 2000 *The Scientific Endeavor: A Primer on Scientific Principles and Practice* as the source material. In class discussions, we illustrated terminology with historical scientific case studies and recent scientific articles. Then, as a final project, students searched for popular science articles of interest to them, defined scientific terms, summarized the articles and integrated into their summaries how the specific terminology was used in the articles.

But even after a semester in the course, students seemed to have no context for the assignment and no idea how to structure their summaries. They couldn't figure out where to "hang" or tease out the terminology. Students repeatedly asked questions like these:

"So what do *you* want?'

"How many pages should the summary be?"

"Why is *this* an important article?"

"What if the scientific term is not exactly in the article?"

Students often became too wrapped up in the more mechanistic aspects of the assignment and were not working on their critical thinking, reading, and writing skills. We wanted students to do much more with these articles and with their summaries. We imagined a more student-centered, workshop approach that would allow for "lower-stakes" writing and anonymous critique before students wrote the individual projects that would be graded.

In this chapter, we describe the collaborative project undertaken by a writing-across-the-curriculum (WAC) director and a senior biologist. Working together, we created a reading and writing workshop for the first-year honors students in Scientific Inquiry 2700C. Although the biologist, Frank Cantelmo, who describes himself as a tentative writer, had never before asked his science students to work with one another's writing, his own experience in a weeklong faculty-development workshop sponsored by the St. John's University Institute for Writing Studies left him wanting to bring student writing to the seminar table.

MATERIALS AND METHODS

In this new approach, rather than waiting for the end of the semester to ask students to research, read, and summarize scientific articles, about a third of the way into the semester, Frank asked each of his students to choose an article about science from the popular press, summarize the article, and tease out of it one of the scientific terms the class had been studying. To support Frank as he developed a plan for the first in-class writing workshops of these summaries, the WAC director, Anne, read first drafts and the corresponding articles along with him. After talking about the students' drafts, they defined four issues that seemed crucial to students' level of success with the assignment:

- How appropriate was the original article for the assignment?
- Could the student identify who was engaged in the science described in the article?
- Could the student identify and describe the science that was done?
- Could the student choose a term appropriate for the article's science, define the term appropriately, and analyze (in writing) how the term related to the science described in the article?

The in-class workshops emphasized and supported these four tasks, teaching students new ways of reading published writing and their own writing and presenting writing and workshopping as more than editing and mechanics. These workshops were held in a conference room in our Institute for Writing Studies, where the students sat around one large table. Out of their usual classroom and in the Institute for Writing Studies, students had a sense that what they were doing was valued and important. Besides, as Maggie Debellius writes in this volume, "Once students cross the threshold [of the writing center], they're more likely to return" (158), and we wanted to encourage students' ongoing use of the writing center. It's interesting to note that what has actually happened is that a number of former Honors 2700c students have become writing center consultants. They *really* "crossed the threshold."

For the in-class workshops described here (spring of 2008 and fall of 2009), Anne and Frank chose three draft student summaries representative of the successes and struggles of the entire class, and provided all the students with these summaries, the original science articles summarized, and workshopping handouts. Working together across two class periods, students first read the original articles to consider how and why they might summarize these articles and tease out the terminology and/or principles. Students then workshopped the summaries written by their peers and discussed how and why the summaries could be strengthened.

Although they set out intending to focus primarily on students' writing, Anne and Frank came to realize that the project had teaching and learning opportunities they hadn't anticipated. Many students did not understand how to identify articles describing experimental science. Others could not see how popular science articles twist and manipulate facts to the point where the science is no longer accurate. For example, one *New York Times* article they chose for the first semester's workshop from among those students submitted claimed to answer the question of whether hookah smoking is safer than cigarette smoking. As experienced teachers of first-year students, both Anne and Frank knew this topic would intrigue most of the students in class. They also knew most students would not notice how the article faultily compared the way "cigarette smokers took 8 to 12 puffs and inhaled 0.5 to 0.6 liters of smoke over five to seven minutes," while "hookah smokers may take 50 to 200 puffs of up to a liter of smoke each during a single session" (O'Connor 2007).

But we were both surprised in the next semester when students didn't see that it was possible to answer "who is doing the science and what are they doing" when evaluating a first-person essay by a naturalist. By that point, however, Frank had become a confident facilitator of the workshops. In response to the students' confusion he told them, "I did this on purpose. I chose three very different ways of reporting science when I chose the articles for us to look at together." And he went on to explain the spectrum of science from more generalized personal observations to the most rigorous empirical investigations.

While the textual work of this workshop may seem simple to those who frequently teach writing courses, the importance of this model lies in the fact that the science course in which it takes place is *not* designated writing intensive, so students in this core course see writing prioritized beyond the writing classroom. Also striking is the way in which the open classroom conversation of science and writing about science allows Frank to reiterate lessons of content. This is a case study for new and veteran teachers of how workshopping across the disciplines, even in introductory courses, provides more opportunity to teach content, not less opportunity.

THE WORKSHOPS OF THE SCIENTIFIC ARTICLES

On the first class day of workshops, Frank facilitates a whole-class discussion of three scientific articles chosen from all those submitted by students. He hands out the workshopping sheet with guiding questions. Students read the articles and fill out the sheet silently and individually. Then the whole group discusses their answers to the specific questions on the workshopping sheet.

Workshop Handout One: Questions to Keep in Mind While You Are Reading the Three Articles

- Who is doing the science and what are they doing?
- Do you see anything different about these articles regardless of terminology? If so, what?
- What scientific terminology can you tease out of these articles?
- Is it a good choice of an article in order to do the assignment?

Generally, students seem to have a very clear idea of *who* was doing the science and *what* they were doing. In other words, when their attention was explicitly turned to these questions, students had a clear idea of the differences between active "hands-on" research and reporting on research activities.

Students are also able to notice obvious and subtler differences in the articles. They report on articles that range from very personal to very scientific. As they considered Robert DeCandido's 2007 "Searching for Green in Gotham," students recognized it was more like a narrative than a scientific article. They wrote, it "seems buoyant and pleasant,"and "there were metaphors and interesting descriptions" and "a personal piece about a subject of special importance to the author." Compared to the "Gotham" article, Donna Deedy's 2008 report on duck farms had a range of responses. Some said "specific scientific studies," but others remarked that it "seemed full of quotations from angry citizens" and that it had "less scientific evidence" and more "opinion and non-scientific commentary."

In a different semester, students contributed articles ranging from Henry Fountain's 2009 "Solar Living Without Compromising on Lifestyle" to John Broder's 2009 "Polar Bear Habitat Proposed for Alaska." Students noted that the articles ranged from the "rambling vs. very to the point" in writing style and had varied intended audiences, from "the general public to the scientific community." There was relative agreement on Paul Voosen's 2009 "Biodiversity a Bitter Pill in 'Tropical' Mediterranean Sea," an article about changes in the species living in the Mediterranean. Students expressed that it was "very dense and descriptive" and a "more scientific" article than those about solar living and polar bear habitats. They felt it contained "excessive information" meant for readers "who already have the supporting vocabulary, background knowledge, etc." And yet one student noted it was actually a very good choice for the assignment because it included information about "a legitimate agency researching implications of man."

There were significant similarities in the terminology students were able to tease out of the articles. Terms like *cause and effect, induction, paradigms, risk assessment, assumptions, model, selective reporting, sampling, bias, soft science, control groups, peer review, conflict of interest, correlation,* and *experimental bias* indicated a certain level of scientific and critical-thinking sophistication made possible by the specific workshopping approach employed.

Almost all students agreed the articles were well suited to do this assignment but for different reasons. For example, the "Gotham" article may have been an example of soft science whereas an article on DDT that same semester had a number of scientific correlations and robust statistics. In the other semester, many students noted how long the "Biodiversity a Bitter Pill" article was but said it was "rich with environmental info," "full of information," and has numerous terms that are applicable."

WORKSHOPS OF THE STUDENT SUMMARIES

On the second day of workshopping, Frank hands out the three student summaries and a workshopping sheet with guiding questions. Students fill out the sheet silently and individually. Then the whole group discusses their responses.

Workshop Handout Two: Questions to Keep in Mind While You Are Reading the Student Analyses

- What are the students doing well?
- What are they still struggling with?
- What would make these summaries better?

Overall, when asked what the students were doing well in three different drafts, most felt their peers were summarizing quite effectively. For example, here is the first paragraph of a student's three-paragraph summary of "Solar Living, Without Compromising Lifestyle":

> The Solar Decathlon is a Department of Energy competition to design and build an efficient and livable solar-powered house. This competition lasts for ten days and includes twenty student teams from universities in the United States, Canada and Europe. Each team assembles its house on the National Mall in Washington. All of the projects are judged on electrical use, architectural design, engineering skill, comfort and marketability. Each team needs to create a home that can maintain comfortable air temperatures, produce a sufficient amount of hot water and provide enough electricity for entertainment.

Summarizing the original article may very well be the one task of this assignment easily adapted from previous writing experiences in a variety of other courses and disciplines. What both Frank and Anne were pleased to see and hear, however, was that students could also identify varying levels of quality in the summaries. For example, students' comments to one another included "worded interestingly, verb choice, not structured in a boring way," "very clear and concise, focuses on the environmental aspect and not so much of the business aspect," "the summary was great because it included specific examples of each of the [decathlon] teams," "you get to the point of the article," while "the summary doesn't encompass the article," "the summary has a lot of facts but seems to ramble on, not structured well," and "I feel as if much of the 'meat' of the article was left out" showed that students could see some summaries were stronger than others.

The second question, which asked students to consider what their classmates were still struggling with, opened up an even more interesting conversation. The students could see how difficult it was for the summary writers to identify and then elegantly incorporate into their writing a scientific principle appropriate to the original article. On their workshopping sheets students noted their peers' difficulties: it would be better "if there was a longer explanation of how the term related to the article," "not sure the term used is one of the best," "use of term could be expanded," "need to be more definitive." Students commented that the writer should include "explanation/examples of the term" and "explain the relevancy better."

In the student summary of "Solar Living without Compromising Lifestyle," the writer began by clearly defining the term—"Applied Research: Applied research is done to solve a specific problem and often leads to new or improved technology"—and then returned to discuss the same term at the end of the summary.

> The teams that participated in the Solar Decathlon used applied research to solve environmental issues by building solar-powered houses. The participants recognized the problems we have in our environment including air pollution and abuse of energy. Each of the twenty teams had to do research and gather information for this event otherwise they wouldn't know how to design or build the solar houses.

In the first workshops we facilitated, the question "What would make these student summaries better?" led students to comment on one another's grammar and editing. But Frank did not want the workshops to be about sentence editing only, and he used this conversation to once again articulate that to the students. Yet there was, and continues to be, value in having students see one another's errors. At the end of the workshops in which these conversations took place, students said they would be sure to have someone read over their work because they heard their peers criticize careless editing including spelling, typos, and punctuation mistakes. In later workshops, Frank has heard less of this—in part, he thinks, because he has better articulated that students are writing for their classmates and they have thus become more attentive to proofing before they share their work. He has also become better at convincing them that these workshops should not focus on grammar and editing.

But editing help was not all the students offered one another. In response to the question about what would make the summaries better, students also readily shared valuable writing hints everyone in the class would be able to utilize in their final graded summaries: "link the term to the purpose of the experiment," "some exchanging of word choices," "include more names from the article," "I feel like these are all boring," and "more detail of what the article included."

Varied examples of student summaries encourage the class to make comparisons and feel comfortable doing it. In one workshop, for example, a student noted that one summary set a standard that others did not yet meet. The summary of "L.I. Duck Farms Struggle with Water Regulation," this student observed, contained multiple references to the key terms *cause and effect* in different paragraphs, while the summary of "Can a Maligned Pesticide Save Lives" used the term *paradigm* just once. Similarly, two different summaries of "Biodiversity a Bitter Pill in 'Tropical' Mediterranean Sea" had weaknesses the students learned from. One student writer did not offer the detail or tone of the original article, which, as they had noted, was longer and included more scientific detail than other articles. And while another student clearly showed the relationship of a key term to the article, the term (*biodiversity*) was in the article's title, so the student took on none of the intellectual challenges that would have come from identifying other terms—like *sampling, cause and effect,* or *migration*—that were also present in the science of the article.

WORKSHOP REFLECTIONS

Frank asks his students to read popular-press articles about science precisely because he hopes they will learn to critically think about what they read and what they experience in their everyday lives through a scientific lens using scientific principles. For the students to think critically in these ways, he believes they should learn correct application of scientific terminology like *experimental bias, selective reporting, cause and effect, assumptions,* and *conflict of interest.*

This assignment is difficult precisely because students must understand the scientific principles well enough to identify them in the articles they read—even when the principles are not specifically named. They must also understand the principles well enough to explain their relevance to the science reported in the article. The workshops allowed Frank to clarify differences between *cause and effect* and *correlation,* to clear up confusion about uses of words—*ad hominem,* for example—and to refine students' understanding of the differences between words like *precision* and *accuracy.* This content teaching would not have happened were it not for the freewheeling workshop conversations about the varied terminology that could be teased out of the articles.

In workshops, the students seemed to embrace the role of inquirer, learning to look for what might not be obvious or explained within the published articles and within their classmates' writing, even when they weren't quite sure what it was they were looking for. Working together they could build on what one another noticed, helping one another see what wasn't quite explained or what seemed to be missing or overlooked. They could learn more sophisticated ways of considering the quality of their own and their classmates' summaries. They could learn more about how to read between the lines of published science.

That students, in their reflections on the workshops, described the workshops as "personal" was striking to us. Frank had always had small, personalized classes. Even in semesters before the workshops, students had been allowed to choose their own articles for this assignment. What we've come to believe is that with the workshops, students *feel more engaged* in the work at hand and with one another. In their minds, more engaged equals "more personal." We think this has implications for working with student texts in the classroom because sharing writing that does not seem to the professor to *be* "personal" (here, writing about science and not one's experiences) may still feel "personal" to students.

Students in Frank's Scientific Inquiry courses had not, before this workshop approach was instituted, seen one another's choice of articles and they had not seen one another's summaries, so they had also never before seen the variety of writing styles that he accepted in articles and in summaries. Students came to understand that they should value the choices they were making in their reading and their writing because their individual choices were also valued by the biologist. Finally, and perhaps most important, students realized there were many good choices of articles to summarize and ways to summarize but they should be making those choices in informed ways and for different reasons.

Prior to this workshop, Frank assumed students routinely look at or comment on one another's writing in other classes. But he learned they don't. Frank has come to believe that, regardless of the discipline or class, students need to have openness about both published articles and their own writing and be willing to revisit both in a low-stakes environment. And, he has come to value what Joseph Harris notes in this collection—that faculty might create "seminar" situations in classes where they could "frame a lesson on writing for everyone in the class" (147) by having students look at one another's writing. Frank saw how the workshops allowed students to revisit their original reading and writing premises, and he became convinced that the revisiting promoted by in-class workshops could produce a very rich and rewarding process for students and faculty alike.

ACKNOWLEDGMENTS

The authors would like to thank St. John's University for allowing them to participate in the 2007 Summer Faculty Writing Institute in Rome, Italy, where their collaboration and work on this project began. Many thanks go to the students in Frank Cantelmo's spring 2008 and fall 2009 Honors 2700c Scientific Inquiry classes at St. John's University who have graciously allowed us to reprint their writing here: Francesca B., Jordan Baum, Adam Czerwin, Molly Dies, Benjamin Donaghy, Brendan Doy, Frank Emmanuele, Joanna Erickson, Zachary Hubbard, Erin Jordan, David Law, Katherine L'Esperance, Sean McGrath, Jennifer Morrisey, Pooja Patel, Elizabeth Stylianou, and Justine Woods.

20

BRINGING OUTSIDE TEXTS IN AND INSIDE TEXTS OUT

Jane Mathison Fife
Western Kentucky University

Reading a text not just for *what* it says but for *how* it responds to the challenges of a particular rhetorical situation is a powerful ability to have and not an easy one to acquire. It is the core of what I try to help my students toward through my teaching. This statement sounds obvious and straightforward. But as I reflect on the fifteen-plus years I have taught writing, I realize my growth as a teacher has centered around my increasing understanding of the gap between how I perceive model texts and how my students perceive them—and my ability to find ways to bridge that gap. I remember that in my first years of teaching I handed out model papers with no discussion of them at all because I assumed it would be clear to my students how these models were successful fulfillments of the assignment we were working toward in class. Over the years, student texts have become more central to my pedagogy as I've learned to bring them in more often and use them more effectively to increase my students' awareness as writers. The student texts I bring into class are both "outside" texts, written by students outside the class, and "inside" texts, written by students in the class as assignments for the class. (In their essay for this volume, Doug Downs, Heidi Estrem, and Susan Thomas use the terms "far" and "near" to label the same distinction; their terms emphasize well the continuum of distance beyond the classroom.)

To develop students' understanding of assignment goals and writing strategies to meet those goals, as well as to expand their sense of what is possible for student writing in terms of content, quality, and circulation, I draw on a variety of outside student texts—both from previous classes and from student texts published elsewhere: on our department Web site, in our textbook, and in local and national journals that publish the work of undergraduate writers. The student texts we focus on shift from outside to inside as activities in the class move from analyzing textual features to giving feedback on students' own writing. These inside texts range, as the course progresses, from very early drafts and outlines, to intermediate drafts, and, finally, to finished products. My courses end with some form of showcase for completed inside texts with an eye toward appreciation rather than revision. Additionally, our department's English 100 Conference, which shares work submitted by students in first-year writing classes, brings some of these inside texts outside the classroom, thus expanding the traditional role for writing produced in these classes. My first uses of student writing that crossed the boundaries of the classroom focused on bringing outside texts in as models to discuss so my current students could improve their texts inside the bounds of the classroom. As student texts have become more central to my teaching, though, I have put increasing emphasis on expanding the use of inside texts within the classroom (beyond seeing the text as a focus for revision) and creating more opportunities to take them outside the classroom, making student texts more visible and—to use Bruce Horner's term from this book—revalued.

INITIAL INTRODUCTIONS: GETTING AN IDEA
OF THE TYPE OF TEXT

The first time I bring in student texts during work on a particular assignment is to introduce the core purpose of that assignment—its make-or-break features, if it has them. For example, students need to understand that a researched argument must synthesize material from multiple sources instead of serially summarizing articles to accumulate information. Similarly, a rhetorical analysis must engage with the rhetorical strategies of a piece instead of focusing solely on the content or ideas. A literacy narrative ought to draw the reader in with rich details of the author's experiences as well as suggesting, even if this suggestion is subtly implied, the insight that should be drawn from this particular selection and arrangement of experiences. Kennedy and Smith's 2006 *Reading and Writing in the Academic Community* offers student examples of these and other genres. I supplement these outside texts with still more outside texts—but a little "nearer" in Downs, Estrem, and Thomas's terms (this volume)—written by my students in previous semesters. Instead of discussing all the features on the assignment rubric, we focus on the main purpose of the assignment. Often I've found students have trouble catching onto the assignment's purpose if it conflicts with conceptions they bring with them from previous courses, a phenomenon noted by Jennie Nelson (1990).

In our initial encounter with a model text, I want students to find its defining features. I ask students to read these texts before the class meeting, but in class I give them time to look back over the model after I have given them an explanation of what we're looking for. For example, to introduce them to the genre of annotated bibliography, I project the sample from our composition program Web site as we discuss the features of the genre. Some students follow along on their own computer screens (of course, the activity also works well with hard copies). I explain that the three parts I look for in the annotation are the summary, the evaluation of the source's credibility, and the statement about how the student will use it in an argument. After identifying these parts in the first annotation, I ask students to find them in the next several, calling on students to supply the answers. This activity is quick but helpful. I used to think my own pointing out of the components of a text should be sufficient, but I realized that distinguishing a text's features is something students grasp more quickly when they identify them actively. This same type of activity works with the central characteristics of whatever genre we're working on.

SUGGESTING POSSIBILITIES: TEXTS TO INITIATE INVENTION

Once students have a good idea of an assignment's goals, they still struggle to find a topic that both interests them and fits the parameters of the assignment; therefore, they can benefit from student texts from previous semesters as examples of ideas that were developed well for a particular assignment. Especially as they grapple with the goal of making a claim with their paper instead of just talking about a topic, seeing multiple examples of what past students have done can spur invention. I used to describe verbally some projects students had worked on in the past, but now I also share a set of essay introductions or abstracts from previous students in the course. Before I give them the handout, I ask them to brainstorm a list of some ideas for their papers. Then we discuss the excerpts from previous projects after I emphasize that sharing these examples is intended to expand their conception of what is possible instead of restricting their ideas. After I point out a few examples and give them time to look over the list more closely, I ask them to go back to their brainstormed list of ideas for this assignment. We go around the room, with each student sharing a topic or research question, and other students suggesting additional questions or approaches to the topic that would be interesting to pursue. Seeing the breadth of options represented by this sampling of partial texts initiates invention more effectively than do the one or two complete texts we look at first to understand the purpose of the assignment.

READING FOR THE DETAILS: USING CONTRASTIVE TEXTS TO ILLUMINATE WRITING STRATEGIES

Sometimes a textual feature that is hard for students to identify when looking only at a good model stands out in stark relief when contrasted with weaker models. In a writing-in-the-disciplines course with a focus on researched arguments, we compare three essays of varying quality with attention to where the writer summarizes, paraphrases, or quotes source material, and where he or she analyzes or interprets it to draw conclusions. We look at a very weak paper from a "free papers" Web site, along with another paper from our textbook that includes minimal commentary on its sources (Rosenwasser and Stephen 2009, 227–30), and an essay from our composition program's Web site with more extensively developed interpretation of source material (Meisinger 2005). I ask students to work in groups with these three texts using highlighters to mark all the writing that reflects ideas or interpretations from the authors in contrast to ideas that simply come from the source material. Once they have finished highlighting the texts, I ask them to refer to the highlighting to identify the argument the author is making about the sources. The student text from the "free papers" Web site has virtually no highlighted material, the mediocre example in the textbook has very little highlighting (and most of what is highlighted is not very clearly contrasted with the source ideas), and the stronger example has easily as much writing highlighted as not. This activity really brings home to them how important interpretive commentary is to making clear what the writer is saying and not just what the sources say. After they have highlighted each writer's commentary versus source material, we discuss the three student essays to find what the writers' points about their sources are. They realize the importance from a reader's perspective of seeing statements that reveal the author's position on the sources without any ambiguity.

STUDENT TEXTS FROM PUBLISHED VENUES: RAISING EXPECTATIONS AND SENSE OF POSSIBILITIES

I want all my students to be aware that they can find audiences for their writing beyond the classroom. In my first-year composition class we look at sample texts written by first-year students that were published in our campus newspaper and a local online magazine started by students (though not an official school publication). We also focus on our annual English 100 Conference as a venue for sharing their writing. In class we discuss sample student texts from previous years published on the conference Web site, making it visible to students that this writing is high quality, but not unattainable for many of them. Additionally, most of my classes include the requirement that one of the papers they write be targeted to a public audience of their choice.

While I make students aware of possible venues in my first-year composition classes, students in my upper-level classes are charged with presenting on articles from student publications to inform the class—myself included—of these available venues. The presentations (sometimes individual and sometimes group, depending on how much time we have for them in class and the variety of publication venues appropriate to writing from that course) involve students projecting information about the publication's submission guidelines as they explain the types of texts it publishes. *Young Scholars in Writing*, described in this volume by Downs, Estrem, and Thomas, is often one of the publications included. Additionally, they show us samples of published student texts—either from an online publication or in print form. The students point out a few features of the text that they found striking or exemplary, and indicate the range and type of texts published by mentioning a few other examples. They provide a handout detailing their findings about the publication and its submission guidelines and preferences so everyone in class can develop a file of publication opportunities. I don't require that all my students submit something to be published, but I do ask that they develop one text for a public audience and make their rhetorical decisions accordingly—even if they would deliver their text to the audience via a self-published blog or YouTube video.

WHEN AN INSIDE TEXT DEFINES KEY GOALS: THE WRITER'S MEMO AS WORKSHOP TOUCHSTONE

When students bring in their own drafts for feedback, I ask that they always supply a writer's memo telling their readers what they are trying to accomplish and where they need feedback. While these memos work well in concert with an assignment rubric to let the students define their specific goals and concerns in relation to the existing criteria, they take on even more prominence when the central purpose of an assignment is for students to define their own audience and rhetorical goals when writing for a chosen public audience. I ask that students include in the memo how complete the draft is, what they intend as its thesis or goals, what they think is working well, what they think needs improvement, and several specific questions they have for reader feedback. Several students have told me this procedure is different from what they have encountered in creative writing classes at our university, where the usual practice requires that the writers not influence the readers with a statement of their intentions before they read the draft. I, however, want students to know what the intentions of the writer are in order to help the writer gauge how well they have fulfilled them. I ask students to share these memos with their readers before they read their drafts, and I ask readers to keep the goals and questions of the writer in mind as they read and respond. I emphasize that if they ever felt that peer review was a wasted process because they didn't get useful feedback, they can now change that dynamic by offering specific questions they really want to have answered and pushing their readers for more detail if their responses are too general to be helpful.

SPOTLIGHTING STUDENT TEXTS FOR WHOLE-CLASS MOMENTS IN GROUP DRAFT WORKSHOPS

While I am not going to describe what seem to me the standard features of the small-group workshops in my courses, I will describe one aspect I include that I think may not be as widespread. As I circulate around the room listening to students offer feedback, many of them have questions for me. Often they may be very straightforward, and I can provide a simple answer. But when the question is one that reflects an interesting rhetorical choice or a confusion that many other students may have, I project the student text onscreen so that other students can see it as we discuss the merits of different strategies for that situation. This method brings moments of the seminar pedagogy described by Joseph Harris in this book into a class session that is otherwise focused on small-group workshops. Sometimes the spotlight moment might be for sharing a well-done move rather than answering a question. But these momentary views into other texts with commentary about technique add to students' conceptions of effective writing and emphasize the seriousness of the enterprise, undercutting the idea of peer review as busy work.

CLOSING THE LOOP: SHARING "INSIDE" TEXTS
AS FINISHED PRODUCTS

While I have included inside student texts in the form of drafts for in-class group workshops in every writing class I've ever taught, I've only more recently included showcasing of a student-selected finished product in all my classes. I became convinced of the need for and the importance of this move during a recent research project in which I interviewed students who had published their writing in some form outside the classroom. As I talked with Warren, an English major who had presented papers at departmental, university-wide, and national conferences (both one for undergraduates and one primarily attended by faculty), he spoke about his disappointment with the lack of opportunities to share his writing in the classroom. Warren felt strongly about encouraging other students to circulate their work in the classroom and beyond, noting that a major complaint about his education "is that it is very insulated from other students." He said that while students do a lot of writing in their major classes, generally "there's not any kind of peer review or anything like that, so nobody knows what anyone is saying, especially the 70% of the class that doesn't talk."

Warren's observation is similar to Downs, Estrem, and Thomas's claim, in this book, that "we often encourage or require students to circulate drafts, but far less often their *finished* texts, to in turn affect and shape each other's scholarly inquiry" (122). To remedy this lack of focus on finished student scholarship, Warren suggested a class anthology in an advanced composition class, which the professor eagerly coordinated. Warren was pleased with the collection: "It was so much fun reading other people because you don't get to read them. Nobody reads them out loud. I like filling that sort of vacuum between students with something like that." Sharing texts within the classroom may not seem like a significant public audience from a professor's perspective, but it can be a crucial influence for students eager to hear more from each other and develop confidence about putting their ideas out for response from a larger public. Such sharing of finished writing within the classroom can expand what Bruce Horner (in this volume) terms the "potential use value" of student writing within the academy, thus contributing to the revaluing of student writing Horner calls for.

Before talking with Warren, I had included sharing of finished work in some of my classes, but not all of them. Since that interview, I have expanded that practice to all my classes. In my writing-in-the-disciplines class, students give presentations about their major research project, not reading the whole paper, but talking us through their research questions, conclusions, and any interesting twists along the way. Students in advanced composition classes choose their best piece from the term to read for us during our final two class sessions. Students in Argument and Analysis share the argument they composed for a public audience. To offset feelings of anxiety about presenting common among first-year students, I don't require that they share their work, but I do offer them a few points extra credit if they choose to do so, and many of them do.

MOVING THE INSIDE TEXTS OUTSIDE THE CLASSROOM

Some students in our first-year writing classes have the opportunity to share their work with an even wider audience at our English 100 Conference—which is held on the last Friday of classes during the fall semester. While the benefit to the students who present is clear, students who attend also get an expanded sense of possibility for student writing as something that can initiate conversations in addition to something that is graded to earn course credit. Additionally, faculty expectations can be enriched: after the conference I typically hear surprise from other faculty at the quality of papers written by first-year students. This awareness—that first-year composition classes can produce good writing—needs to be extended. Some faculty who never attend the conference tell me they've spent far too many hours already reading freshmen papers and they can't endure the thought of willingly listening to any more of them on a Friday afternoon. When faculty imagine taking inside texts outside the classroom, the image can be unpleasant, like a departmental assessment session. But when the discussion focuses not on evaluating what has been written but on how our expectations and values for student texts shape how we teach, we might find new possibilities for learning from student texts. (See Nicole Wallack's essay in this volume for a description of this kind of professional-development session.) While most of this essay, and this volume, focuses on the *whys* and *hows* of using student texts in the writing class, my experiences with some dismissive faculty attitudes about student writing suggest that if we hope to make such work more valued, we need to find ways to bring student texts to the table in discussions beyond the classroom.

ACKNOWLEDGMENTS

Comments from Warren come from an interview conducted as part of an HSRB-approved study. I've used a pseudonym, as per the informed consent agreement. I'd like to thank Warren and all the other students I've interviewed. Their insights have shaped both my research and my teaching.

21

EMBRACING UNCERTAINTY
The Kairos of Teaching with Student Texts

Rolf Norgaard
University of Colorado at Boulder

With new technologies making it easier to get student texts into the undergraduate writing classroom, student writing is making an appearance not just as an occasional example, but as the ongoing focus of instruction. As the essays in this volume demonstrate, students' own writing can now serve in a variety of ways as *the* classroom text. Yet the centrality of student writing offers fresh challenges even to the veteran teacher, to say nothing of the risks it presents to those new to the classroom. With student texts at the forefront, what we gain in relevance we also reap in uncertainty. We now share our classroom, with our teaching texts coming as much from the students as from ourselves. Gone are the certainties of traditional writing pedagogies: fixed readings and predictable responses to them, not to mention the well-rehearsed lecture or lesson plan. A pedagogy focused on work in progress makes for an engaged, student-centered classroom, yet it requires major shifts in curricular orientation and teaching practice. Although the essays in this volume address many issues accompanying such shifts—from revaluing student texts, to their effective and ethical circulation, to changing classroom practice—I believe that a fundamental prerequisite for any such shift lies in our own willingness to embrace the uncertainties that come with teaching with student texts.

This essay, by way of a conclusion to the volume, argues that those very uncertainties can be our best allies as we refashion our pedagogies to teach and learn on the page. Four challenges loom:

- *How do I handle uncertainty?* A writing classroom centered on student texts requires, first, that we think beyond the usual rationales for using those texts and come to appreciate how such texts make timely or opportune teaching possible.

- *How do I handle evolving texts?* The use of student texts asks that we continually refashion the workshop or seminar environment as the texts themselves shift and mature.

- *How do I handle student perspectives?* Along with their texts, students also bring into class their expectations, anxieties, and fears—perspectives we must address if our pedagogical partnership with students is to succeed.

- *How do I handle myself?* Teaching with student texts should prompt us to rethink the workshop roles we ourselves play.

It's routine to think that we as teachers bring writing pedagogies to bear on student texts. I submit that we'd be well served by considering how sustained and intensive use of student texts in the classroom can—and should—refashion those pedagogies.

HOW DO I HANDLE UNCERTAINTY?

When we bring student writing into the classroom and allow it to take center stage, we are doing far more than introducing one more element to the mix; we are fundamentally shifting the dynamics of our teaching. As we value student texts in new and different ways, we are thrown back on a different set of pedagogical resources. Student texts—and the comments of students on those texts—require that we respond in the moment and think on our feet. Working with these texts places a premium on our improvisational readiness to engage the unexpected and seize its opportunities.

Student texts can thus make our classroom teaching opportune and timely—in a word, *kairotic*. A fundamental rhetorical concept, *kairos* represents the opportune occasion for speaking, writing, and, yes, teaching. It refers to the way a given context for communication both calls for and constrains one's speech. Sensitive to *kairos*, a teacher takes into account the contingencies of a given place and time, and considers the opportunities within this specific context for words to be effective and appropriate. Although we as teachers can have a hand in shaping those contingencies, students themselves do much to make the classroom a rich space for opportune teaching by bringing in drafts that reflect their immediate struggles as writers. Teaching becomes opportune when we listen to and address the class not as students taking a writing course but as writers working in a community of writers. Teaching becomes opportune when a student comment becomes not so much a response to our teaching as an invitation for all to share in teaching—and learning.

Classrooms become timely spaces for teaching when we are willing to entertain and work out the very ideas that students bring through the door. It's challenging—especially if we hope to challenge our students in return. We're thinking through a range of papers right along with the students. In a sense, we are mentally writing and revising them ourselves. We'll need to think critically on our feet as we ferret out the opportunities and challenges in each draft, and as we respond to the unexpected question or pursue the imaginative, even oddball comment. We'll need to anticipate difficulties in the execution of an argument and consider a variety of possible solutions to those challenges. Yet what seems to be the chief drawback of teaching with student texts—the unexpected insights and dilemmas we may uncover—can be its greatest advantage. As we work with student texts in the classroom, students see us and others engaging their ideas, responding to their words. They see us and others sharing in their inquiry, encouraging intellectual risk taking because we ourselves are playing with and refining ideas. Our approach to drafts can send a message that all writing worth reading grows from a willingness to take risks.

One of the most promising ways to seize the opportunities in student texts is to focus on the rewards of writing for readers. Whether discussed in a small-group workshop or in a seminar setting, student work in progress transforms the solitary, silent writing process into a genuine dialogue between authors and readers. The quiet shuffle of papers—whether handed in or handed back—is replaced by conversation and shared inquiry. Students can no longer write to an audience of one, the teacher, but now must meet the demands of a larger and more real audience, one that includes their peers but can also extend well beyond the classroom.

Such classes do more than provide immediate feedback to the author. They encourage the author to acknowledge, question, or clarify the reactions of readers. In a sense, workshops and seminars verbalize—and thus make available—the hidden dynamics of reader response. In so doing, they help writers hone and refine their editorial sixth sense. By making the responses of readers available to the author, they also establish intellectual context. This was the case when a student in one of my courses was writing on the role of online medical information in reshaping doctor-patient interactions. Although taken by her analysis, students were nevertheless skeptical about several assertions. Thanks to the workshop, the author found that the questions and counterarguments she needed to engage were immediate, not abstract. They came from skeptical readers in the same classroom, who worked with her and other writers on each new draft. This process transforms writing into shared inquiry. It's not enough for papers to parade knowledge; they must tackle genuine questions at issue and win the respect, if not the belief, of intelligent readers.

Because those readers include the writer's own peers, classroom discussion takes on fresh relevance and credibility. Students often find their peers surprisingly tough and demanding as critics. In fact, many student writers say their greatest challenge lies in persuading their classmates that they have thought clearly and written effectively. This reaction is part of a workshop's chemistry. When students are required to meet standards of clarity and persuasion set in part by other students, they take their writing seriously. At the same time, they learn writing is a communal act, dependent always on the nature and disposition of the audience addressed.

When students learn on the page, they do more than sit in class and turn in assignments; they become involved in an apprenticeship. When I think back to teachers and writers who have had considerable influence on me, I recall looking over their shoulders. They invited me to inhabit their minds and imaginations, to observe hidden steps in their thinking as they engaged an intellectual problem or revised a text to let a muffled idea speak more clearly. I may not remember the specific writing task but I do recall their conceptual moves, their habits of mind. I learned as an apprentice—by doing and by working next to someone who does it well.

To teach well ourselves, we ought to emulate how our own best teachers brought us along as apprentices. Workshops and seminars centered on student work in progress can transform the classroom into an apprenticeship. This happens when teachers no longer speak to, but rather *with*, students, and when students themselves begin to speak with and teach others, ourselves included. When I discuss a student's draft and engage comments on it from other students, I try to avoid cookie-cutter answers—be they general platitudes or specific corrections. Just the other day I was working with students on a formal prospectus for a semester-long research project. I find I'm most productive for these writers and for others reading their work when I voice not rules but rather explain underlying conceptual and discursive moves. These moves are rarely articulated for the novice writer, yet their mastery is necessary for joining disciplinary communities. In the case of the prospectus, we focused on how to frame a question at issue, how to create a discursive and intellectual space for their own research contribution, and how to lend authority to their voices even as they call on the authoritative voices of other researchers. I try to verbalize what's behind my response as a reader and the problem-solving strategies I might invoke as a writer or editor. For students to gain confidence as writers and discerning readers, they need an opportunity to explore and refine the hidden moves that occur as they read the drafts of other students and work on their own. Because workshops ask students to shuttle back and forth between actual writing and an array of potential strategies, we can model those moves for them—and they can test the moves on us. In so doing, we acquaint them with both the skills they need and the habits of mind those skills require.

Student texts make teaching opportune.

HOW DO I HANDLE EVOLVING TEXTS?

New technologies give the appearance of having eased, if not solved, the practical issues of logistics that can make or break a writing workshop. Would that were the case. Whether students are operating in a Gutenberg universe of printed texts or in the latest digital environment, they still need specific strategies for circulating and reading drafts, for responding to and commenting on them, and for collaborating with each other. What's more, as student work evolves over time, moving from short preliminary explorations to longer drafts, we likewise need to refashion the workshop or seminar environment. Evolving texts require an evolving classroom pedagogy.

The evolution of student texts in the classroom begins well before those texts are first circulated for peer review. Drafts don't appear out of thin air, but are instead prepositioned. The inventional moments that lead to those drafts are framed by the assignment design, the place of that assignment in an overall arc of rhetorical and compositional opportunities, and the evaluative tools and frameworks (rubrics, grading criteria) that themselves shape our classroom comments and our more formal graded responses. If we are unhappy with the texts that students bring into a workshop, or with the discussion those texts elicit, we might look to our own assignments as moments of invention that shape the classroom. By openly discussing the purposes and rhetorical challenges behind an assignment and the evaluative criteria that shape our collective responses, we are likely to improve the drafts that the assignment first elicits and the discussion that ensues.

The effectiveness of bringing student texts into the classroom can easily hinge on the arrangements we put in place regarding their circulation and the reading assignments we provide to guide their engagement with each others' work. Although we may expect students to read all their classmates' drafts, we can usefully focus their reading in particular ways. One option is to assign each paper a group of three or four editors. These editors then have a special responsibility for contributing to or even guiding the discussion of that paper. Another option is to assign particular reading roles to groups of students in the class. For example, one group of students may pay particular attention to evidence and support, while other groups may focus on matters of audience or style. These reading roles can be rotated so that, in the course of several weeks, all students will have had a chance to come at a draft from a variety of perspectives. Whatever option you choose, I encourage responsible reading and constructive criticism by putting readers on the line in class, lest the authors of the drafts feel they're the only ones with a stake in the discussion.

The value of focusing on student texts is that we can help model for students how to engage in and offer appropriate feedback on work in progress. For editing groups to be effective, I've found it is crucial for me to model for the entire class how readers and writers can collaborate effectively, and what sorts of issues should be foregrounded at different stages of the writing process. For example, students may be tempted to focus on surface errors because they are easy to identify, when attention to larger rhetorical issues—purpose, audience, claims, lines of reasoning—may be far more productive. I often save class sessions devoted to group work for the middle or end of the term, when I am confident that members of the class have begun to internalize strategies for reading drafts critically and commenting on them constructively. As students work on papers over the course of the term, it's appropriate that they gradually assume more responsibility for commenting on drafts, even orchestrating the discussion. In a sense, over time I seek to make myself dispensable. One of our goals should be to help students prepare for a life of writing and reading after the course is over. When students learn to work on their own with a circle of discerning readers, and to hone their own editorial sensibilities through that engagement, they can assume the authority and responsibility that mature and maturing writers deserve. I've also found it helpful to integrate group work back into the class as a whole. I often ask authors of the drafts being discussed to report back to the entire class on what they have learned by talking to readers in their editing group and on any unresolved questions the discussion raised. These "author reports" help each student develop a revision plan. Moreover, by capturing the advice they have received in their own words, they are more likely to "own" that advice. Perhaps most importantly, such author reports place the focus on the rich potential of their future work, and not on any inadequacies in the drafts they have already submitted.

As work in progress moves from early exploratory drafts to revised full drafts, the dynamics of the workshop can and should change, for the intellectual and interpersonal tasks are now different than they were during the early phases of the writing process. We're no longer exploring ideas but responding to the way in which writers have made good on the promises of early drafts. We're no longer considering the potential shape of a case but evaluating its actual credibility. As drafts mature, so does the workshop environment itself, providing a fresh chance to rethink the essay's focus.

Rethinking is essential to revision, and to the very spirit of using student texts as teaching tools. Without it, revision becomes both superficial and mechanical. As student drafts grow in maturity and complexity, moving from preliminary sketches to full drafts, we need to encourage students to play out and explore the consequences that words and ideas have. As they develop their case, their perspective may mature or even change. It would be a shame if it didn't. Longer, more complex drafts will likely raise unforeseen difficulties that force them to think anew. We should treat these difficulties as welcome opportunities to convey the excitement and rewards of substantive revision. Even conclusions to an essay can serve as an invitation to revise. When students try to pull together their case in an essay's concluding moments, they often discover the essence of that case. Conclusions thus inspire new beginnings, a chance to rework the essay in light of an eleventh-hour insight.

Although the dynamics of the workshop change as we move through revision cycles and the academic term itself, as do the specific rhetorical concerns we address, we should never lose the sense of exploration and discovery that workshop discussion can inspire. What students are likely to remember five months or five years later are not specific strategies so much as an appreciation for shared inquiry. That in itself will keep them writing and encourage them to write well.

HOW DO I HANDLE STUDENT PERSPECTIVES?

Because writing workshops or seminars require close collaboration between us and our students, and among students themselves, it's helpful to consider them as students do, from the back of the classroom or the far end of the seminar table. By understanding the expectations, and perhaps the fears, that students bring into the classroom, we can work with interpersonal dynamics in ways that promote intellectual discovery. I've found that many students enter my classroom with assumptions that inhibit learning. The success of the course often hinges on changing the subtle attitudes and behaviors those assumptions promote.

The first of these unproductive assumptions has to do with their preoccupation with themselves. Any writer's worst enemy is self-absorption, an unwillingness to look beyond oneself or to look at one's work in new ways. We can help expand students' intellectual and personal horizons by encouraging them to switch roles, to inhabit the minds and imaginations of others. We can ask them, in short, to learn how to write by thinking like a reader. Moreover, by asking them to read and discuss the work of their peers with growing critical discernment, we help them learn by acknowledging that they can also teach.

This role switching encourages them to extend their own imaginations emotionally and intellectually. They learn to inhabit other positions, other roles. In so doing, they become better acquainted with themselves—with their opinions and unexamined assumptions. Perhaps most importantly, this role switching reduces the fear that comes with self-absorption, the fear of being exposed. Workshops are intimate affairs. Students accustomed to lectures may experience some anxiety in the small class that affords them no chance to hide. I remember a student from several semesters ago who confided that she was terrified of sharing her work. She's far from alone. As students try out other roles, they do become exposed, but in ways they may not expect. Yes, workshop discussion may expose flaws in their writing and thinking for all to see, but through constructive suggestions and support they are also exposed to new perspectives on their writing, and to intellectual and emotional resources within themselves, and within the classroom community, that they otherwise might not have found. At the end of that semester, as we were saying our good-byes and inquiring about summer plans, this student turned to the class and in a moving expression of gratitude and solidarity, said she had never felt so supported—intellectually and emotionally—as in this writing class. That support came not from superficial praise but from a deep critical engagement with each other's ideas as thinkers and with each other's challenges as serious writers.

A second assumption is that students will readily expect us to dispense right answers. Their pursuit of those answers can take a variety of forms. Some students may simply hunger for approval, always adapting their ideas to what they perceive to be the correct response. Others may commit themselves a bit prematurely to a "right answer" and cling to it with amazing tenacity. Still others, taken aback by the intellectual demands of the course, may content themselves with recycling conventional opinions and resist genuine inquiry into them.

What's wrong with right answers is that premature closure can close minds. A writing workshop that foregrounds the students' own work in progress isn't about answers themselves, but about the process by which we arrive at and justify answers—answers that may still call for refinement or even fundamental modification. The habits we'll want to instill in our students should focus on the process by which thinkers arrive at positions, not on any one particular position.

Here are some ways I seek to promote inquiry. I try to focus as much on questions at issue as on the claims that reply to them. I discuss not rules but rationales, not solutions so much as problem-solving strategies. As students develop their own papers, I am vigilant in not letting my own personal opinions sway them. I am eager to ask the inconvenient question of anyone's argument. In short, I encourage students to earn their conclusions by explaining why simply asserting them falls short. And if, in working toward those conclusions, some students become committed to one right answer, I help them focus on their readers, whose skeptical questions can help them sharpen their support of that conclusion and perhaps even improve upon their answer.

A third assumption students bring into the class is that disagreement is, well, disagreeable. Students unaccustomed to the frank and spirited dialogue that can energize the workshop may shy away from any hint of criticism when commenting on drafts. They'll like everything, lest someone not like their own work . . . or not like them. I try to challenge this behavior from the first day—not by asking them to disagree and criticize, but by showing them why and how disagreement can be productive. When a student offers a critical remark, I take special pains to demonstrate why such a comment might improve a paper more than friendly but evasive praise. I try to communicate through my own teaching that criticism, when constructive, represents respect; I care enough about students' ideas to pay close attention to them.

Disagreements among students can lead to new insights and probing discussions of writing strategies. But those disagreements can confuse or overwhelm even the most receptive author. I often encourage students to ask someone else in the class to take notes on the discussion when their paper comes up for review. This way, they can return to a record of the discussion when their minds have cleared and their nerves have settled down. I also make a point of turning to the authors after we've discussed each draft to help them sort out the advice they've received and to see if any issues or questions have gone unaddressed. By lending a bit of closure to the discussion of each paper, I'm able to highlight the two or three key points the author ought to focus on for the next revision.

When encouraging perceptive critical comments, it's equally important to convey to students that disagreement, in itself, remains insufficient. Finding problems with an essay is only part of their job; negotiating solutions to those problems is the other, more important responsibility. We should encourage students to collaborate with the authors in revising the argument, adjusting the essay's voice, or rethinking the support now offered to accommodate unanticipated counterarguments. Criticism always should include one or two specific suggestions for revision and improvement.

A final assumption students bring into the classroom is that a positive comment will get them off the hook. Of course, students appreciate positive comments, and we ourselves are anxious to offer them. But rarely have I heard much said about how to make something of those positive comments in the classroom. It's not enough for us or our students to offer appreciative remarks. We must use them, pursue them, if they are to be of any genuine help. If students offer vague statements of approval, I'll ask them to be more specific, to point to a particular passage in the essay that demonstrates why they liked something, to clarify the principle behind why that passage worked, and to consider how that principle might apply to other papers in the class. Each author deserves more than our criticism—or even our praise. They deserve the thoughtful analysis that lies behind our judgments. The best way to encourage this behavior, of course, is for us to exemplify it in our own classroom comments.

HOW DO I HANDLE MYSELF?

I trust my remarks thus far about teaching workshops or seminars focused on student texts have revealed the many dimensions and concerns that shape—often in the same, contradictory moment—our dialogue with students. Yet all too often this variety seems not to apply where it matters most—in our presentation of ourselves as teachers. There's no one way to teach a writing workshop or seminar; there are many, even for the very same teacher. Those who teach well adopt not one but many roles. Role playing is particularly germane to writing workshops, oddly enough most especially to those focused on analysis and argument. One might think of those concerns, so central to academe, as being staid, even stuffy. But there's plenty of drama to be had.

The workshop or seminar dramatizes a theater of the mind. It is a stage on which students voice and play out their inquiry—an inquiry that might otherwise remain silent, solitary. Shared inquiry demands dialogue, and dialogue is the essence of drama. As we help students pursue a line of inquiry, as we ask skeptical questions that seem to challenge the very conclusions to be drawn, as we give advice about tone and phrasing and listen to and answer our students' questions about their own logic and rhetorical strategies, we are setting ideas in action, dramatizing the dialogue that always occurs between reader and writer.

When leading or responding to workshop discussion, I find it useful to invent roles for myself that will elicit and deepen that dialogue. Those roles may differ from course to course, week to week, often from student to student. I invent a different teaching persona for a class of engineers than I do for a class of English majors. But my intent remains consistent: to question preconceived notions that may limit how students approach their subject, their audience, even themselves. I may adopt a different guise from week to week, according to the stage of their work. I may be supportive or demanding, depending on what it takes to help their papers mature. Even the individual interactions I have with students influence how I dramatize myself. I may be self-deprecating to an insecure student who needs the reassurance that I've made the very same mistakes myself. Or I may add a bit of irony and wit to clarify a point to a student self-confident enough to appreciate humor with an edge.

Is it insincere to play different roles? Hardly. In fact, it may be the most appropriate expression of our sincerity. Only by inventing those roles can we respond to immediate situations, particular needs, and unanticipated opportunities—in short, the *kairos* of the classroom. Inquiry is a moving target, and we must constantly refashion our teaching to keep up with it and spur it on. Inquiry also involves risk. It demands a certain adroitness of mind, a willing spontaneity, a capacity to improvise. Ideally, our own teaching should be inquiry's most eloquent model. Teachers who stick to one role—through one class, one term, a whole career—make inquiry predictable, a dogma rather than a delight.

Much of the drama that can occur in a writing workshop or seminar shaped by student texts lies in revealing the connection between page and principle. When we and our students comment on an essay, we are attending to what's on the page. And yet if we are to make sense of teaching and learning on the page, we also must attend to general but unspoken principles and strategies. In a sense we are forever shuttling back and forth between the concrete and the abstract, between immediate application and theory. That middle ground is *techne*—craft, knack, know-how—and it becomes the stage on which the workshop's drama plays itself out. *Techne* is associated with the creative process, with the very "making" (*poesis*) of knowledge. Of Aristotle's three categories of knowledge—practical knowledge, productive knowledge, and theoretical knowledge—the writing workshop focused on student work in progress seems to lie chiefly in the domain of productive knowledge, as does rhetoric itself. But we should not constrain the possible range of these workshops. The *techne* we offer in the writing workshop may start with the available means of persuasion, with the possibilities for addressing the particular contingency the author may face. But the *techne* we share with our students is in fact far more than rules, or instrumental techniques, or even rhetorical strategies. Rather, the writing workshop or seminar offers, at its heart, a complex model of knowledge and a dynamic, highly collaborative process of knowledge acquisition and production.

If we make those connections between page and principle compelling for our students, we enhance their ability to draw those connections themselves, as they compose and share their own knowledge. In so doing, we also make principles more than ghostly abstractions, and strategies a matter of practical problem solving. I recall working with a bright civil engineering student on her analysis of the construction practices commonly used for highway guardrails and the hidden safety concerns those practices pose. The classroom discussion sought to clarify some confusing moments in her rather technical paper. We could only do so by shuttling back and forth between the specific details of her analysis and more general strategies for communicating technical material. Such connections are the substance of our teaching—not the page alone, not disembodied principles. Only through our teaching can we lend those connections substance and value.

There's a further dimension to the drama we can create when leading a workshop or seminar. In addition to linking page to principle, we should set the various papers the students are writing into a sort of colloquy. Those papers can vary enormously—in subject matter, style, and quality. Yet if shared inquiry is our goal, each paper we discuss can and should help illuminate someone else's essay. It's relatively easy to run a workshop by discussing first one paper and then another. But how predictable, how dull. What's more, this sort of sequencing confines each paper, and each author, in a solitary space that impedes collaborative learning. The art of teaching a workshop or seminar lies in dramatizing the hidden connections among papers so that no matter what paper we have before us, we also are talking about other papers as well. Our teaching should help the papers echo and resonate with each other. With each paper we discuss, we also are reminding the class of a paper we just reviewed, or anticipating the paper we will turn to next. In that sense we are discussing not just a series of individual texts but also a larger text that is the sum—indeed often more than the sum—of all the papers.

Much of the drama in teaching a workshop shaped by student work in progress lies in how we explore our own minds in public. We are making and modeling aesthetic, emotional, and logical judgments—at one and the same time delving into the inquiry pursued by our students and exemplifying the appropriate nature of that inquiry. A fundamental outcome of any writing workshop should be the development of informed judgment, or what in rhetorical terms has been called *phronesis*—practical wisdom. The development of *phronesis* can be thought of as the cardinal virtue of an effective writing workshop or seminar—the virtue from which all other virtues flow. Can this rich, practical wisdom be taught? Although practical wisdom may be difficult to teach directly, much less addressed as a line in a lesson plan, I nevertheless believe that rhetorically informed workshops and seminars can lead to that wisdom. As we impart the *techne* of making productive knowledge and encourage the inquiry that will spur and sustain that effort, we can hope students will recall, perhaps months or years later, how our collaborative writing class-room instilled a practical wisdom that has come to enrich their lives as writers and critical thinkers.

The prospect of exploring our own minds in public can unnerve even the most hardened classroom veteran. It's easy to feel that we can't afford to get it wrong, that we're likely to make a mistake, or that we're sure to come up against some difficulty we can't immediately resolve. The worst thing we can do is fear those possibilities. If fear prevents the flowering of the mind, it can also prevent teaching from flowering. If we fear making mistakes, students will take their cue from us and fear taking the intellectual risks we tell them are so educational. Here, what seems to be the chief drawback to the workshop can actually serve as our key resource: teaching in a lively workshop invites us to share in the very inquiry we are asking students to pursue. An interesting and entirely unexpected comment from an art history student recently helped the whole class see our way more clearly through the revision of a paper on the visual rhetoric of editorial cartoons. To take advantage of the comment, I had to reconsider the advice I had just given. And gladly so. For the comment did more than improve the paper; it reminded all of us that revision means we should always be willing to take a fresh look. Such instances of classroom *kairos* demand on our part the high-est intellectual rigor, creative imagination, and generosity of response. Only by exploring our own minds and sharing the risk of being wrong can we let students recognize and develop the habits of mind that pro-mote inquiry.

We all hope to be challenged by our students (or at least we say we do). But little do we realize that to be *challenged* by them we must also be willing to be *changed* by them. The drama of the workshop begins when we are willing to be taught by our own students. The many workshop or seminar roles we play help dramatize for our students the process of seri-ous, imaginative inquiry. That inquiry should extend to our own teach-ing. The essays in this volume exhibit the best of that inquiry. One of the secret rewards of teaching a writing workshop or seminar that places stu-dent texts at its center is that the process constantly invites us to question and revise our own classroom practice. By embracing the uncertainties of teaching with student texts, we learn even as we teach.

AFTERWORD
Notes toward an Informed Practice

Charles Paine
University of New Mexico

John D. Miles
Wofford College

"Practice" is used here to denote a recurrent sense of goal-directed activities with some common object, carried out with a particular technology and involving the application of a particular knowledge. A practice is a usual mode or method of doing something and cultural practices exist in all domains.

Sylvia Scribner

Hence the teaching which they gave to their pupils was rapid but unsystematic; for they conceived that they could train their pupils by imparting to them not an art [techne] but the results of an art, just as if one should claim to be about to communicate knowledge for the prevention of pain in the feet and then were not to teach the cobbler's art and the means of providing suitable foot-gear, but were to offer a selection of various kinds of shoes; for he has helped to supply his need but has not imparted an art to him.

Aristotle

We have written these notes to help readers, especially those who are new to teaching writing or new to teaching with student texts, use the essays collected here to guide them toward their own "informed practices." The twenty-one chapters in *Teaching with Student Texts* constitute more than a repertoire of "classroom moves" (as we put it in the introduction)—more than "a selection of various kinds of shoes" (as Aristotle put it more than 2300 years ago). An *informed* practice (roughly what Aristotle called a *techne* or "art") is guided by a know-how for getting things done. Some contemporary cognitive psychologists call this know-how a "framework" or "mental model." Sylvia Scribner calls it simply "practice": an activity guided by specific situations, goals, and a general knowledge framework.

Just as writing itself should be conceived as a practice that allows writers to make intelligent choices in the context of various situations, teaching writing with student texts, we think, should be conceived as a practice that improves when a teacher possesses a "mental model" for deciding which choices among many will lead to the desired goals in a specific situation.

These notes can serve as an alternative thematic table of contents that points to several chapters whose approach and ideas might help readers gain an overall sense of this informed practice of teaching with student texts. We also venture into some territory not explicitly covered by our authors.

PICTURING THE CLASSROOM WHERE STUDENT TEXTS ARE CENTRAL

For those who are new to teaching writing or teaching writing with student texts, we suggest two chapters that provide an overall sense of what a writing class that makes student texts central looks like, Joseph Harris's "Workshop and Seminar" (chapter 12) and Rolf Norgaard's "Embracing Uncertainty" (chapter 21). Both authors offer useful frameworks for making informed choices about TWiSTing. (Like some of our authors, we will use this acronym to save space.) These two chapters help explain *why*, as the new teacher we quoted in the first sentence of the introduction explained, "It changes everything." Harris's and Norgaard's chapters provide a big-picture sense for how this practice can transform a writing course.

Harris distinguishes the seminar from the workshop. This distinction might strike some readers as merely common sense, but to our knowledge the distinction is original, and we feel it is important. A workshop, Harris suggests, focuses on strategies to improve a particular student text, on the question "How can we help this writer revise?" A seminar focuses on understanding writing generally—how writing works, the choices writers can make and why they might choose one over others, on the question "What can we learn as writers from this text?" Harris does not advocate one format over the other, nor does he suggest that teachers maintain a clean distinction between the two. He argues for "both/ and" approaches, a constant blending of the two that is consciously considered by the teacher. The workshop/seminar distinction helps us *see* the choice and guide us in making the right choice.

As Rolf Norgaard cautions, making the transition to TWiSTing requires teachers to reorient their general approach and specific teaching practices. This shift "offers fresh challenges even to the veteran teacher, to say nothing of the risks it presents to those new to the classroom" (229). Authors in this collection focus mostly on the benefits, but Norgaard focuses as much on the challenges as the rewards. Norgaard explains why TWiSTing presents a challenge to both students and teachers, and he offers a framework for considering choices that will serve new teachers as well as seasoned veterans. In sum, he provides a broad but detailed sense of such a writing classroom, describing what can work well and what can fail, as well as a framework for improving the chances of success.

VALUING STUDENT TEXTS

Although it is usually necessary, responding to and evaluating (grading) writing is just one way to value, or honor, student writing. As Bruce Horner explains in "Revaluing Student Writing (chapter 1), when the value of student texts is reduced to "exchange value"—an exchange of writing for advice, encouragement, displaying knowledge and ability, or a grade—students reasonably come to the conclusion that their writing for this classroom is just "notwriting." Horner challenges us to rethink how we value student writing so that it might obtain a genuine use value when students engage with and rework academic knowledge. They get the message that writing is valuable because it accomplishes something and that their writing matters

All the contributors to this volume, as Horner explains, "are united in aiming to treat student texts as sites for students' and teachers' collaborative engagement in legitimate academic inquiry: as real writing, not 'notwriting.'" (22). Most offer explicit strategies for encouraging students to revalue student writing as writing that matters. For instance, Patrick Bruch and Thomas Reynolds (chapter 6) discuss how teaching in a department of writing studies encourages faculty to see and use student work in ambitious ways. Chris Warnick ("Texts to Be Worked On and Worked With," chapter 14) describes his methods for helping his students analyze the work that writing can do. He wants his students to be able to "do theory." By this he means he wants them to learn how to build "an analytical framework, an idea or concept that we can do work with and put to further use" (163). Michele Eodice and Kami Day ("Learning from Coauthoring," chapter 17) describe their emphasis on coauthoring, a relationship among writers that requires writers to describe, reflect on, and articulate their choices. Jane Fife ("Bringing

Outside Texts In and Inside Texts Out," chapter 20) describes a multilayered process in which texts by students from other classes and by students in the same class are used to help students develop consciously held sets of values and consider those against others' values, which may or may not coincide with their own. Nicole Wallack ("Revealing Our Values," Chapter 2) describes a similar scene, a summer seminar in which teachers from high school and college work together with student texts to interrogate their differences about what should be valued and encouraged in student texts. The goal is not for one group to sway the other toward their values but for both to move toward mutual understanding and appreciation.

Other authors focus on assessment. They describe approaches that help students recognize that how writing is assessed—how it is valued—varies from situation to situation. TWiSTing helps bridge the gap between teachers' (and others') values, students' values, and students' perceptions of teachers' (and others') values. When students examine *how* writing is assessed, and when they realize *that* writing can be and is assessed differently by different audiences and in different situations, they learn not just how writing works, but also how assessment—or valuing—works. This in turn can help them make better, more informed choices, and they gain increasing control over their choices. Chris Anson, Matthew Davis, and Domenic Vilhotti ("What Do *We* Want in this Paper?" chapter 3) describe a classroom technique that has students participating in building the rubric by which their work will be valued. Asao Inoue ("Teaching the Rhetoric of Writing Assessment," chapter 4) describes his first-year writing classroom in which students constantly wrangle with the question "What counts as good writing in this situation?"

ETHICS, REPRESENTATION, AND PEDAGOGY

Three essays caution that reading student texts involves not just pedagogical but ethical choices. These contributions in particular remind teachers that while student texts are in many ways uniquely useful, we need to consider the *student* in student texts, we need to keep in mind that there is always a person or persons behind—and often in—those texts. We urge anyone who teaches with student texts to consider these challenges and strategies.

Paul Anderson and Heidi McKee ("Ethics, Student Writers, and the Use of Student Texts to Teach," chapter 5) focus explicitly on ethical issues, demonstrating why it is important that writing teachers and scholars give student authors and their texts the same respect they give published authors. They caution that TWiSTing "exposes students (and the persons whom they may represent in their writing) to potential, albeit unintended, embarrassment, ridicule, and hurt" (60). Anderson and McKee alert teachers to possible ethical consequences from using student texts that we may not have considered. Their article has already moved us, at least, to alter the way we teach and the way we present student authors to professional colleagues. As the authors explain, the benefits of bringing student texts to the table must always be weighed against potential harm to the students. At the end of their essay, they offer a helpful and important set of guidelines for recognizing and avoiding any ethical lapses.

Mariolina Salvatori and Patricia Donahue ("The Figure of the Student in Composition Textbooks," chapter 11) argue that whenever we focus on a student text, we value it in certain ways and we position the student writer in certain ways. Therefore, we should carefully consider the ways we "read" student texts because our reading protocols serve to represent students themselves in particular ways. Through their examination of mid-twentieth-century and recent composition textbooks, Salvatori and Donahue show that the field of rhetoric and composition (in its publications and in the classrooms informed by those publications) has failed to treat student authors as authors. We need to devise ways to give them their due.

In "The Writer/Text Connection" (chapter 16), Muriel Harris addresses these issues by encouraging us to keep in mind that writers and their texts are fundamentally inseparable. Drawing on a long and productive career that has been informed by her work with and in writing centers, Harris offers suggestions for ways of interacting with students during conferences or other situations in which teachers, tutors, and mentors find themselves sitting next to student writers.

THE WORK STUDENT TEXTS DO

The first step in carrying out any informed practiced is understanding (at least generally) what you intend to accomplish. TWiSTing affords a powerful means for engaging writers in the study of writing. But teachers should remember a well-known principle in teaching writing, that what we *say* about student texts is less important than what we *do* with them. While TWiSTing shows our students that we value and honor their writing, their ideas, and the challenges they face, teachers need to be mindful about *what* they value and honor.

Student texts can be used to illustrate the moves, strategies, principles, and forms of critical reading and writing, and they can also engage writers in more basic issues in writing. They can be used to illustrate and inquire into the conventions used in specific genres and for specific audiences, the stylistic and tonal choices writers make (sentence combining, adding flair, levels of formality), and even surface features (such as grammar and other issues of mechanical correctness). For instance, by focusing on a sentence, passage, or paragraph written by a student (rather than those written by handbook writers), a writing class might explore such conventions and strategies as thesis sentences, paragraph topic sentences, quoting, citing and documenting, and even grammar. But if the classroom becomes a place where student texts are explored only or primarily for conventions and mechanical issues, we are sending the powerful, even if unintended, message that those are the things we value above all others. We thus urge teachers to carefully consider their overall goals and the kind of work they make student texts do.

Of course, these more basic issues should be covered in most classes where students are writing. Most teachers cannot (or choose not to) simply ignore them, leaving them to writing-center tutors or others. To address such issues, we suggest a teaching move that Chris Anson calls the "by the way" approach (2010). Here teachers might take the time to note a student's use (or lack of use) of a convention or style, or a student's stylistic tic or lapse in grammatical correctness. They can divert attention for a while with an introduction such as "By the way, what do you think of . . . ?" Teachers might even take some time to explain the issue, or they might have students engage in group work to explore other possibilities or to practice identifying and correcting errors. In this way teachers can have it both ways: they can help students learn about the conventions and mechanics of writing, *and* they can maintain the goal of valuing students' ideas.

FINDING AND SELECTING STUDENT TEXTS

An informed practice suggests an equally informed choosing of student texts. Margaret Marshall's description of her graduate practicum for writing teachers provides insights that inform those choices ("Writing to Learn, Reading to Teach: Student Texts in the Pedagogy Seminar," chapter 15). Of course, our choices should be informed by the specific issues students are facing at a particular time. The point is pretty straightforward: student texts can help illustrate any aspect of writing, from the most mundane to the most nuanced. Most (although not all) of the contributors to this book describe working with texts that come from students who are very close (in time and space) to the students in the classroom, but there are other sources for student texts to consider.

"Inside" versus "Outside" Texts

At the end of this section we provide a list of places to find student texts. We make a distinction between the first item in the list and all the others. This first type we call "inside" texts because they come from participants who are there in the room (real or virtual), doing the work of the class. All others we call "outside" texts.

We have found that, for our classrooms and our students, inside texts afford certain fundamental advantages over outside texts—although we encourage teachers to mix it up a bit, using at least some outside texts. When outside texts are used—when the writer is *not* present and students know he or she is not present—students tend to be less careful about their criticism. For instance, they rarely bother to find and articulate the text's positive attributes, but instead run immediately to its failings. If a teacher is using an outside text and wants students to make thoughtful criticism, the teacher usually has to specifically ask for that, and students often respond with *pro forma* thoughtfulness that can be difficult to sustain.

We have found that this is true even when the text is pretty well written and even when the class or group is composed of mature, highly educated individuals. For instance, Chuck teaches a class for his university's master's degree in public health, where every student holds a PhD, MD, or MA. He also facilitates a variety of faculty workshops about writing-across-the-curriculum or writing-in-the-disciplines (WAC/WID) classroom strategies and National Institutes of Health grant writing. In all these situations, when the participants understand that a text comes from someone who is not present, the amount of criticism increases and its thoughtfulness decreases. Often, at least one participant will get a little nasty and even comment snidely about the writer. If participants who are well reared in the culture of higher education act this way, we can hardly blame younger, less-experienced students for doing the same.

But even though the level of thoughtfulness wanes when the class knows the writer is not present, outside texts offer some advantages. The lack of thoughtfulness and care means less hesitancy, so outside texts can help you get the class's critical juices flowing for brainstorming lists of criteria and principles of good writing. We think it also gives inexperienced or diffident writers a sense of expertise, the sense that they can look at a text and make judgments about it, and even back those judgments up with principles. This practice of using outside texts can be an excellent way to begin discussing texts.

However, for generating careful, thoughtful, helpful criticism of texts, we have found that using inside texts, with students understanding that the author is sitting somewhere in the class, offers several clear advantages. The tone and direction of the class is noticeably different. Students become careful about offering criticism, sometimes even (too) hesitant. When a class moves midsession from an outside to an inside text, it's as if a switch is flipped—a "reverence switch." Students become more respectful of the text, the author, and the entire process. They almost suddenly find it easier to discern the positive attributes, what works. Rather than mostly pronouncing what's wrong with a text, they suddenly become very good at suggesting strategies for improvement.

"Model" versus "Interestingly Problematic" Texts

What sort of student text is most useful to work with—a superbly written and flawless text, a pretty good B-plus text, a middling text, or the full range of texts that students write for a class representing the full range of abilities? It depends on the class and on the teacher's goals. A teacher who uses model (or very high quality) texts could bring just one student text to the table during the semester. This strategy can work well, for instance, in a large lecture classes when there is little time for focusing on writing (see Bean, Drenk, and Lee 1982). However, a "model" text suggests "no room for improvement," and since we, like most writing teachers, focus almost always on the craft of revision, we prefer to use texts that invite students to suggest revision.

For that reason, we usually look for what Anson, Davis, and Vilhotti in this volume call "interestingly problematic" texts (35–45). There are good reasons for bringing to the table texts that are below average or even not passing. Doing so helps make the class a place where student writing—all student writing—is circulated and has social value. If, as we believe, writers often learn best from writers who are not too distant from them in time, space, and abilities, then students who are struggling might learn some things better from another student who is facing similar challenges. But even well-prepared and high-achieving students can learn from below-average or nonpassing texts. Some of the more nuanced moves of academic writing are thrown into starker relief and become more visible when they appear in such texts.

A List of Places to Locate and Select Student Texts

Our list moves from work that is close to students in terms of time, space, and abilities, to work that is further removed from where students are. The list also proceeds from work that tends to be "drafty" and "in process" to work at the end of the writing process, after editing, polishing, and then selection for publication (after which more revising and polishing occur). The essays in this volume focus slightly more on the kind of student texts that appear near the top of this list of places to turn to find and select student texts.

- *Same course, same section.* Students examine texts that come from their colleagues—that is, what we and many of our authors call "inside texts." Texts come from those sitting in the same classroom, usually working on the same or very similar assignment. Anne Ellen Geller and Frank Cantelmo ("Workshopping to Practice Scientific Terms," chapter 20) and others examine students' lower-stakes writing, which has helped them focus their students' attention on higher-order issues such as critical thinking and reading. And Maggie Debellius (chapter 13) describes how, at the start of a course, she sets a productive tone and agenda for students in writing workshops.

- *Same course, different section.* Students examine texts that come from students taking the same course but in a different section, usually working on the same or very similar assignment.

- *Same course, different semester.* Students examine texts that come from students who took the class during a different semester. A variety of strategies are described by Laurie McMillan ("Students Write to Students about Writing," chapter 7), Jane Fife "("Bringing Outside Texts In and Inside Texts Out, chapter 20), and others in this book. In McMillan's course, students who are finishing a semester address students who will be taking the same course in the next semester and explain what they can expect in the class. This practice, McMillan explains, is a valuable reflective activity for the writers, and it helps the future students understand this class will be different from what they were expecting (and dreading).

- *Different course, same semester.* Students examine texts written by students who are taking a different course altogether. For instance, students from an advanced composition or a teaching practicum might exchange work with students in a first-year writing course. Or, students taking a graduate-level course in the history of the Civil War might exchange work with students taking a similar advanced undergraduate course.

- *Locally published student work.* Some writing programs publish exemplary student texts—either in a stand-alone document or inserted into a custom edition of the textbook they are using. The work that appears in such publications is usually showcased as excellent. Although Karen McDonnell and Kevin Jefferson ("Product as Process: Teaching Publication to Students," chapter 9), discuss their use of a local publication in an unusual classroom setting (a class on editing the publication itself), their practices and conclusions, as they point out, can be generalized to almost any writing class. And the Internet now offers exciting possibilities for making student texts public—as both Scott Warnock (chapter 7) and Scott Rogers, Ryan Trauman, and Julia Kiernan (chapter 18) discuss in their essays.

- *Nationally published student work.* Some publishers offer anthologies of student work, usually at no charge to the students for programs that use the publisher's textbook. Better yet, there are several nationally distributed publications of student work, such as *Young Scholars in Writing,* which is described by Doug Downs, Heidi Estrem, and Susan Thomas ("Students' Texts beyond the Classroom: *Young Scholars in Writing*'s Challenges to College Writing Instruction," chapter 10).

- *Student work from textbooks.* In the last decade, writing textbooks have been increasing the number of student texts that appear in textbooks. Jane Fife (chapter 19) describes how she combines student work from previous classes with student work from textbooks. But as Mariolina Salvatori and Patricia Donahue show (chapter 11), while textbooks are a ready source for such sample student texts, they are often faked (written by the textbook authors), and there are important issues teachers should consider before using them.

TEACHING WITH STUDENT TEXTS, BECOMING BETTER TEACHERS

Bringing students' texts to the table helps teachers achieve their goals in two principal ways. First, it provides a chance to get formative feedback for students and teachers. Students learn or even help determine what counts as good writing. Of course, all the authors in this collection argue in various ways that TWiSTing helps students become better writers and transforms the classroom. But like many of our contributing authors, we believe this practice also helps us become better teachers.

Providing Formative Feedback for Both Students and Teachers

Student texts can help teachers communicate what they really value, what for them counts as good writing, and what criteria they will use to evaluate student work. The activity of TWiSTing can also set the scene for collaborating to determine values and standards. Students want and deserve to know the criteria we will use to grade their work. And so long as we take the time to align our values about what makes writing good with our grading criteria, we should oblige them. To make their grading criteria more transparent, many college teachers have turned to rubrics (or scoring guides)—by which we mean here *any* explanation or system, whether in narrative or grid form, whether a single phrase or a short treatise, designed to convey expectations and evaluation criteria and to aid in providing feedback. Although rubrics can be very effective, no writing-assignment rubric can completely capture what constitutes good writing (writing is too complex). The rubric's principles are best understood when fleshed out and illustrated with actual texts that allow students and teachers together to examine the rubric through the student text, and the student text through the rubric.

But even when a teacher has designed a strong rubric and discussed it with students, many students still will not spend sufficient time working with the rubric as they invent, draft, and revise. In fact, some students, especially those who enjoy writing, tend to get lost in the process of writing and forget to pay attention to rubrics. That enthusiastic student may then be disappointed by the grade. However, bringing student texts and the rubric together during class time can humanize a rubric—that is, show students that following the rubric is not a mechanical matter but can serve as a heuristic for getting engaged with the writing project. No matter how formal or informal an explanation of criteria a teacher provides, that explanation can be enhanced and clarified when it is discussed side by side with student texts.

The process of making grading criteria and values more transparent can thus become a two-way street. Pursuing such a deep collaboration, writing teachers learn about who their students are and about their interests, strengths, and challenges. Teachers gain insights into how well they have communicated their values and what still needs to be communicated. We suggest further that teachers should collaborate with students on values and criteria—as described, for instance, by Anson, Davis, and Vilhotti (chapter 3). When teachers bring a student text to the table and examine it through the lens of their tentative criteria, they put those values on the table as well, sometimes gaining new insights about what makes writing good. Teachers can adapt their rubrics and even change their mind. That is, teachers and students can collaborate on values and criteria. In this sense, then, students and teachers collaborate to build a shared, perhaps negotiated, set of values about what constitutes good writing.

Becoming a Better Teacher

> If, therefore, on consideration, it appears to you that, in view of such original conditions, our system is adequate . . . , then the only thing which would remain for all of you, or those who follow our instruction, is that you should pardon the lack of completeness of our system and be heartily grateful for our discoveries. (Aristotle 155)

This sentence from Aristotle's *Sophistical Refutations* completes the passage quoted in the opening epigraph. We cite these words with tongues only partly in cheek, because we editors find ourselves indeed "heartily grateful" to the authors in this volume for sharing their discoveries and contributing to this collection, which we hope will serve as a valuable resource for teachers who use writing to teach.

So we end this afterword—and this book—with an observation about the long-term benefits of TWiSTing for teachers, and with final thoughts about ourselves as learners in this drama. Many of our authors describe how making student texts central to their work makes them better teachers—more reflective and informed, more intellectually engaged, just plain better. We suggested in the introduction that TWiSTing can be a reflective and transforming move in pedagogy. It inevitably transforms us, too. As Rolf Norgaard writes in this book, "The drama . . . begins when we are willing to be taught by our own students. . . . By embracing the uncertainties of teaching with student texts, we learn even as we teach" (242). Indeed, as editors of this book—and we speak here for all three of us—we have found that our work with this varied and insightful group of authors has transformed our teaching. We hope our readers will undergo similar transformations.

REFERENCES

Acker, Stephen, and Kay Halasek. 2008. Preparing high school students for college-level writing: Using ePortfolio to support a successful transition. *Journal of General Education* 57: 1.

Adler-Kassner, Linda, Robert Crooks, and Ann Waters, eds. 1997. *Writing the community: Concepts and models for service-learning in composition.* Urbana, IL: NCTE.

Albion, P. R., and P.A. Ertmer. 2004. Online courses: Models and strategies for increasing interaction. Paper presented at AusWeb04at Sea World Nara Resort, Australia. http://ausweb.scu.edu.au/aw04/papers/refereed/albion/paper.html.

Allison, Libby, Lizbeth Bryant, and Maureen Hourigan, eds. 1997. *Grading in the post-process classroom: From theory to practice.* Portsmouth, NH: Boynton/Cook.

Anson, Chris M. 1999. Talking about writing: A classroom-based study of students' reflections on their drafts. In Bowman Smith and Yancey, 59–74

———. 2007. Beyond formulas: Closing the gap between rigid rules and flexible strategies for student writing. In *Closing the gap*, ed. Karen Keaton Jackson and Sandra Vavra, 147–64. Charlotte: Information Age.

———. 2010. Guaranteed thinking: Writing to learning in all disciplines. Workshop presented at the University of New Mexico, Albuquerque, NM.

Aristotle. 1955. *On sophistical refutations, on coming-to-be, on the cosmos.* Trans. D. J. Furley. Cambridge, MA: Harvard University Press.

Baron, Dennis. 2009. *A better pencil: Readers, writers, and the digital revolution.* New York: Oxford University Press.

Bartholomae, David. 1985. "Inventing the university. In *When a writer can't write: Studies in writer's block and other composing problems,* ed. Mike Rose, 134–65. New York: Guilford.

———. 1995. Writing with teachers: A conversation with Peter Elbow. *College Composition and Communication* 46: 62–71.

Bartholomae, David, and Anthony Petrosky. 1986. *Facts, artifacts, counterfacts: Theory and method for a basic reading and writing course.* Portsmouth, NH: Boynton/Cook.

Bawarshi, Anis S. 2003. *Genre and the invention of the writer: Reconsidering the place of invention in composition.* Logan: Utah State University Press.

Bazerman, Charles. 1995a. *The informed writer: Using sources in the disciplines.* 5th ed. Boston: Houghton Mifflin Company.

———. 1995b. Response: Curricular responsibilities and professional definition. In Petraglia 1995a, 249–59.

Bean, John C., Dean Drenk, and F. D. Lee. 1982. Microtheme strategies for developing cognitive skills. In *Teaching writing in all disciplines,* ed. C. Williams Griffin, . San Francisco: Jossey-Bass.

Beaufort, Anne. 2007. *College writing and beyond: A new framework for university writing instruction.* Logan: Utah State University Press.

Bergmann, Linda S., and Janet S. Zepernick. 2007. Disciplinarity and transfer: Students' prceptions of learning to write. *WPA* 31: 124–49.

Berlin, James. 1989. Rhetoric and ideology in the writing class. *College English* 50: 477–94.

Bettes, Nicole. 2008. Log 17. Learning log, Johnson County Community College.

Bishop, Wendy. 1998. *Released into language.* 2nd ed. Portland, ME: Calendar Islands Press.

Bleich, David. 1997. What can be done about grading? In Allison, Bryant, and Hourigan, 1535.

Bloom, Lynn Z. 2003. The good, the bad, and the ugly: Ethical practices for (re)presenting students and student writing in teachers' publications. *Writing on the Edge* 70: 67–82.

Bly, Carol. 2001. *Beyond the writer's workshop.* New York: Anchor.

Bowman Smith, Jane, and Kathleen Yancey, eds. 1999. *Student self-assessment and development in writing.* Cresskill, NJ: Hampton.

Brandt, Deborah. 2001. *Literacy in American lives.* New York: Cambridge University Press.

———. 2009. When people write for pay. *JAC 29*: 165–97.

Bridwell-Bowles, Lillian. 1992. Discourse and diversity: Experimental writing within the academy. *College Composition and Communication* 43: 349–68.

———. 1995. Freedom, form, function: Varieties of academic discourse. *College Composition and Communication* 46: 46–61.

Broad, Bob. 2003. *What we really value: Beyond rubrics in teaching and assessing writing.* Logan: Utah State University Press.

Broder, John M. 2009. Polar bear habitat proposed for Alaska. *New York Times,* October 22.

Brooks, Cleanth. 1947. *The well-wrought urn.* New York: Harvest.

Brooks, Cleanth, and Robert Penn Warren. 1949. *Modern rhetoric (with readings).* New York: Harcourt.

———. 1958. *Modern rhetoric.* 2nd ed. New York: Harcourt.

Brooks, David. 2001. The organization kid. *Atlantic Monthly,* April, 40–54.

Bruffee, Kenneth A. 1984. Collaborative learning and the "Conversation of mankind." *College English* 46: 635–52.

Carrick, Tracy Hamler, and Rebecca Moore Howard, eds. 2006. *Authorship in composition studies.* New York: Wadsworth.

Carter, Shannon. 2008. *The way literacy lives: Rhetorical dexterity and basic writing instruction.* Albany: State University of New York Press.

Child, Ryann. 2008. Response to Lakoff. Unpublished essay, Duke University.

Coles, William E., Jr. 1978. *The plural I.* New York: Holt.

Coles, William E., Jr., and James Vopat, eds. 1985. *What makes writing good: A multiperspective.* Lexington, MA: Heath.

Collison, George, Bonnie Elbaum, Sarah Haavind, and Robert Tinker. 2000. *Facilitating online learning: Effective strategies for moderators.* Madison, WI: Atwood.

Conference on College Composition and Communication. 2000. Guidelines for the ethical treatment of students and student writing in composition studies. http://www.ncte.org/cccc/resources/positions/ethicalconduct.

———. 2003. Guidelines for the ethical conduct of research in composition studies. http://www.ncte.org/cccc/resources/positions/ethicaltreatmentstud.

Crowley, Sharon. 1998. *Composition in the university: Historical and polemical essays.* Pittsburgh: University of Pittsburgh Press.

Day, Kami, and Michele Eodice. 2001. *(First person)²: A study of coauthoring in the academy.* Logan: Utah State University Press.

DeCandido, Robert. 2007. Searching for green in Gotham." *New York State Conservationist,* December, 2–9.

de Certeau, Michel. 1984. *The practice of everyday life.* Trans. Steven Rendall. Berkeley: University of California Press.

Deedy, Donna. 2008. L.I. duck farms struggle with water regulation." *New York Times,* 25 February.

Dombeck, Kristin, and Scott Herndon. 2004. *Critical passages: Teaching the transition to college composition.* New York: Teachers College Press.

Donahue, Patricia. 2007. Introduction. *Reader* 56: 6–10.

Dorman, Wade, and Susann Fox Dorman. 1997. Service-learning: Bridging the gap between the real world and the composition classroom." In Adler-Kassner, Crooks, and Waters, 119–32.

Downs, Douglas, and Elizabeth Wardle. 2007. Teaching about writing, righting misconceptions: (Re)envisioning "first-year composition" as "introduction to writing studies." *College Composition and Communication* 58: 552–84.

Draghi, Nicole. 2008. Unpublished essay exam, Marywood University.

Dryer, Dylan B. 2008. An "unconventional" textbook: Re-working pedagogy in the self-eeflective classroom. In Lu and Horner, 126–45. .

Durst, Russel K. 1999. *Collision course: Conflict, negotiation, and learning in college composition.* Urbana, IL: NCTE.

Ede, Lisa, and Andrea Lunsford. 1984. Audience addressed/audience invoked: The role of audience in composition theory and pedagogy. *College Composition and Communication* 35: 155–71.

———. 1985. Let them write—together." *English Quarterly* 18: 119–27.

Edmundson, Mark. 1997. On the uses of a liberal education: As lite entertainment for bored college students." *Harpers,* September, 39–50.

Edwards, Heather. 2008. Unpublished essay exam, Marywood University.

Elbow, Peter. 1973. *Writing without teachers.* New York: Oxford University Press.

———. 1981. *Writing with power: Techniques for mastering the writing process.* New York: Oxford University Press.

———. 1991. Reflections on academic discourse: How it relates to freshmen and colleagues." *College English* 53: 135–55.

———. 1995. Being a writer vs. being an academic: A conflict in goals." *College Composition and Communication* 46: 72–83.

———. 1999. Ranking, evaluating, and liking: Sorting out three forms of judgment." In *A sourcebook for responding to student writing,* ed. Richard Straub, 175–96. Cresskill, NJ: Hampton.

———. 2002. The role of publication in the democratization of writing. In *Publishing with students: A comprehensive guide,* ed. Chris Weber, 2–8. Portsmouth, NH: Heinemann.

———. 2006. Do we need a single standard of value for institutional assessment? An essay response to Asao Inoue's "Community-based assessment pedagogy." *Assessing Writing* 11: 81–99.

Ellis, Jonathon. 2006. Extending Emily Groves: Features of AIM in relation to the voyeur and the narcissist." *Young Scholars in Writing* 4: 94–96.

Ellis, Megan, Taylor Maine, Chris Moguchy, Karissa Wilcox, and Andrea Wright. 2007. Rhetorical analysis of "Just walk on by." Rhetorical analysis, Johnson County Community College.

Erickson, Better LaSere, Calvin B. Peters, and Dian Weltner Strommer. 2006. *Teaching first-year college students.* San Francisco: Jossey-Bass.

Faigley, Lester. 1992. *Fragments of rationality: Postmodernity and the subject of composition.* Pittsburgh: University of Pittsburgh Press.

Flores, Juan F. 2006. The first letter in individual: An alternative to collective online discussion. *Teaching English in the Two-Year College* 40: 430–44.

Fountain, Henry. 2009. Solar living, without compromising on lifestyle." *New York Times,* 13 October.

France, Alan W. 1993. Assigning places: The function of introductory composition as a cultural discourse. *College English* 55: 593–609.

Freed, Lynn. 2005. Doing time: My years in the creative-writing gulag." *Harper's,* July, 65–72.

Freedman, Aviva. 1995. The what, where, when, why, and how of classroom genres. In Petraglia 1995a, 121–44.

Fulwiler, Toby. 1982. The prsonal connection: Journal writing across the curriculum. In *Language connections: Writing and reading across the curriculum*, ed. Toby Fulwiler and Art Young, 15–31. Urbana IL: NCTE.

Galonsky, Alex. 2008. Response to Lakoff. Unpublished Essay, Duke University.

Gere, Ann Ruggles. 1987. *Writing groups: History, theory, and implications*. Carbondale, IL: Southern Illinois University Press.

Goodburn, Amy. 2001. The ethics of students' community writing as public text. In Isaacs and Jackson, 26–34.

Graff, Gerald. 2003. *Clueless in academe: How schooling obscures the life of the mind*. New Haven, CT: Yale University Press.

Graff, Gerald, and Cathy Birkenstein. 2006. *They say, I say: The moves that matter in academic writing*. New York: Norton

Graves, Roger. 2001. Responses to student writing from service learning clients. *Business Communication Quarterly* 64: 55–62.

Groves, Emily W. 2005. The emerging new discourse of the away message system. *Young Scholars in Writing* 3: 5–10.

Hall, Donald. 1982. *Writing well*. 4th ed. New York: Little, Brown.

Hanna, Donald E., Michelle Glowacki-Dudki, and Simone Conceicao-Runlee. 2000. *147 practical tips for teaching online groups*. Madison, WI: Atwood.

Harrington, Susanmarie, Rebecca Rickly, and Michael Day. 2000. Introduction. In *The online writing classroom: Instructional and information technology*, ed. Susanmarie Harrington, Rebecca Rickly, and Michael Day, 1–15. Cresskill, NJ: Hampton Press.

Harris, Joseph. 1994. From the editor: The work of others. *College Composition and Communication* 45: 439–41.

———. 2006. *Rewriting; How to do things with texts*. Logan: Utah State University Press.

Harris, Muriel. Forthcoming. Assignments from hell: The view from the writing center. In *What is college-level writing?* Vol. 2, ed. Patrick Sullivan, Howard Tinberg, and Sheridan Blau. Urbana, IL: NCTE.

Hawisher, Gail. 1992. Electronic meetings of the minds: Research, electronic conferences, and composition studies. In *Re-imagining computers and composition*, ed. Gail Hawisher and Paul LeBlanc, 81–101. Portsmouth, NH: Boynton/Cook.

Hayes, Sandy. 2006. Technology tool kit: Improving writing: Online bulletin boards. *Voices from the Middle* 14.2: (62-64).

Heilker, Paul. 1997. Rhetoric made real: Civic discourse and writing beyond the curriculum." In Adler-Kassner, Crooks, and Waters, 71–77.

Herrington, Anne, and Marcia Curtis. 2000. *Persons in process: Four stories of writing and personal development in college*. Urbana, IL: NCTE.

Hill, Charles A., and Lauren Resnick. 1995. Creating opportunities for apprenticeship in writing." In Petraglia 1995a, 145–58.

Hindman, Jane E. 2001. Personal writing. *College English* 64: 34–40.

Hjortshoj, Keith. 2001. *The transition to college writing*. Boston: Bedford.

Honebein, Peter C. 1996. Seven goals for the design of constructivist learning environments. In *Constructivist learning environments*, ed. B. G. Wilson, 11–24. Englewood Cliffs, NJ: Educational Technology Publications.

Howard, Rebecca Moore. 2000. Applications and assumptions of student self-assessment. In Bowman Smith and Yancey, 35–58.

Howe, Neil, William Strauss, and R. J. Matson. 2000. *Millennials rising : The next great generation*. New York: Vintage, 2000.

Hudson, James M., and Amy Bruckman. 2004. "Go away": Participant objections to being studied and the ethics of chatroom research. *Information Society* 20: 127–39.

Hull, Glynda A., and Mark Evan Nelson. 2005. Locating the semiotic power of multimodality. *Written Communication* 22: 224–261.

Huot, Brian. 2002. *(Re)articulating writing assessment for teaching and learning.* Logan: Utah State University Press.

Hwang, David Henry. 1989. *M. Butterfly.* New York: New American.

Inoue, Asao B. 2004. Community-based assessment pedagogy. *Assessing Writing* 9: 208–38.

Irmscher, William F. 1979. *Teaching expository writing.* New York: Holt.

Isaacs, Emily J., and Phoebe Jackson, eds. 2001. *Public works: Student writing as public text.* Portsmouth, NH: Boynton/Cook.

Johnson, Ruth, Beth Clark, and Mario Burton. 2007. Finding harmony in disharmony: Engineering and English studies. *Young Scholars in Writing* 5: 63–73.

Jolliffe, David. 1998. *Inquiry and genre: Writing to learn in college.* Upper Saddle River, NJ: Prentice Hall.

Jonassen, David H. 1991. Objectivism versus constructivism: Do we need a new philosophical paradigm? *Educational Technology Research and Development* 39: 5–14.

Kennedy, Mary Lynch, and Hadley M. Smith. 2006. *Reading and writing in the academic community.* Upper Saddle River, NJ: Prentice-Hall.

Lakoff, George. 2002. *Moral politics.* 2nd ed. Chicago: University of Chicago Press.

Larson, Richard. 1999. Revision as self-assessment. In Bowman Smith and Yancey, 97–103.

Lee, Jeffrey. 2000. *The scientific endeavor: A primer on scientific principles and practice.* Upper Saddle River, NJ: Pearson Benjamin Cummings.

Leverenz, Carrie. 1996. Collaboration, race, and the rhetoric of evasion. *JAC* 16: 297–312.

Levine, S. Joseph. 2007. The online discussion board. In *Teaching strategies in the online environment,* ed. Simone Conceição, 67–74. San Francisco: Jossey-Bass.

Lindemann, Erika. 2001. *A rhetoric for writing teachers.* 4th ed. New York: Oxford University Press.

Loomis, Ormond H. 2006. Program anthologies, classbooks, and zines: An examination of approaches to publishing first-year students' work. PhD diss., Florida State University.

Lu, Min-Zhan, and Bruce Horner, eds. 2008. *Instructor's manual for writing conventions.* New York: Penguin Academics.

Lunsford, Andrea, and Robert Connors. 1999. *The new St. Martin's handbook.* New York: St. Martin's.

Lunsford, Andrea. 2008. *The St. Martin's handbook.* 6th ed. New York: St. Martin's.

Macrorie, Ken. 1985. *Telling writing.* Portsmouth, NH: Boynton/Cook.

Maimon, Elaine P. 1979. Talking to strangers. *College Composition and Communication* 30: 364–69.

Maine, Taylor. 2008. Reflection. End-of-semester portfolio reflection, Johnson County Community College.

Malcolm, Katherine. 2008. Composing some "necessarily messy" teaching practices for *writing conventions.* In Lu and Horner, 170–87.

Malone, Anne Righton, and Barbara Tindall. 1997. Dear teacher: Epistolary conversations as the site of evaluation. In Allison, Bryant, and Hourigan, 125–140.

Martell, James. 2008. Unpublished essay exam, Marywood University.

Martin, Deb, and Diane Penrod. 2006. Coming to know criteria: The value of an evaluating writing course for undergraduates. *Assessing Writing* 11: 66–73.

Mauriello, Nicholas, and Gian S. Pagnucci. 2001. Can't we just Xerox this?" The ethical dilemma of writing for the World Wide Web. In Isaacs and Jackson, 44–52.

McDonnell, Matthew. 2008. Unpublished essay exam, Marywood University.

McKee, Heidi A. 2008. Ethical and legal issues for writing researchers in the age of media convergence. *Computers and Composition* 25: 104–22.

McKee, Heidi A., and James E. Porter. 2009. *The ethics of internet research: A rhetorical, case-based process.* New York: Peter Lang.

Meisinger, Sarah. 2005. Ethical problems in business and their solutions. General education and composition at Western Kentucky University: Sample papers. http://www.wku.edu/ composition/300s3.htm.

Meyer, Katrina A. 2007. Does feedback influence student postings to online discussions? *The Journal of Educators Online* 4(1). http://www.distance-educator.com/dnews/Article15296.phtml.

Miller, Susan. 1991. *Textual carnivals: The politics of composition.* Carbondale, IL: Southern Illinois University Press.

Moguchy, Chris. 2008. Letter of reflection. End-of-semester portfolio reflection, Johnson County Community College.

Moran, Charles. 2001. Publishing student writing. In Isaacs and Jackson, 35–43.

Murray, Donald. 1993. *Writing to learn.* 4th ed. Belmont, CA: Wadsworth.

Myers, D. G. 2006. *The elephants teach : Creative writing since 1880.* Chicago: University of Chicago Press.

National Commission for the Protection of Human Subjects of Biomedical and Behavioral Research. 1979. The Belmont report. Washington, DC: U.S. Government Printing Office. http://www.hhs.gov/ohrp/humansubjects/guidance/belmont.htm.

Nelson, Jennie. 1990. This was an easy assignment: Examining how students interpret academic writing tasks. *Research in the Teaching of English* 24: 362–96.

Nelson, Nancy. 2001. Writing to learn: One theory, two rationales. In *Writing as a learning tool: Integrating theory and practice,* ed. Paivi Tynjala, Lucia Mason, and Kirsti Lonka, 23–36. Boston: Kluwer.

New London Group. 1996. A pedagogy of multiliteracies: Designing social futures. *Harvard Educational Review* 66: 60–92.

O'Connor, Anahad. 2007. The claim: Hookahs are safer than cigarettes. *New York Times,* 11 September.

Ohmann, Richard. 1976/1996. *English in America: A radical view of the profession.* Hanover: Wesleyan University Press.

O'Leary, Claire Elizabeth. 2008. It's not what you say but how you say it (and to whom): Accommodating gender in the writing center conference. *Young Scholars in Writing* 6: 60–72.

Ondaatje, Michael. 1993. *The English patient.* New York: Vintage.

Ong, Walter J. 1975. The writer's audience is always a fiction. *PMLA* 90: 9–21.

Orwell, George. 1946/2005. Politics and the English language. In *Why I write.* New York: Penguin.

Parent, Richard. 2007. The accidental author: Does our worldwide electronic publication of student works promote our scholarship at the expense of their authorship? *Reader* 56: 44–53.

Petraglia, Joseph, ed. 1995a. *Reconceiving writing, rethinking writing instruction.* Mahwah, NJ: Lawrence Erlbaum.

———. 1995b. Writing as an unnatural act. In Petraglia 1995a, 79–100.

Prosser, Jon. 2000. The moral maze of image ethics. In *Situated ethics in educational research,* ed. Helen Simons and Robin Usher, 116–32. London: Routledge.

Quinn, Noah. 2008. Letter of reflection. End-of-semester portfolio reflection, Johnson County Community College.

Rankin, Elizabeth. 1990. From simple to complex: Ideas of order in assignment sequences. *JAC* 10: 126–36.

Resnick, Daniel P., and Laura Resnick. 1977. The nature of literacy: A historical exploration. *Harvard Educational Review* 47: 370–85.

Rijlaarsdam, Gert. 2008. The yummy yummy case: Learning to write—observing readers and writers. Paper presented at Writing Research Across Borders Conference, Santa Barbara, CA.

Robillard, Amy. 2006. *Young scholars* affecting composition: A challenge to disciplinary citation practices. *College English* 68: 253–70.

Rosen, Evan. 2008. Fascination leads to generalization. Unpublished essay, College of Charleston.

Rosenwasser, David, and Jill Stephen. 2009. *Writing analytically*. 5ᵗʰ ed. Boston: Thomson/Wadsworth.

Sacchi, Catherine. 2006. "Are you talking to me? Personal pronoun usage in tutoring across the disciplines. *Young Scholars in Writing* 4: 51–63.

Salvatori, Mariolina, and Patricia Donahue. 2005. *The elements (and pleasures) of difficulty*. New York: Pearson.

Scholes, Robert, Nancy R. Comley, and Janice Peritz. 2000. *The practice of writing*. 5ᵗʰ ed. Boston: Bedford.

Scribner, Sylvia. 1997. The practice of literacy: Where mind and society meet. In *Mind and social practice: Selected writings of Sylvia Scribner*, ed. Ethel Tobach et al., 190–205. New York: Cambridge University Press.

Sedaris, David. 2000. *Me talk pretty one day*. New York: Little, Brown.

Shalit, Ruth. 1998. The man who knew too much. *Lingua Franca* 8: 31–40.

Shamoon, Linda. 1998. International e-mail debate. In *Electronic communication across the curriculum*, ed. Donna Reiss, Dickie Selfe, and Art Young, 151–61. Urbana, IL: NCTE.

Shor, Ira. 1987. *Critical teaching and everyday life*. Chicago: University of Chicago Press.

Sirc, Geoffrey. 2004. Box-logic. In *Writing new media: Theory and applications for expanding the teaching of composition*, ed. Anne Frances Wysocki, Johndan Johnson-Eilola, Cynthia L. Selfe, and Geoffrey Sirc, 111–46. Logan: Utah State University Press.

Simpson, Jeanne. 2008. Personal communication.

Slevin, James F. 2001. *Introducing English: Essays in the intellectual work of composition*. Pittsburgh: University of Pittsburgh Press.

Sommers, Nancy. 2008. The call of research: A longitudinal view of writing development. *College Composition and Communication* 60: 152–64.

Spidell, Cathy, and William Thelin. 2006. Not ready to let go: A study of resistance to grading contracts. *Composition Studies* 34: 35–68.

Spigelman, Candace. 2000. *Across property lines: Textual ownership in writing groups*. 2006. Urbana, IL: NCTE.

Staples, Brent. 2007. Just walk on by. In *The Blair reader: Exploring contemporary issues*, ed. Laurie G. Kirszner and Stephen R. Mandell, 450–53. Upper Saddle River, NJ: Prentice Hall.

Starke-Meyerring, Doreen, and Melanie Wilson, eds. 2008. *Designing globally networked learning environments: Visionary partnerships, policies, and pedagogies*. Rotterdam: Sense.

Stover, Andrea. 2001. Redefining public/private boundaries in the composition classroom. In Isaacs and Jackson, 1–9.

Strakhov, Dmitri. 2008. Unpublished essay exam, Marywood University.

Strasser, Emily. 2007. Writing what matters: A student's struggle to bridge the academic/personal divide. *Young Scholars in Writing* 5: 146–50.

Straub, Richard. 1996. The concept of control in teacher response: Defining the varieties of "directive" and "facilitative" commentary. *College Composition and Communication* 47: 223–51.

Straub, Richard, and Ronald Lunsford. 1995. *Twelve readers reading: Responding to college student writing*. Cresskill, NJ: Hampton.

Strickland, Kathleen, and James Strickland. 1997. Demystifying grading: Creating student-owned evaluation instruments. In Allison, Bryant, and Hourigan, 141–55.

Stygall, Gail. 1998. Women and language in the collaborative classroom. In *Feminism and composition studies: In other words*. Eds. Susan Jarratt and Lynn Worsham, 318–41. New York: MLA.

Sullivan, Patrick, and Howard Tinberg, ed. 2006. *What is "college-level" writing?* Urbana, IL: NCTE.

Summerfield, Judith, and Geoffrey Summerfield. 1988. *Texts and contexts: A contribution to the theory and practice of teaching composition.* 2nd ed. New York: Random.

Taczak, Kara, and William H. Thelin. 2009. (Re)envisioning the divide: The impact of college courses on high school students. *Teaching English in the Two-Year College* 27: 7–23.

Tagg, John. 2003. *The learning paradigm college.* Bolton, MA: Anker.

Tchudi, Stephen. 1997. Introduction: Degrees of freedom in assessment, evaluation, and grading." In *Alternatives to grading student writing,* ed. Stephen Tchudi, xi–xvii. Urbana, IL: NCTE.

Trimbur, John. 1989. Consensus and difference in collaborative learning. *College English* 51: 602–16.

———. 1991. Literacy and the discourse of crisis. In *The politics of writing instruction: Postsecondary,* ed. John Trimbur and Richard Bullock, 277–95. Portsmouth, NH: Boynton/Cook.

———. 1996. Response: Why do we test writing? In *Assessment of writing: Politics, policies, and practices,* ed. Edward White, William Lutz, and Sandra Kamusikiri, 45–48. New York: MLA.

———. 2000. Composition and the circulation of writing. *College Composition and Communication* 52: 188–219.

Ugoretz, Joseph. 2005. Two roads diverged in a wood: Productive digression in asynchronous discussion. *Innovate* 1(3). http://www.innovateonline.info/index.php?view=article&id=30.

Varmer, Anita. 2008. Politics of difference in the writing center. *Young Scholars in Writing* 6: 30–38.

Voosen, Paul. 2009. Biodiversity a bitter pill in "Tropical" Mediterranean Sea. *New York Times,* 22 September.

Vygotsky, Lev. 1978. *Mind in society: The development of higher psychological processes.* Cambridge, MA: Harvard University Press.

Wall, Beverly C., and Robert F. Peltier. 1996. "Going Public" with electronic portfolios: Audience, community, and the terms of student ownership." *Computers and Composition* 13: 207–17.

Wardle, Elizabeth. 2007. Understanding "transfer" from FYC: Preliminary results of a longitudinal study. *WPA* 31: 65–85.

Warnock, Scott. Online writing teacher. onlinewritingteacher.blogspot.com.

Whateley, Jennifer. 2007. Composition's Frankenstein debate: Are composition students organ donors or authors in their own right? *Reader* 56: 34–43.

Williams, Joseph. 2005. *Style: Ten lessons in clarity and grace.* 8th ed. New York: Pearson.

Williams, Raymond. 1980. *Problems in materialism and culture.* London: Verso.

Yancey, Kathleen Blake. 2004. Made not only in words: Composition in a new key. *College Composition and Communication* 56: 297–328.

INDEX

Acker, Stephen, 33
Across Property Lines (Spigelman), 61
Albion, Peter, 99
Anderson, Paul V., 5, 58, 136, 246–47
Anson, Chris M., 8, 39–42, 51–52, 246, 253–54
argument, 164, 165–66
Aristotle, 240, 243, 254
assessment
   criteria, 48-49
   rhetorics of, 46–50
   technology, 47
asynchronous, 96–99, 106
Atlantic Monthly, 156
audience, 190, 194
authorship, 19–20, 136, 165
Authorship in Composition Studies (Carrick and Howard), 61

Baron, Dennis, 174
Bartholomae, David, 21, 152–53
Bartholomae-Elbow debate, 152–53
Bawarshi, Anis, 10, 13–15
Bazerman, Charles, 17
Bell Curve, The (Murray), 149
Belmont Report, The (National Commission), 63
Bettes, Nicole, 192
Beyond the Writer's Workshop (Bly), 159
"Biodiversity a Bitter Pill" (Voosen), 214–15, 217
Bishop, Wendy, 157
Bleich, David, 49–50
Bly, Carol, 155, 159
Broder, John, 214
Brooks, Cleanth, 129, 130–35, 137, 138, 140–41. *See also* Robert Penn Warren
Brooks, David, 156, 159–61
Bruch, Patrick, 58, 245
Bruffee, Kenneth, 156–58
Burton, Mario, 123–24

"Can a Maligned Pesticide Save Lives" (Glausiusz), 217
Cantelmo, Frank R., 144, 152, 211, 251
Carter, Shannon, 194
Child, Ryann, 148–49

citation, 135–36, 140–41
Clark, Beth, 123–24
Coles, William E, Jr., 2, 11
collaboration, 20, 115, 124, 174
   in classroom setting, 190–92, 197–99
Collision Course (Durst), 64
Collison, George, 106
"Community-Based Assessment Pedagogy" (Inoue), 48
computer assisted instruction, 203
"Concept of Control in Teacher Response, The" (Straub), 48
Conference on College Composition and Communication, 72
constructivism, 8, 35, 97, 107
craft, 240, 241–42, 243
Critical Teaching and Everyday Life (Shor), 2

Davis, Matthew, 8, 42–44, 246, 250, 253–54
Day, Kami, 143, 245
Day, Michael, 106
de Certeau, Michel, 18
Debelius, Maggie, 142, 152, 212, 251
DeCandido, Robert, 214
Deedy, Donna, 214
digital tools, 97–99
"Doing Time" (Freed), 154
Donahue, Patricia, 5, 59, 247, 252
Donovan-Kranz, Eileen, 109
Downs, Douglas, 59, 114, 115, 220, 252
Durst, Russel, 64

editorial board, 109–11, 116
Edmundson, Mark, 156,160–61
Elbaum, Bonnie, 106
Elbow, Peter, 25-26, 46, 49-50, 108, 146. *See also* Bartholomae-Elbow debate
Elements(and Pleasures)of Difficulty, The (Salvatori and Donahue), 141
Ellis, Jonathan, 123
Ellis, Megan, 194
Eodice, Michele, 143, 245
Erickson, Better, 121
Ertmer, Peggy, 99
Estrem, Heidi, 59, 114, 221, 224, 226
exchange value, 7, 15–18, 121, 245
experimental writing, 180

Facts, Artifacts, Counterfacts (Bartholomae and Petrosky), 21
Feister, Steven, 149
Fife, Jane, 144, 245–46, 251, 252
"Finding Harmony in Disharmony" (Johnson, Clark, and Burton), 123–24
(First Person)² (Day and Eodice), 194
Flores, Juan, 105
Fountain, Henry, 214
France, Alan, 18
Freed, Lynn, 154
Fulwiler, Toby, 97

Galonsky, Alex, 149
Geller, Anne Ellen, 144, 152, 251
Goodburn, Amy, 72, 136
Graff, Gerald, 163–64
Grobman, Laurie, 120
Groves, Emily, 123
"Guidelines for the Ethical Treatment" (Conference on College Composition and Communication), 72

Haavind, Sarah, 106
Halasek, Kay, 33
Hall, Donald, 136
Harper's, 154, 156
Harrington, Susanmarie, 106
Harris, Joseph, 135–37, 142, 183, 225, 244
Harris, Muriel, 143, 247
Hawisher, Gail, 106
Hayes, Sandy, 99
Hjortshoj, Keith, 122
Horner, Bruce, 5, 170, 221, 226, 245
Huot, Brian, 48, 49–50

identity, 116, 134, 147, 165, 191
Inoue, Asao B., 8, 110, 113, 246
Inquiry and Genre (Jolliffe), 201
"Inquiry Contract" (Joliffe), 202
institutional context, 143, 171–72
instruction, whole-class, 142–43, 175, 179
IRB Boards, 136, 141
Irmscher, William, 48
"It's Not What You Say but How You Say It (and to Whom)" (O'Leary), 124

Jefferson, Kevin, 58–59, 118, 252
Johnson, Ruth, 119–20, 123–24, 126
Jolliffe, David, 201, 202
"Just Walk on By" (Staples), 194–97

kairos, kairotic (opportune), 144, 230–31, 240, 242
Kiernan, Julia E., 95, 143–44, 252

"L.I. Duck Farms Struggle with Water Regulation," 217
labor, 115, 130, 154, 163
Lakoff, George, 148–50, 151
Larson, Richard, 46
Learning College Paradigm (Tagg), 197
Learning in Groups (Garth), 191
Lee, Jeffrey, 210
Leverenz, Carrie Shively, 155, 157
Levine, S. Joseph, 97, 107
Lindemann, Erika, 48
literacy narratives, 86, 172, 178, 180
low-stakes, 96, 97, 101, 105, 106
Lunsford, Ronald, 48

Macrorie, Ken, 11, 158
Maimon, Elaine, 103
Maine, Taylor, 194–97
Marshall, Margaret J., 142–43, 152, 248
Martin, Deb, 46
McDonnell, Karen, 58–59, 118, 252
McKee, Heidi A., 5, 58, 136, 246–47
McMillan, Laurie, 58, 251
Meier, Deborah, 163–64
message board texts, 96–99
Meyer, Katrina, 102
Miles, John D., 5
Miller, Susan, 10–11
Modern Rhetoric (Brooks and Warren), 129, 131, 136, 140
Moguchy, Chris, 194–97
"Moral Maze of Image Ethics, The" (Prosser), 71–72
Moral Politics (Lakoff), 148–49
multimodal, 201-02
Murray, Charles, 149

National Commission for the Protection of Human Subjects of Biomedical and Behavioral Research, 63
Nelson, Jennie, 221
New London Group, 200
New York Times, 151, 212
Norgaard, Rolf, 5, 144, 244–45, 254

O'Leary, Claire, 119–20. 123, 124, 126
On Sophistical Refutations (Aristotle), 254
"On the Uses of a Liberal Education" (Edmundson), 156, 160–61
Online Writing Teacher (Warnock), 100
opportune (*kairos*), 144, 230–31, 240, 242
"Organization Kid, The" (Brooks), 156, 159
Orwell, George, 158–59

Paine, Charles, 5
pedagogy seminar, 142–43, 171, 173, 178, 180
peer review, 80-82, 99-100
Penrod, Diane, 46
Peters, Calvin, 121
Petrosky, Anthony, 21
phronesis (practical wisdom), 241–42
Plural I, The (Coles), 2
"Polar Bear Habitat Proposed for Alaska" (Broder), 214
"Politics and the English Language" (Orwell), 158–59
"Politics of Difference in the Writing Center" (Varmer), 125
practical wisdom, 241–42
Prosser, Jon, 71–72
Public Works: Student Writing as Public Text (Isaacs and Jackson), 61
publishing, 115–17

Quinn, Noah, 198

Reading and Writing in the Academic Community (Kennedy and Smith), 221
Rewriting: How to Do Things With Texts (Harris), 136–37
Reynolds, Thomas, 58, 245
rhetorical dexterity, 194, 199
Rickly, Rebecca, 106
Riljaarsdam, Gert, 127
risk taking, 97, 231
Robillard, Amy, 121
Rogers, Scott, 95, 143–44, 252
role playing, 239–41
Rosen, Evan, 165–70
Rosenwasser, David, 136
rubrics, 48–49, 253–54

St. Martin's Handbook, The (Lunsford), 138
Salvatori, Mariolina Rizzi, 5, 59, 247, 252
Scientific Endeavor, The (Lee), 210
Scribner, Sylvia, 243
"Searching for Green in Gotham" (DeCandido), 214
Sedaris, David, 154, 155
service learning, 12–13, 71–72, 74
Shalit, Ruth, 64
Shor, Ira, 2
Simpson, Jeanne, 188
Slevin, James, 15
"Solar Living Without Compromising on Lifestyle" (Fountain), 214–16
Spigelman, Candace, 61, 120
Staples, Brent, 194

Stephen, Jill, 136
Strasser, Emily, 119–20, 123, 124
Straub, Richard, 48
Strommer, Dian, 121
student
    assumptions, 121, 169, 173, 236–38
    editor, 58–59, 109–10, 115
    learning, 47, 142–43, 171, 178
student-centered pedagogy, 152–53, 202–03, 228
Stygall, Gail, 155, 157
Style (Williams), 97
Sullivan, Patrick, 32

Taczak, Kara, 33
Tagg, John, 197
Tchudi, Stephen, 49
"Teaching about Writing, Righting Misconceptions" (Downs and Wardle), 78
techne (craft), 240, 241–42, 243
Telling Writing (Macrorie), 158
Thelin, William, 33
theme writing, 11–12, 16
Theory of Justice, A (Rawls), 149
This American Life, 201
Thomas Susan, 59, 114, 224, 226, 252
Tinberg, Howard, 32
Tinker, Robert, 106
Trauman, Ryan, 95, 143–44, 252
Trimbur, John, 9, 10, 14–16, 17, 155–56

Ugoretz, Joseph, 98–99
Uncertainty, 144, 299
use value, 7, 15, 17–18, 226, 245

Varma, Anita, 119–20, 123, 125, 126
Vilhotti, Domenica, 38–39, 246, 250, 246, 253–54
Voosen, Paul, 214
Vopat, James, 11

Wallack, Nicole B., 7, 8, 108, 171, 246
Wardle, Elizabeth, 78–79
Warnick, Chris, 142, 152, 175–76, 180, 245
Warnock, Scott, 58, 252
Warren, Robert Penn, 129, 130–35, 137, 138, 140–41. *See also* Cleanth Brooks
Well-Wrought Urn, The (Brooks), 131
Wilcox, Karissa, 194
Williams, Joseph, 97
Williams, Raymond, 12, 19
Women in Graffiti, 206–07
Wright, Andrea, 194
Writing Analytically (Rosenwasser and Stephen), 136

writing groups, 2, 155, 157
Writing On the Edge (Brooke and Good-
  burn), 136
writing studies classes, 78–79
Writing Well (Hall), 136
"Writing What Matters" (Strasser), 124

Writing Without Teachers (Elbow), 2, 146

Yancey, Kathleen Blake, 201
Young Scholars in Writing, 115, 118–20, 224,
  252

CONTRIBUTORS

JOSEPH HARRIS is an associate professor of English at Duke University, where he teaches courses in academic writing, critical reading, and creative nonfiction. From 1999–2009, he was the founding director of the Thompson Writing Program at Duke—an independent, multidisciplinary program noted for its approach to teaching writing as a form of critical inquiry. He is the author of *A Teaching Subject: Composition since 1966* (Prentice Hall 1997) and *Rewriting: How to Do Things with Texts* (Utah State University Press 2006).

JOHN D. MILES is an assistant professor of English and director of the writing center at Wofford College. Prior to graduate school, he taught high-school English for seven years in North Carolina. His research interests include indigenous rhetorics, writing assessment, and writing pedagogy. Currently he is at work on a longitudinal study of student writing at Wofford.

CHARLES PAINE is an associate professor of English at the University of New Mexico, where he teaches first-year writing, professional writing, and the history of rhetoric. A member of the executive board of the Council of Writing Program Administrators, he has written *The Resistant Writer* (SUNY Press 1999) and a first-year writing textbook, *Writing Today* (Longman 2010). From 1998–2008, he served as director of UNM's core writing division.

PAUL V. ANDERSON is the Roger and Joyce L. Howe Director of the Howe Center for Writing Excellence and a professor of English at Miami University, Ohio. He has served on the university's institutional review board and as a consultant to the United States Office for Protection from Research Risks (now the U.S. Office for Human Research Protections). In addition to ethics, his research concerns the contribution writing makes to learning, writing in the disciplines, digitally mediated collaboration, assessment, and technical and scientific communication.

CHRIS M. ANSON is University Distinguished Professor and Director of the Campus Writing and Speaking Program at North Carolina State University. A scholar of writing, language, and literacy, he has published fourteen books and over ninety articles and book chapters, and has spoken at or conducted faculty-development sessions across the United States and in twenty-one other countries.

PATRICK BRUCH is an associate professor of writing studies at the University of Minnesota, Twin Cities. His current research examines the definitions, promises, and perils of the writing studies movement in composition studies.

FRANK R. CANTELMO is an associate professor of biological sciences and environmental studies at St. John's College, St. John's University, in Queens, New York. He teaches a variety of courses in ecology, sustainability, and resource management. He is currently environmental advisor to the Holy See at the United Nations.

MATT DAVIS is a PhD student in rhetoric and composition at Florida State University. His research interests cluster around classroom pedagogy and pedagogical theory, literacy studies, technology and digital culture, and collaborative learning and writing.

KAMI DAY recently retired from Johnson County Community College, where she spent the last ten years of her twenty-year teaching career. She has published articles and chapters on coauthoring, learning communities, plagiarism, and faculty scholarship, several of which were coauthored with her partner, Michele Eodice. Their book, (*First Person)²: A Study of Co-authoring in the Academy*, was published by Utah State University Press in 2001.

MAGGIE DEBELIUS is the director of the writing center and associate director of the writing program at Georgetown University, where she also teaches in the English department. She is the author, with Susan Basalla, of *So What Are You Going to Do with That?: A Guide to Postacademic Careers* (University of Chicago Press).

PATRICIA DONAHUE is a professor of English at Lafayette College, where she teaches courses in rhetoric, discourse theory, literary theory, and Renaissance poetry. She is also the founding director of the college writing program, which she directed for twenty-three years. In 2003–04 she was selected as a Carnegie Scholar for her work in reading across the curriculum. With Mariolina Salvatori, she has coauthored several essays and presentations, in addition to *The Elements (and Pleasures) of Difficulty* (Pearson 2005).

DOUG DOWNS is an assistant professor of rhetoric and composition in the Montana State University department of English. His research interests center on research-writing pedagogy and facilitating undergraduate research both in first-year composition (he has worked extensively with Elizabeth Wardle on writing-about-writing pedagogies) and across the undergraduate curriculum.

MICHELE EODICE is the director of the Learning, Teaching and Writing Program, the Conoco-Phillips Writing Center, and the Writing across the Curriculum Program at the University of Oklahoma. She is also a past president of the International Writing Centers Association. She has published articles about coauthoring, writing-center work, and plagiarism, several of which were written with coauthors, including Kami Day. Their book, (*First Person)²: A Study of Co-authoring in the Academy*, was published in 2001 by Utah State University Press. She is coauthor of *The Everyday Writing Center* (Utah State University Press 2008).

HEIDI ESTREM is an associate professor and director of the First-Year Writing Program at Boise State University. She teaches a range of writing courses, from first-year writing to graduate courses for new instructors of writing. Her research interests consistently bring her back to students.

JANE MATHISON FIFE teaches writing and directs the writing center at Western Kentucky University. Her research interests include composition pedagogy, responding to student writing, digital literacies, and the circulation of writing within and beyond the academy. Her work has appeared in *Pedagogy, College Composition and Communication, Composition Studies, Dialogue*, and edited collections.

ANNE ELLEN GELLER is an associate professor of English, and director of writing across the curriculum in the Institute for Writing Studies, at St. John's University in Queens, New York. She is coauthor of *The Everyday Writing Center* (Utah State University Press 2008).

MURIEL HARRIS, professor emerita of English and Writing Lab director (retired) at Purdue University, serves as editor of the *Writing Lab Newsletter*. Her scholarship focuses on writing-center theory, pedagogy, and administration, as she is an ardent proponent of the individualized instruction that writing-center tutorials offer.

BRUCE HORNER is Endowed Chair in Rhetoric and Composition at the University of Louisville, where he teaches composition, composition theory and pedagogy, and literacy studies. His books include *Writing Conventions* (Penguin 2008), coauthored with Min-Zhan Lu, and *Cross-Language Relations in Composition*, coedited with Min-Zhan Lu and Paul Kei Matsuda (Southern Illinois University Press 2010).

ASAO B. INOUE is the assessment expert for the College of Arts and Humanities and codirector of first-year writing at California State University, Fresno. He has published on classroom and large-scale writing assessment, particularly validity and racism studies. His current project investigates racism in various writing assessment technologies.

KEVIN JEFFERSON teaches writing and humanities courses for the School of Writing, Rhetoric and Technical Communication at James Madison University.

JULIA E. KIERNAN is a PhD candidate in rhetoric and composition at the University of Louisville, where she has taught courses in first-year writing, technical writing, and professional writing. Her primary areas of scholarly interest include early modern women's rhetorics, Canadian multilingual student writing practices, and writing-center pedagogy and theory.

MARGARET J. MARSHALL currently serves as director of university writing and professor of English at Auburn University. From 1999 to 2005, she directed the English composition program at the University of Miami and taught the graduate pedagogy seminar there. Her research focuses on the rhetorics of educational discourse.

KAREN MCDONNELL splits her time at James Madison University between teaching for the School of Writing, Rhetoric and Technical Communication and consulting one-to-one with writers in the university writing center.

HEIDI A. MCKEE is an assistant professor in the department of English at the University of Miami, Ohio. Her teaching and research interests include digital writing and rhetoric, composition pedagogies, qualitative research methodologies, and ethical research practices. She served as founding coordinator of Miami's Digital Writing Collaborative, and she serves on Miami's institutional review board. With Dànielle Nicole DeVoss, she coedited *Digital Writing Research: Technologies, Methodologies, and Ethical Issues.* With James Porter she coauthored *The Ethics of Internet Research: A Rhetorical, Case-Based Approach.*

LAURIE MCMILLAN is the writing coordinator and an associate professor of English at Marywood University. She has published essays on feminist rhetoric, pedagogy, and multimodal writing. She is currently working on a book project, *Feminism's Critical Turn,* that explores contemporary experimental literary criticism.

ROLF NORGAARD serves as associate director of the Program for Writing and Rhetoric at the University of Colorado at Boulder. He has published widely on the rhetorical dimensions of writing instruction. In 2006 he received the Boulder Faculty Assembly Award for Excellence in Teaching, the highest campus wide teaching award.

THOMAS REYNOLDS is an associate professor of writing studies at the University of Minnesota, Twin Cities. His research interests include literacy studies, composition and popular culture, and basic writing theory.

SCOTT L. ROGERS is a PhD candidate in rhetoric and composition at the University of Louisville working on a dissertation that tracks intersections of composition scholarship and trauma studies. His other interests include cultural rhetorics, critical literacy, and the rhetoric of designed spaces.

MARIOLINA RIZZI SALVATORI is an associate professor of English at the University of Pittsburgh, where she teaches undergraduate and graduate courses in literacy, pedagogy, and hermeneutics. She is particularly interested in the transactions of knowledge and the relations between teachers, students, and texts made possible by different theories of reading. She was selected as a Carnegie Scholar in the Scholarship of Teaching and Learning for 1999–2000.

SUSAN THOMAS is a senior lecturer in English and higher education at the University of Sydney, Australia, where she designed and implemented a first-year writing program and helped establish the Sydney Writing Hub. She is currently working on a WAC program and fostering stronger writing partnerships with area high schools and corporations.

RYAN TRAUMAN is a PhD candidate in rhetoric and composition at the University of Louisville. His academic interests center on digital writing technologies. He also works with the center for digital storytelling in Denver, and the Digital Media and Composition Institute at The Ohio State University.

DOMENICA VILHOTTI taught composition and earned an MA in American and British literature at North Carolina State University. She maintains an interest in constructivist instruction and composition pedagogy. As a former corps member and literacy specialist with the Teach for America organization, she is currently applying her knowledge of composition studies and student-centered assessment as an AP language and composition instructor at Mastery Charter School in Philadelphia.

NICOLE B. WALLACK is director of the Columbia University Undergraduate Writing Program. She is also an associate of the Institute for Writing and Thinking at Bard College. Her most recent publication is "Focused Freewriting: Things to Do with Writing Prompts" in *Writing-Based Teaching: Essential Practices and Enduring Questions* (SUNY Press 2009). Currently she is working on a manuscript, *Crafting Presence in American Essays*, which examines the development and cultural functions of essays in American public life since the 18th century.

CHRIS WARNICK is an assistant professor of English at the College of Charleston, where he teaches a variety of undergraduate and graduate writing courses. His most recent publication is a chapter in *Working in the Archives: Practical Research Methods for Rhetoric and Composition*.

SCOTT WARNOCK is an assistant professor of English and director of the Drexel University Freshman Writing Program; he also coordinates online and hybrid composition courses. He wrote *Teaching Writing Online: How and Why* and has published in many journals and anthologies. He also helped create Waypoint writing assessment software.